God's Plan for Humanity
Volume 5

God's Biblical Festivals
Pentecost to Purim

Second Edition

James Malm

ISBN: 978-1-7753510-6-1

Copyright 2018 James David Malm
All Rights Reserved

Unless otherwise noted
all scripture quotes are from the King James Bible

Dedication

This work is dedicated to the Great God whose house is eternity; the Father and Sovereign of all that exists and the sum of all Truth, Wisdom, Love, Justice and Mercy.
May God's house be filled with children whose chief joy is to be like Him!

Visit Our Website
theshininglight.info

Table of Contents

Introduction 7

An Overview of the Biblical Festivals and Appointed Times 12

Tithes and Festival Offerings.. 18

How to Observe the Weekly and Annual Sabbaths 23

Pentecost 41

Pentecost 42

Pentecost; Hearts of Stone Hearts of Flesh.. 49

Peter's Message on the Day of Pentecost... 62

Pentecost and Ruth.. 69

The Millennium.. 81

The Memorial of Trumpets 89

How Lucifer Became Satan and God's Plan for Man 90

The Transition from Pentecost to the Feast of Trumpets 95

The Memorial of Trumpets... 107

The Great Ezra Revival 118

The Fast of Atonement 121

Introduction 122

Godly Fasting... 124

Psalms of Repentance for Passover and Atonement............................. 135

Satan's Final End 148

The Day of Atonement... 156

The Feast of Tabernacles 173

Introduction 174

Branches and Booths... 177

Ecclesiastes.. 188

Ezekiel 37 and the Resurrection to Flesh... 226

God the Light of the World 231

The 70 Feast of Tabernacles Sacrifices 239

The Living Waters of the Holy Spirit... 244

The Eighth Day 269

The Feast of The Eighth Day 270

The Tree of Life	284
Purim	**303**
Introduction	304
Outline	310
Esther	313

Introduction

Our articles on the Biblical Festivals reflect our best understanding at this time (2018). They are not the complete and ultimate understanding of the subject, and without any doubt God will reveal much more as time goes by. It is up to us to search out and accept new revelation with great joy, and to correct any errors as they are discovered.

God gave His Biblical Calendar at creation, adding the High Days, Appointed Times and Festivals to his people in Egypt and at Sinai, and Moses recorded these things as Holy Scripture.

A good understanding of the meaning of these things has been sealed up until these very last days (Dan 12:9).

In Palestine there is an early harvest in the spring, and a later harvest in the fall.

When God brought Israel out of Egypt and they entered into and began to cultivate the land, they were commanded to observe certain annual Holy Days and Festivals.

These Holy Days and Festivals were set up as Harvest Festivals to celebrate the ingathering of the early and the latter harvests of the land.

These Harvest Festivals rejoiced over the local harvests, and were illustrative allegories of God's plan for mankind and the spiritual harvests of humanity into the Family of God the Father.

There were three annual Harvest Festivals in which Israel was commanded to present themselves before God and to rejoice over the bounty that God had provided.

Deuteronomy 16:16 Three times in a year shall all thy males appear before the Lord thy God **in the place which he shall choose; in the feast of unleavened bread, and in the feast of weeks** [Pentecost], **and in the feast of tabernacles:**

Exodus 23:14 Three times thou shalt keep a feast unto me in the year.

23:15 Thou shalt keep **the feast of unleavened bread**: (thou shalt eat unleavened bread seven days, as I commanded thee, in the time appointed of the month Abib; for in it thou camest out from Egypt: and none shall appear before me empty:)

Three offerings are required each year, one offering during each of the three pilgrim Festivals

23:16 And **the feast of harvest, the firstfruits** [Pentecost] of thy labours, which thou hast sown in the field: and **the feast of ingathering, which is in the end of the year**, when thou hast gathered in thy labours out of the field.

The Feast of Unleavened Bread and the Feast of Tabernacles [Ingathering] are each seven days in length and ONE Offering was commanded by God to be given at some point during each of these two Feasts, and ONE Offering was to be given at the Feast of first fruits called Pentecost. No offerings were commanded to be given on the Fast Day of Atonement or on the Feast of Trumpets.

Although organizations may request money offerings on other occasions - example the offering for the tabernacle construction - there are only three God commanded offerings each year.

There are three key points in understanding the meaning of the Biblical Festivals.

1. They are physical Harvest Festivals for specific times of the year, which are allegories of God's spiritual harvest of mankind.

The actual reaping of the spring harvest began with the first Wave Sheaf cutting and Offering during the Feast of Unleavened Bread and the spring harvest was not reaped in the autumn at the Feast of Trumpets.

The Covenant people were commanded to come before God at the place that God chose, three times each year; first to the tabernacle and then later after the Temple was built the people gathered at the temple in Jerusalem for these Festivals and the first Sheaf beginning the early harvest was cut and offered to God at the Temple in Jerusalem on the day after the weekly Sabbath during the Feast of Unleavened Bread, then after this Feast the people returned home to reap the early harvest.

It is very important to realize that the Feast of Unleavened Bread is called the early harvest because it was the first harvest to be reaped at the beginning of the year.

Jesus Christ was the first to be reaped from the earth just as the Sabbath ended and Sunday began during the Feast of Unleavened Bread and the chosen first fruits will be reaped at the end of the sixth day - picturing the end of 6,000 years - of the Feast of Unleavened Bread, because the Feast of Unleavened Bread is an allegory of the early harvest of fleshly men from the earth to spirit.

The Feast of Unleavened Bread is the early harvest feast because it is the first harvest to be reaped and was reaped in the spring at the beginning of the year. If it was reaped in the fall, it would not be the early harvest: It would be the later fall harvest!

The spiritual corollary is that the early resurrection to spirit takes place during the Feast of Unleavened Bread; NOT on any of the Fall Festivals which have to do with the main harvest of humanity.

2. Both the Feast of Unleavened Bread Festival and the later fall harvest of the Feast of Tabernacles [Ingathering] are seven day Feasts. The scriptures give us the principle to understand by telling us that:

2 Peter 3:8 But, beloved, be not ignorant of this one thing, that **one day is with the Lord as a thousand years, and a thousand years as one day.**

This means that each of the seven days of these two Festivals must represent one thousand years; and in no case can a full seven day Festival represent only one thousand years.

Using the scriptural criteria it becomes clear that the early six day harvest festival followed by a Holy Annual Sabbath, which harvest is reaped in the spring, represents a six thousand year early harvest of humanity into the Family of God, followed by a millennial Sabbath with our Creator; while there will also be a seven thousand year later main harvest of the main bulk of humanity represented by the Feast of Tabernacles.

We can now see that the Feast of Unleavened Bread with its seven days, represents God calling out a kind of early first fruits from humanity for six thousand years, which is then capped by a resurrection to spirit of the early harvest at the end of the sixth day of Unleavened Bread followed by a millennial Sabbath which all flesh then living will spend with their Creator and during that 1,000 years all humanity then living will also be brought into the family of God completing the seven day [seven thousand year] early first fruits harvest.

After the resurrection to spirit of the early harvest of the Feast of Unleavened Bread, the seven last plagues are poured out and then the Millennial Kingdom of God will be established over all the earth on the Feast of Pentecost, just as the theocracy of Mosaic Covenant Israel was established on Pentecost and the New Covenant was firmly established in part on the same Feast of Pentecost in the first century.

The fall Feast of Tabernacles is also a seven day Feast representing a seven thousand year main harvest period when those who have not known God will be resurrected to flesh (Ezek 37), and most will be brought into the family of God in the reaping of the main harvest of humanity represented by the Feast of Ingathering called Tabernacles.

The scriptures also teach us about the intervening period between the post tribulation Pentecost and the Fall Festivals.

Definitions:
   1. Ekklesia

In Acts 19:32, 41, Ekklesia is translated "assembly" and refers to an unlawful gathering, a mob. In the same context it has reference to a "lawful assembly" in Acts 19:39. The word Ekklesia appears in reference to the faithful believers who live by the Word of God more than 100 times in the

Greek NT Scriptures, but **only in these three instances in Acts 19 is the word correctly translated assembly!**

In reference to a religious gathering, the English word "church" is always substituted for the correct translation; at the express command of King James.

The translators were forbidden to render the true meaning of the word, except in the three above instances and were required by the King to substitute the word "church." Rule 3 of the "Rules to be observed in the Translation of the Bible" specifically says: "The old Ecclesiastical [Roman Catholic] words [were] to be kept," meaning the word **Ekklesia was to be replaced with "church" and was** not to be correctly translated as a gathering. The translators obeyed the King and that version is rightly called the King James Version!

King James wanted to keep his authority over the corporate church of England and would not permit the translators to correctly inform the people that the Ekklesia was NOT a corporate body.

2. **When the word LORD** is written fully in capitols, it was directly translated from the Hebrew word YHVH

3. **Appointed Times** are commanded observances which are not Holy Days, and on which work may be done.

4. **Sabbaths or Holy Days** are Holy Days on which no work of any kind may be done [including cooking and buying and selling food and drink, or anything else]. Acts of mercy and those activities specifically commanded by God for the occasion are lawful. All necessary preparations should be made before the Sabbath or Holy Day. See the appropriate section below.

5. **Days:** It is important to know that God defines days in the scriptures as beginning and ending at sunset (Genesis 1, "evening" meaning sunset); not by today's midnight to midnight method

An Overview of the Biblical Festivals and Appointed Times

The Appointed Times

The New Moons are not Holy Days; they are Appointed Times [like Passover and Wave Offering Sunday] to acknowledge God as Creator with worship [Bible Studies] and rejoicing before Him and to sanctify and dedicate each new month to God.

Work may be done on New Moons but we are also commanded to worship God. This is best done by a Bible Study as was customary in ancient Israel (2 Kings 4:23)

The first visible light of the New Moon as seen from Jerusalem; Sets Apart and Consecrates, each biblical month; which is essential for correctly dating the observance of all other Biblical Appointed Times, Holy Days and Festivals on their proper God commanded dates. The current Rabbinic Molad Calendar is based on darkness and not the Biblical LIGHT and is full of other contrary to scriptural rules; any Rabbi will tell you that it is not scriptural.

The Biblical Calendar and New Moons are fully explained in "The Biblical Sabbath and Calendar" course.

The Biblical Spring Festivals picture the early Spring Harvest of the First Month

Passover pictures the sacrifice of the Lamb of God, the Creator who gave up his God-hood to become flesh: Jesus Christ.

The Wave Offering during the Feast of Unleavened Bread depicts Christ's ascension to God the Father after his resurrection as the Sabbath ended and Sunday began, to become a spiritual High Priest forever, restoring the Melchisedec order.

The Feast of Unleavened Bread pictures the calling out of a kind of first fruits to God for six thousand years, during which men like Abel, Noah, Abraham, Moses, David, Elijah, Daniel, John Baptist and so many others were called out to God and given the Holy Spirit in faith that Jesus would complete his mission to atone for sin; followed by a one thousand year millennial Sabbath in the presence of the Creator during which the remainder of the early harvest of first fruits will be brought into the family of God. to complete a full seven thousand year early harvest.

Pentecost pictures the establishment of the Covenants of God; first the Mosaic Covenant and then in a small way the New Covenant on Pentecost 31 A.D., with its complete fulfillment establishing a kingdom of God over all the earth and expanding the New Covenant to all flesh (Joel 2:28).

At the end of the millennium Satan is loosed for a short time and after that the fall main Feast of Tabernacles harvest of humanity begins.

The Fall Festivals

The Feast of Trumpets

The first of the Fall Festivals is "**The Feast of Trumpets.**"

The blasting of the trumpets on this day celebrates the victory over Satan as foretold in Ezekiel 38-39 and Revelation 20, and calls on God to remember his promises of a resurrection to physical life of all the remaining dead [Ezek 37), for the harvest of the Ingathering of Nations [The Feast of Tabernacles].

This Feast is on the seventh New Moon of the year and represents the dedication of the entire seventh month and all of its fall harvest events to God.

The High Holy Fast Day of Atonement

After the Feast of Trumpets and just before the Feast of Tabernacles, the Fast of Atonement pictures the sincere repentance of the main harvest of humanity and the judgment and final removal of Satan forever as the ultimate source of sin, decay and death; on a day of fasting and sincere repentance.

The Feast of Tabernacles

The Feast of Ingathering - called the Feast of Tabernacles - pictures the ingathering of the main harvest of humanity into the Family of God.

Revelation 20:12 And I saw the dead, small and great, stand before God; and the books were opened: and another book was opened, which is the book of life: and the dead were judged out of those things which were written in the books, according to their works.

The Feast of the Eighth Day

The Eighth Day is a Holy Day attached at the end of the Feast of Tabernacles picturing God and man going forward into eternity in a new beginning after the harvest of humanity to spirit has been completed.

Purim

Purim, is not a Festival or Appointed Time commanded by God; however it commemorates historic events with profound religious significance. The Book of Esther is Holy Scripture recorded for our instruction and contains important lessons for all godly people.

The Difference between the Festivals of the FIRST and SEVENTH Months

The spring beginning of the first month was commanded by God to Israel in Egypt, which supposes that they did not begin the year at that time while in Egypt.

AFTER they entered Palestine and began to cultivate the land; the command to offer a Wave Offering at the beginning of the barley harvest during the Feast of Unleavened Bread kicked in.

To offer the Wave Offering at the commanded time, the first month must be sanctified by the sighting of the first light of the new moon at Jerusalem where God had placed His name; when the barley would be ripe enough for harvest, because the whole nation was gathered together at Jerusalem [after God chose Jerusalem] to keep the Feast of Unleavened Bread.

The Festivals of the First Month are associated with the spring harvest and are an instructional allegory of God's plan for an early harvest of spiritual first fruits.

The Festivals of the Seventh Month used the completion of the FALL main harvest in Palestine as an allegory of the coming remaining Main Harvest of Humanity; and have nothing to do with any millennium or reaping of the spiritual harvest of first fruits!

The Festivals of the FIRST month are about the early harvest; and the Festivals of the SEVENTH month are about the latter main harvest of humanity.

That is a FUNDAMENTALLY BASIC to understanding the Biblical Festivals of God!

The Biblical Fall Festivals Picture the Latter Main Harvest of the Seventh Month

The Fall Festivals of God picture the main harvest in Judea as a type of the main harvest of humanity and have nothing whatsoever to do with the early spring first fruits harvest resurrection of the early harvest of spiritual first fruits, or the millennium.

In the past the Feast of Trumpets was equated with the trumpets of Revelation and the resurrection of the first fruits. This was an obvious error, because a spring harvest is reaped in the Spring and is NEVER reaped in the autumn; and the seventh month refers to the main fall harvest of humanity.

The EARLY harvest of first fruits is not reaped on any fall High Day; the early harvest must be reaped in the spring, or it would not be an early harvest, it would be a fall harvest!

Nor can the seven day Feast of Tabernacles picture a one thousand year millennial period (2 Peter 3:8).

The Fall Festivals have absolutely nothing to do with the early harvest of first fruits; the Fall Festivals are about the main fall harvest of humanity into the family of God.

Those who thought that they are celebrating the resurrection of the first fruits on the fall Feast of Trumpets, or celebrating the Millennium at the Feast of Tabernacles are entirely mistaken, being contrary to scripture.

Tabernacles is a seven day Festival, and Peter inspired by God tells us that one day [NOT SEVEN DAYS] is as one thousand years. The seven day Feast of Tabernacles pictures a seven thousand year reaping of the main harvest of humanity.

This background information is important to understand the Biblical Festivals of God in general including the Feast of Trumpets.

The Intermediate Feast Days

The weekly Sabbath Day and the first and seventh days of the Feast of Unleavened Bread are High Holy Days; on which no work of any kind may be done.

The weekly Sabbath Day and the first day of the fall Feast of Tabernacles along with the attached Feast of the Eighth Day are High Holy Days on which no work of any kind may be done.

Except for the weekly Sabbath, the intermediate days of the Feast of Unleavened Bread and the intermediate days of the Feast of Tabernacles are not High Holy Days and work may be done on them provided we also assemble for worship services.

We are to assemble on every day of these two seven day Feasts and rejoice before God; however necessary work - like cooking, shopping and washing - may be done on the intermediate days [except the Holy Days and the Weekly Sabbath].

The High Holy Days

The weekly Sabbath, the first and last days of the Feast of Unleavened Bread, the first day of the Feast of Tabernacles and the Feast of the Eighth Day are High Holy Days.

On the weekly Sabbath and annual Holy Days no work of any kind may be done except that which God has commanded for that day; and acts of mercy.

The Appointed Time of Passover represents the sacrifice of the Lamb of God for the sins of the world. Passover day ends at sunset ending the 14th day of the first month. The first High Holy Day of the Feast of Unleavened Bread begins as the sun sets on the 14th day and begins the 15th day of the first month.

After sunset ends Passover day, we are to begin the High Holy Day with a "Night To Be Much Observed;" to discuss and expound the exodus from Egypt. Later assemblies are also to be held during the daylight portion of the High Holy Day, and teachings on coming out of Egypt as an allegory of coming out of bondage to sin are to be presented along with the spiritual meaning of this Feast.

The Feast of Unleavened Bread is seven days long. Holy Convocations [assemblies] are to be held on every day of the Feast. Work may be done on the intermediate days [except the weekly Sabbath] as mentioned above.

The Seventh Day of the Feast of Unleavened Bread is a High Holy Day, on which we are to assemble and hear the Song of Moses expounded, and to hear messages on the power of God and His victory over Egypt; and messages on the gift of God's victory over bondage to sin.

The seven day Feast of Unleavened Bread is about coming out of bondage in Egypt, and is an allegory of God calling out an early harvest of lives from bondage to Satan and sin; over the first six thousands of history [the first six days of the Feast] to be trained and tested.

Those who faithfully follow their Lord to live by every Word of God will be resurrected to spirit as an early harvest of lives at the end of the sixth day of the Feast of Unleavened Bread, picturing the end of six thousand years; which will be followed by a one thousand year Millennial Sabbath of peace pictured by the seventh day High Day.

Tithes and Festival Offerings

The First Tithe

The law commands that the people tithe a tenth of all their increase to the Levites who must then tithe a tenth of that to the priests (Numbers 18:24-28).

The tithe to the Levites is to support them in their work doing the menial things of the tabernacle - later the temple; and Moses set the Levites as teachers of the people in the synagogue system.

In Psalm 74:8 David prophecies that an enemy will destroy the synagogues from the land, which implies that synagogues existed in the time of David. The synagogue system was created as schools where the Levites could teach the Word of God to all people. After the Babylonian captivity Ezra restored the synagogue system to Judah.

In addition, such functions as Levitical choirs were also added by David.

A tithe of the tithe received by the Levites is to be given to the priests to pay for the sacrifices commanded to be offered on behalf of the whole nation including the Daily, the Sabbath and New Moon, and the Festival sacrifices. In addition the priests were to receive wages for offering sacrifices on behalf of individuals in the form of a portion of the personal sacrifices.

David set up courses of priests to serve one by one at the tabernacle, later the temple; and because the vast majority of personal individual sacrifices were made at the Festivals and because of the Festival work load, all priests were to serve at all of the Festivals.

The tithe from the people was to be a tenth of their increase which means that all expenses incurred to earn that income are to be deducted before tithing.

For example travel expenses to and from work, work clothes and cleaning - dry cleaning, education and training, and any other expenses needed to earn the income; like customer entertainment expenses to make a sale, work tools, and raw materials for resale as more finished products.

Further since God gave each family a plot of land, which many do not have today it is permissible to deduct a reasonable amount for housing costs.

That covers the Levitical tithe

Festival Tithes

God also commanded that every person in the land who is able, were to journey to the place where God had placed his name, i.e. the tabernacle or temple; three times a year

Deuteronomy 16:16 Three times in a year shall all thy males appear before the LORD thy God in the place which he shall choose; in the feast of unleavened bread, and in the feast of weeks, and in the feast of tabernacles: and **they shall not appear before the LORD empty:**

To pay for these three annual journeys to the Holy Place, another tithe on our increase is commanded

Deuteronomy 14:22 Thou shalt truly tithe all the increase of thy seed, that the field bringeth forth year by year. **14:23** And thou shalt eat before the LORD thy God, in the place which he shall choose to place his name there, the tithe of thy corn [grain], of thy wine, and of thine oil [a festival tithe of all of our increase], and [we are also to bring the first fruits of the particular harvest to the spring summer and fall Festivals] the firstlings of thy herds and of thy flocks; that thou mayest learn to fear the LORD thy God always

The purpose of appearing as a nation before God was to learn about God. Festival sermons are to be about God, His Word, His Law, His Wisdom and His Greatness; to bring the people to, and keep them close to God; and to exhort them to live by every Word of God.

14:24 And if the way be too long for thee, so that thou art not able to carry it; or if the place be too far from thee, which the LORD thy God shall choose to set his name there, when the LORD thy God hath blessed thee: **14:25** Then shalt thou turn it into money, and bind up the money in thine hand, and shalt go unto the place which the LORD thy God shall choose: **14:26** And thou shalt bestow that [Festival tithe] money for whatsoever thy soul lusteth [lawfully desires] after, for oxen, or for sheep, or for wine, or for strong drink, or for whatsoever thy soul desireth: and thou shalt eat there before the LORD thy God, and thou shalt rejoice, thou, and thine household,

It is self-evident that some people were left at home; the unclean, the very young or very aged, the seriously ill and their care givers and those needed to care for the flocks and herds; but the intent was and is, that as many as possible attend the three annual pilgrim Festivals.

The three annual Festivals were for the people to appear before the LORD to learn of Him; to worship God and to exalt Him and to rejoice with their God.

The Festival tithe was to be spent in attending these Festivals and feasting before the LORD as an allegory of a spiritual feast on the Word of God; and in great rejoicing over the physical harvests; as an allegory of feasting on the Word of God and looking forward to the wondrous spiritual harvests of humanity that these physical harvests represent in the plan of God.

We are to rejoice; NOT because - as some wrongly think - that we will get ours and dominate others in the Kingdom of God, but because we shall be laborers bringing in the sheaves of humanity into the family of God! Saving humanity!

When someone is well off, they are NOT to spend their Festival tithe on tourist activities and non God centered activities, instead they are to share with their less well off brethren.

14:27 And the Levite that is within thy gates; thou shalt not forsake him; for he hath no part nor inheritance with thee.

Festival Offerings

In addition to our Festival tithes for us to eat and rejoice with before God, and the Festival sacrifices of the priests on behalf of the whole nation; the people are commanded to bring an offering to God on each of the three pilgrim festivals, that is three times a year.

Deuteronomy 16:17 Every man shall give as he is able, according to the blessing of the LORD thy God which he hath given thee.

These offerings could be, but were not primarily gifts of money to be given to the Levites or to the priests; they were the animal "Freewill and Thank Offerings" of rejoicing which were to be killed and then eaten by the offeror and shared with families and with the Levites. Therefore they are not commanded to be offered on the Fast of Atonement or the Feast of Trumpets, but on the three specifically commanded Harvest Festival occasions.

Offerings may also be given on occasions of great rejoicing such as the dedication of the temple, but are only COMMANDED for the three specific Harvest Festivals each year. (See also 2 Chr 31:14 Hezekiah's reformation, the return from exile: Ezr 1:4-6; Ezr 2:68; Ezr 7:16; Ezr 8:28; Ne 7:70-72 and the Eze 46:11-12 millennial temple).

The meaning of these Freewill and Thank Offerings is far deeper than merely casting some money into a basket.

These Festival offerings had to be killed in the Temple before God [although they were NOT sacrifices but offerings]; they had to be eaten inside the temple; and they had to be shared with family, friends and the Levites!

The Freewill and Thank Offerings were a physical allegory of a festive spiritual family meal, with God the Father at the head of the table, and his family gathered about him; in harmony and at peace, eating and rejoicing in the presence of God, as an example of eating [internalizing] the Word of God! There is so much more meaning to the Festival Offerings than mere mammon!

These Festival Freewill and Thank Offerings are not sacrifices to God; they are voluntary Free Will Offerings, brought on occasions of celebration or spiritual significance; to be eaten WITH God and with the people of God in rejoicing. The animal offered was to be killed in the temple and was then eaten as a festive banquet in the temple.

That is how things are to be done when we have a physical temple, yet today there is no physical temple. Nevertheless the Festivals should be observed today in this New Covenant spiritual dispensation with great rejoicing and an emphasis on spiritual feasting on the Word of God.

In Conclusion

We have no physical temple today and cannot kill and eat our Freewill and Thank Offerings before the LORD, yet we can and should feast together spiritually on the Word of God.

Yes, do give a Freewill Offering of money in place of an animal meal offering at the temple, but remember that the money offering is only a token of the Thank and Freewill Offerings to be made and eaten before the LORD in the temple; and understand that the meaning of the Freewill and Thank Offerings, is rejoicing together with God and eating [internalizing] the nature of God, to live by every Word of God in harmonious fellowship with God and all other faithful godly persons!

After Jesus Christ comes he will build the third Temple (Ezekiel 40 - 48) and the physical sacrifices and offerings will be renewed. The descendants of loyal Zadok will be called into the New Covenant of Jeremiah 31:31; and as New Covenant physical priests and will officiate in the physical duties of this third Temple. At that time Jesus Christ will clarify every detail of the Temple service and every detail of the spiritual meaning of that Temple service and God's sacrificial system.

In the millennium it will not be possible for every person of the billions on earth to go to Jerusalem three times a year [look at the problems Mecca has with a few million at the Hajj once each year and add to that the sacrifices and offerings], but our LORD will resolve that problem; perhaps by having the nations send different representatives each year to each Festival while most people in the nations keep the Festivals in their own countries as the Ekklesia does today.

How to Observe the Weekly and Annual Sabbaths

It is lawful to do those things that God has commanded us to do on the Sabbath, since God is also the maker of the Sabbath and can therefore tell us what he wants us to do on HIS Sabbath; for this reason the Priests may fulfill their God commanded duties on the Sabbath.

Matthew 12:5 Or have ye not read in the law, how that on the sabbath days the priests in the temple profane the Sabbath [by doing the work commanded by God], and are blameless?

Since the Sabbath was made for the good of man, we may also do acts of compassion and mercy; however we are NOT to use the "ox in the ditch" emergency excuse, to justify and excuse habitual Sabbath breaking.

We are not to travel on the Sabbath to the extent that it becomes a tiring labor, nor are we to buy gas, food, drink and lodgings on Sabbath. We are to use the Preparation Day to properly prepare for the Sabbath Day.

We are not to do any cooking on the Sabbath (Ex 16:22-24) nor to do our own things, speak our own words, or to even think our own thoughts. We are to be totally dedicated to our God on his Holy Sabbath Day (Is 56 and Is 58).

We are to do no work at all on God's Holy Sabbath, except for that which God himself commands to be done, we are to focus on studying God's Word, discussions of, teaching and learning godliness and prayer, and acts of mercy for the health of others; nor shall we be responsible for any other person or creature being required to do any work on the Sabbath Day.

To pay others to serve us in a restaurant is no different than to pay others to work at any other service. To pay anyone else to do what we would not do ourselves is HYPOCRISY! We are to avoid all appearance of evil (1 Thess 5:22).

Exodus 20:10 But the seventh day is the sabbath of the LORD thy God: **in it thou shalt not do any work, thou, nor thy son, nor thy daughter, thy manservant, nor thy maidservant, nor thy cattle, nor thy stranger that is within thy gates** [subject to our responsibility]:

Cooking, Buying and Work on the Weekly Sabbath and Annual Holy Days

This scripture is often used by unlearned persons to justify cooking on God's Holy Sabbaths.

Speaking of the very first Feast of Unleavened Bread when Israel was leaving Egypt, God allows food preparation on the Holy Days as an extraordinary emergency measure.

Exodus 12:15 And in the first day there shall be an holy convocation, and in the seventh day there shall be an holy convocation to you; no manner of work shall be done in them, **save that which every man must eat, that only may be done of you**.

This statement that food may be prepared during the Feast of Unleavened Bread has been used to justify food preparation on all subsequent and all other annual Holy Day and Weekly Sabbaths by some. Is that a valid assumption?

This verse actually refers to the very First "Feast of Unleavened Bread" with its two High Holy Days ONLY: allowing food to be prepared and eaten on that very FIRST Feast of Unleavened Bread ONLY.

Some extrapolate from this verse that food may also be prepared and eaten on all subsequent Feasts of Unleavened Bread Holy Days and all other High Holy Days.

It is necessary to understand that this particular scripture is a history of Israel coming out of Egypt.

After that FIRST Passover, all leftovers had been burned and there was no prepared food available when Israel began the march out of Egypt; later when they had been crossing the Red Sea throughout the sixth day - just before the seventh and Holy Day - of that Feast there was also not time to prepare food ahead of the seventh day High Holy Day.

As a singular emergency act of mercy, God permitted food to be prepared and eaten on this one emergency "ox in the ditch" occasion.

Nowhere else in all scripture is such a liberty [to prepare food on a Sabbath or High Day] permitted. This is simply a record of a special allowance, a special act of mercy; made for a special situation.

This one time act of mercy is an act of merciful exception to the rule, and does NOT justify breaking the commandments for the weekly Sabbath and subsequent annual High Day Sabbaths!

To cook or buy food or drink on God's weekly and annual Sabbaths except for a very special and extreme extraordinary emergency in SIN!

We must quickly repent and turn from this sin of using Holy Time for our own purposes and pleasures, before we are corrected as physical Israel / Judah were corrected anciently and will be corrected again for the same sin!

The fact that the Passover was the preparation day for the first annual Sabbath of the Feast of Unleavened Bread, on which it was well understood that no work including cooking was to be done; is made clear by the faithful who rushed to entomb Jesus BEFORE the High Day of Unleavened Bread began at sunset that evening.

John 19:31 The Jews therefore, **because it was the preparation** [the preparation day for the first Holy Day of the Feast of Unleavened Bread], that the bodies should not remain upon the cross on the sabbath day, (for **that sabbath day was an high day,**) besought Pilate that their legs might be broken, and that they might be taken away.

SERVILE WORK

In Leviticus 23 the statements regarding the High Holy Days refer to commands not to do any servile work. This has been taken to mean something different than the "do NOT do ANY work" of the Sabbath command; and has been used to try and justify cooking and doing other work on the Annual High Days.

The word "abodah" is translated in the KJV as "servile". The related word "abidah" means to "work of any kind".

In reality, far from justifying some types of work like cooking, the term "servile work" is a redoubling of the command to do no work of ANY kind at all; for emphatic emphasis! Thou shalt not do any [abodah] work and thou shalt not do any servile work [or any kind abidah].

No work of any kind, including food preparation and purchasing, which is NOT to be done on any weekly or annual Sabbath! Only acts of mercy for health and safety and anything specifically commanded by God to be done on the weekly and annual Sabbaths may be done.

We are to properly prepare on the preparation day so that everyone might rest from physical duties, and engage in spiritual pursuits learning about God on His Holy Time

The Weekly Sabbath and the Annual Holy Days are Holy Time. No work of any kind is to be done on them. That means no food preparation or cooking and no buying of food or drink.

Food and drink are to be prepared on the previous day which is the Preparation Day for the Weekly and Annual Sabbaths.

On the weekly and annual Sabbaths we are to do what God has specifically commanded us to do on those days; in addition, acts of mercy are to be done and the days are to be observed by convoking with God as Adam and Eve did and by doing so with other like minded persons.

The Sabbaths are God's time, not our time; and the Sabbaths are for our good to teach us the way to peace and life eternal.

All mankind is obligated to obey their Creator Father and to spend time with Him, and that time is specified by our Creator to be the seventh day; Friday sunset to Saturday sunset! which seventh day is to be observed week by week FOREVER! as time to be spent with God in peace and in rest; learning of Him and acknowledging God as Sovereign Creator in a memorial of the completion of creation in six days, the seventh being a rest from that creation and a memorial of that creation.

Exodus 20:8 Remember the sabbath day, to keep it holy. **20:9** Six days shalt thou labour, and do all thy work: **20:10** But the seventh day is the sabbath of the LORD thy God: **in it thou shalt not do any work, thou, nor thy son, nor thy daughter, thy manservant, nor thy maidservant, nor thy cattle, nor thy stranger that** [anyone that you are responsible for] **is within thy gates: 20:11** For in six days the LORD made heaven and earth, the sea, and all that in them is, and rested the seventh day: wherefore the LORD blessed the sabbath day, and hallowed it.

We are not to work on that day and we are not to require or force anyone else to work on the seventh day Sabbath. No one. Not an employee, a slave, a servant, an animal, or even a beast of burden shall be required to do any work on the Sabbath Day, for God Almighty has decreed that the seventh day shall be a rest for all living things forever!

In **Exodus 31:12**, zeal for keeping the Sabbath is emphasized as one sign between God and his people. This sign is for us, so that we may have this weekly time to spend with God and learn of him: "**that ye may know that I am the LORD that doth sanctify you.**"

Exodus 31:12 And the LORD spake unto Moses, saying, **31:13** Speak thou also unto the children of Israel, saying, **Verily my sabbaths ye shall keep: for it is a sign between me and you throughout your generations; that ye may know that I am the LORD that doth sanctify you.**

Today the Assemblies proclaim the Set Apartness of the Sabbath, and then go out to pollute it on a weekly basis: FOR SHAME! They cook, do menial work around the home and pay others to cook and work for them! For Shame, that the brethren for the most part, speak their own words about business and gossip, and do not discuss the Word of the Eternal!

For this sin, God proclaims that we are cut off from HIM, and from being accounted among his people as a part of his collective bride!

31:14 Ye shall keep the sabbath therefore; for it is holy unto you: **every one that defileth it shall surely be put to death: for whosoever doeth any work therein, that soul shall be cut off from among his people.**

The Called Out of Spiritual Israel shall surely be rejected by Christ (Rev 3:14-22) and vomited out of his body into great tribulation, where they will be strongly corrected for defiling the sanctity of God's Sabbath and Holy Days.

31:15 Six days may work be done; but **in the seventh is the sabbath of rest, holy to the LORD: whosoever doeth any work in the sabbath day, he shall surely be put to death. 31:16** Wherefore the children of Israel shall keep the sabbath, to observe the sabbath throughout their generations, for a perpetual covenant.

Keeping the Sabbath, New Moons and Festivals on God's schedule in the way that God has said; acknowledges the absolute authority of God and His Word.

31:17 It is a sign between me and the children of Israel for ever: for in six days the LORD made heaven and earth, and on the seventh day he rested, and was refreshed.

This was a sign between Israel and God; and we must become Israel in the spiritual sense through living by every Word of God (Jer 31).

All the commandments that God gave to physical Israel are equally applicable to all those of the spiritual Israel of the New Covenant; not only in their physical keeping, but in the keeping of the spirit and full intent of those commandments. For Jesus commanded that we are to live by every Word of God the Father (Mat 4:4).

Even as physical Israel was called out of bondage to become the people of God, so the spiritual New Covenant called out people have been called out of bondage to sin to become the people of God. And even as Israel were required to obey their God, spiritual Israel is also required to obey the same God and keep the same commandments.

If we are to be God's people, just as physical Israel was called to be God's people, we must absolutely obey and live by every Word of the same God and do the will of God. The Sabbath was commanded to Adam at creation, and to ALL humanity as Adam's descendants! Not just to the Jews.

What does God will for us to do on His Sabbaths? What does He want us to do with His Holy time?

Isaiah 58:13

Those who make the seventh day Sabbath [Friday sunset to Saturday sunset] their delight and are zealous to keep it in its full sanctity; who reject doing their own pleasure, like participating in sin by buying food and services in restaurants, those who do not cook or do any work or pay others to work [except for doing what God has commanded to be done on Sabbath, and acts of mercy to care for man and beast], are honoring

God their Father in heaven according to the commandments and shall reap a blessing for doing so.

Brethren, we pollute the Sabbath by even speaking of business! We are to speak of the scriptures and holy things and we are NOT to speak of worldliness and our own words; and yes, we are not to gossip about family things either. Save your own words for other times, and use God's time to speak of him.

58:13 If thou turn away thy foot from the sabbath, from doing thy pleasure on my holy day; and call the sabbath a delight, the holy of the LORD, honourable; and shalt honour him, not doing thine own ways, nor finding thine own pleasure, nor speaking thine own words:

When we think about, and hear, and speak of the whole Word of God; we learn of the wondrous perfection of all God's ways; and by following God the Father and Jesus Christ and longing to be with them, learning of them both and keeping all the ways of God, doing all we can to please God and become like our Father and our espoused Husband on HIS Sabbath Day; they will bless us for learning and keeping the whole Word of God.

To go to a service and then do our own thing, and speak our own words the remainder of the day; is to pollute the Sabbath and is SIN! It is dishonoring God our Father and it is STEALING God's time, which is NOT our time, to do as we want with!

To do our own thing and to speak our own words on Sabbath; is to demonstrate to Christ and the Father that we are only attending for social purposes and to experience an emotional feeling of righteousness, of thinking of ourselves as pretty good godly people!

That is SELF-Righteousness and NOT Godly-Righteousness; for godly righteousness would be focusing on the whole word of God and not on our own pleasures on GOD'S DAY!

Isaiah 58:14 Then shalt thou delight thyself in the LORD; and I will cause thee to ride upon the high places of the earth, and feed thee with the heritage of Jacob thy father: for the mouth of the LORD hath spoken it.

On the Sabbath day we are not to do our own pleasure. We are rather to seek out and make the things of God our pleasure; and we are not to speak our own words.

How many times can you remember going to a Sabbath service where you heard a sermon and then you or your friends talked about nothing except recipes and babies and business and weather, and didn't even discuss the sermon? You were speaking your own words and not discussing the scriptures as God commands us. You were polluting the Sabbath Day!

Now obviously it wouldn't be wrong to say it's a nice day, isn't it? But to do that and to speak of other mundane things and completely neglect discussing the Word of God is sin! It is using God's time for our own purposes.

Brethren, I am not saying that we must speak exclusively of scripture, I am saying that our focus should be on God on God's Day; and today we have gotten so far out of balance, that we discuss our own affairs virtually exclusively and completely neglect discussing the Word of God on HIS Sabbath today.

A sermon should be given and then you should search the Scriptures, discuss the sermon, sharpen each other by discussing these things and trying to learn more and understand better. And you should be able to ask your minister to expound things a little more thoroughly on this point. or that point; that you may not have fully grasped. And you should be able to go to your home or perhaps to the homes of your friends and continue to discuss God's Word and the things of God.

If we are spending more time discussing our own things and doing our own pleasure, then we are spending on the things of God, it is not right.

Isaiah says in verse 13, You should not be finding your own pleasure, nor speaking your own words. You should be thinking of and speaking about the things of God. And the truth is that; what comes out of your mouth is a reflection of what's going on in your mind. And if you are not talking about the things of God, chances are about 95 percent that you are not thinking about the things of God and your mind is not on holy things on God's holy Sabbath Day.

The people complain against God instead of seeking His deliverance, and instead they long for the bondage of Egypt.

This is a lesson that Satan tries his best to discourage us to give up the fight against sin, but if we are faithful to live by every Word of God, God will deliver us.

God tests Israel as to whether they are zealous for his Sabbath or not.

Exodus 16:2 And the whole congregation of the children of Israel murmured against Moses and Aaron in the wilderness: **16:3** And the children of Israel said unto them, Would to God we had died by the hand of the LORD in the land of Egypt, when we sat by the flesh pots, and when we did eat bread to the full; for ye have brought us forth into this wilderness, to kill this whole assembly with hunger.

Then the Eternal rained Bread down from heaven; this being an obvious analogy of the spiritual Bread of Life [Jesus Christ and the Word of God], given to men from God in the spiritual wilderness of this world.

16:4 Then said the LORD unto Moses, Behold, I will rain bread from heaven for you; and the people shall go out and gather a certain rate every day, **that I may prove [test] them, whether they will walk in my law, or no.**

God does not prepare food for the people on the Sabbath, revealing that we should also follow the example of God and NOT prepare food on the Sabbath as per God's example. We are to prepare our food on day BEFORE the Sabbath and Holy Days and not to cook on God's Sabbaths and High Days.

16:5 And it shall come to pass, that **on the sixth day they shall prepare that which they bring in; and it shall be twice as much as they gather daily.**

16:6 And Moses and Aaron said unto all the children of Israel, At even, then ye shall know that the LORD hath brought you out from the land of Egypt: **16:7** And in the morning, then ye shall see the glory of the LORD; for that he heareth your murmurings against the LORD: and what are we, that ye murmur against us? **16:8** And Moses said, This shall be, when the LORD shall give you in the evening flesh to eat, and in the morning bread to the full; for that the LORD heareth your murmurings which ye murmur against him: and what are we? your murmurings are not against us, but against the LORD.

Christ then appears to all Israel in his glory [in a bright cloud].

16:9 And Moses spake unto Aaron, Say unto all the congregation of the children of Israel, Come near before the LORD: for he hath heard your murmurings. **16:10** And it came to pass, as Aaron spake unto the whole congregation of the children of Israel, that they looked toward the wilderness, and, behold, the glory of the LORD appeared in the cloud.

Christ promises Israel quails in the evening and heavenly bread in the morning.

16:11 And the LORD spake unto Moses, saying, **16:12** I have heard the murmurings of the children of Israel: speak unto them, saying, At even ye shall eat flesh, and in the morning ye shall be filled with bread; and ye shall know that I am the LORD your God. **16:13** And it came to pass, that at even the quails came up, and covered the camp: and in the morning the dew lay round about the host.

In the morning Israel found small grains and called it: What's this? And Moses told them that it was the food that God had supplied.

16:14 And when the dew that lay was gone up, behold, upon the face of the wilderness there lay a small round thing, as small as the hoar frost [a grainy pebbly material] on the ground. **16:15** And when the children of Israel saw it, they said one to another, It is manna: for they wist not what it was. And Moses said unto them, This is the bread which the LORD hath given you to eat.

Moses commanded the people to gather up this Bread according to the needs of each person every morning, with double on the sixth day to be used on the Sabbath as well as the sixth day.

16:16 This is the thing which the LORD hath commanded, Gather of it every man according to his eating, an omer for every man, according to the number of your persons; take ye every man for them which are in his tents. **16:17** And the children of Israel did so, and gathered, some more, some less. **16:18** And when they did mete it with an omer, he that gathered much had nothing over, and he that gathered little had no lack; they gathered every man according to his eating.

If the regular daily gathering was left overnight until the following morning it would rot and breed worms [maggots].

16:19 And Moses said, Let no man leave of it till the morning.

Yet some could not follow even these simple instructions for the preparation day and the Sabbath Day, which were given to set apart God's Sabbaths with proper preparations on the day before the Sabbaths.

16:20 Notwithstanding they hearkened not unto Moses; but some of them left of it until the morning, and it bred worms [maggots, flies], and stank: and Moses was wroth with them. **16:21** And they **gathered it every morning**, every man according to his eating: and when the sun waxed hot, it melted [evaporated on the open ground in the sun like the dew].

On the sixth day they were to prepare for the Sabbath by collecting one portion for the sixth day and one extra portion for the Sabbath day.

This was to teach us that we are to follow the example of God and we are NOT to cook and prepare food on any Sabbath or High Day, and that we are NOT to pay others to do this for us!

16:22 And it came to pass, that on the sixth day they gathered twice as much bread, two omers for one man: and all the rulers of the congregation came and told Moses. **16:23** And he said unto them, **This is that which the LORD hath said, To morrow is the rest of the holy sabbath unto the LORD: bake that which ye will bake to day, and seethe that ye will seethe; and that which remaineth over lay up for you to be kept until the morning.**

16:24 And they laid it up till the morning, as Moses bade: and it did not stink, neither was there any worm therein. **16:25** And Moses said, **Eat that to day; for to day is a sabbath unto the LORD: to day ye shall not find it in the field.**

16:26 Six days ye shall gather it; but on the seventh day, which is the sabbath, in it there shall be none.

Yet some did not prepare and went out to gather food to cook on the Sabbath Day; as is done in the Ekklesia today.

16:27 And it came to pass, that there went out some of the people on the seventh day for to gather, and they found none.

Then Jesus Christ was very angry with those people who refused to obey him regarding the Sabbath and Holy Days. Later he sent Israel and then Judah into captivity mainly for breaking his Sabbaths. How much more is he angry with us of spiritual Israel who are supposed to love and live by every Word of God?

16:28 And the LORD said unto Moses, **How long refuse ye to keep my commandments and my laws? 16:29 See, for that the LORD hath given you the sabbath, therefore he giveth you on the sixth day the bread of two days; abide ye every man in his place,**

Jesus Christ told the people that they are not to bake or seethe [boil or simmer]. God's people are not to do any kind of cooking on the Sabbath Day. A simple warming of already cooked food with today's modern conveniences like microwaves is alright, but no cooking from the raw to produce a finished item is allowed because of the work involved.

Ladies and gentlemen, God has given everyone a day off from our labors including cooking and housework, so that everyone may have time to learn about godliness. The principle work of many ladies even today is housework; and God wants to give our ladies the day off, as well as the men.

Exodus 16:23 And he said unto them, This is that which the Lord hath said, To morrow is the rest of the holy sabbath unto the Lord: bake that which ye will bake to day, and seethe that ye will seethe; and that which remaineth over lay up for you to be kept until the morning.

The preparation day is Friday up until sunset. And the Sabbath, the seventh day is Saturday. Sabbath runs from sunset Friday to sunset Saturday. And on the Sabbath Day we are not to do any cooking.

We are not to do any work. We are not to do any traveling. We are simply to take the day off and relax. Spend it with God in prayer, in study, in reading, in thinking about Him, and in discussing the words of God with others, and in teaching our mates and our families, and spending the day totally focused on God, and of course also resting on that day, taking it easy.

One should have the attitude of saying, "This is my day off, I'm glad I don't have to do this or that." It is wrong to have the attitude that "Oh, I can't do this and I shouldn't do that" and taking a negative approach. Take a positive approach and say, "It's my day off, it's my break. I don't have to go out and mow the lawn. I don't have to get up early and go to work. I don't have to bake bread today. I can take it easy and relax."

Now, what about the lady who says, "Cooking relaxes me, I enjoy it." Or the man who says "Working on my car relaxes me, or I enjoy it."

We are to make the things of God our pleasure and we are not to seek out and do our own pleasures, even if we enjoy those things.

After all, why would they be our pleasures if we didn't enjoy them? Of course we enjoy our own pleasures. But we are not to do our own pleasures on God's Sabbath, or on a High Holy Day. We are to dedicate that time to the things of God. On the Sabbath Day, we are not to work, we are not to cook, we are not to engage in travel; and we are not to pay others to serve us either!

What about the person who has to drive 30 or 40 miles to attend a service? The time to walk from the outskirts of the camp to the tabernacle in the wilderness was probably about one hour and one should not spend much more than one hour driving to services on a Sabbath. Be sure to fill up your gas tank on Friday and prepare a little boxed lunch on Friday. Do your preparation on Friday.

If you have to drive a few miles, to associate with the brethren and hear a message, that's fine. Only don't decide you're going to fly to Australia from Britain on a Sabbath or that you are going to take a bus trip across the continent on a Sabbath.

No, absolutely not. No extensive travel and no travel for personal reasons. Travel should be for Godly reasons, should be very, very limited in scope and duration; and should not involve any expense. If you have to buy an extra tank of gas on a Sabbath, the trip is too far. Don't go. Make some kind of other arrangement. It can be done. Things can be worked out. You can work around these things and truly make God's Sabbath a delight.

If you have to drive for four or five hours in each direction to attend the service, such a trip is not a Sabbath rest and is not appropriate. Perhaps it could be arranged to travel on Friday afternoon or Friday evening before sunset and to stay with some of the brethren in the town where the service is being held.

There are different things that can be arranged. Perhaps it would be better to stay at home and simply listen to a tape or a recording. Perhaps one can alternate and one can go one week and then people can come to your town the next week. There are lots of ideas that an inquiring and motivated mind can come up with. But we are not to do our own pleasure on the Sabbath Day.

Nehemiah on buying on the Sabbath

In the time of Nehemiah, some of the Jewish people in Jerusalem had strayed far from God.

In Nehemiah 10:31 they were told by Nehemiah that if the people of the land brought ware [goods] or victuals [food] on the Sabbath Day to sell, we should not buy it of them on a Sabbath or on a Holy Day. And that we should leave the seventh year and the exaction of every debt.

We should be willing to forgive debts especially on the seventh year, which is the Land Sabbath. But on the Sabbath Day, people shall not buy or sell. And the people agreed to that instruction from God in Nehemiah 10:31.

Then after returning from visiting the king, Nehemiah sees a great evil being done in working and buying on the Sabbath, this same wickedness is openly practiced in the major Groups calling themselves God's people today.

It was for this sin [among other sins] that Israel and Judah went into captivity, and it is for the sin of calling the Sabbath holy and then openly polluting it for their own pleasure, that today's Church of God will go into the captivity and correction of the Great Tribulation in the very near future.

Nehemiah 13:15 In those days saw I in Judah some treading wine presses on the sabbath, and bringing in sheaves, and lading asses; as also wine, grapes, and figs, and all manner of burdens, which they brought into Jerusalem on the sabbath day: and I testified against them in the day wherein they sold victuals [food and drink on the Sabbath].

13:16 There dwelt men of Tyre also therein, which brought fish, and all manner of ware, and **sold on the sabbath** unto the children of Judah, and in Jerusalem.

13:17 Then I contended with the nobles of Judah, and said unto them, **What evil thing is this that ye do, and profane the sabbath day? 13:18 Did not your fathers thus, and did not our God bring all this evil upon us, and upon this city? yet ye bring more wrath upon Israel by profaning the Sabbath.**

Nehemiah then enforces the Sabbath.

13:19 And it came to pass, that when the gates of Jerusalem began to be dark before the sabbath, I commanded that **the gates should be shut, and charged that they should not be opened till after the sabbath: and some of my servants set I at the gates, that there should no burden be brought in on the sabbath day.**

13:20 So the merchants and sellers of all kind of ware lodged without Jerusalem once or twice.

Then Nehemiah threatened the sellers. We cannot threaten physical violence today, but we certainly can warn the brethren to avoid the sin of buying food and drink [or anything else] on the Sabbath, and remind them that Almighty God will reject them into great correction and violence if they will not sincerely repent.

13:21 Then I testified against them, and said unto them, Why lodge ye about the wall? if ye do so again, I will lay hands on you. From that time forth came they no more on the sabbath.

Nehemiah as a leader used force to keep the sellers out of the city on the Sabbath; Jesus Christ will use force to correct the wickedness of Sabbath pollution in the very near future.

13:22 And I commanded the Levites that they should cleanse themselves, and that they should come and keep the gates, to sanctify the sabbath day.

Remember me, O my God, concerning this also, and spare me according to the greatness of thy mercy.

Nehemiah writes that he is very zealous for the holy Sabbath Day of the Eternal Creator God. And he asked God to be merciful to him because of his zeal for the Sabbath in keeping out those who would buy and sell on the Sabbath Day.

Brethren we are not to buy on the Sabbath Day. We are not to pay others to serve us on the Sabbath Day. We are not to go in the stores and buy things. We are not to go into restaurants to buy goods and services. We are not to travel. We are not to do heavy cooking. We are not to work. And we are not to be responsible for anyone else having to work on God's Sabbath Day.

The sixth day is the day of PREPARATION for the Sabbath. On the sixth day we are to do all our cooking, cleaning and household labour in preparation for the Sabbath rest.

We are NOT to COOK or PREPARE FOOD (Ex 16:23) on the Sabbath, or to travel (Ex 16:29). We are not to do any work or even to bear burdens on penalty of death and destruction (Jer 17:21-27). For the Sabbath is God's time, not our time, it is HOLY TIME, it is NOT our own. To do our own pleasures is to STEAL from God something that belongs to Him.

It is lawful to seek the things of God on the weekly and annual Sabbaths; To pray and study His Word, to meet together in holy convocation (Lev 23:3) with like-minded believers. To do good (Luk 6:9), by healing or visiting the sick and elderly and to alleviate the suffering of man and beast. It is lawful to cope with genuine emergencies, like fire, broken pipes or the ox in the ditch (Luk 14:5), but beware of using the excuse "this is an emergency" to justify habitual Sabbath breaking. If an ox falls into a ditch many times, one should perhaps repair one's fence! That is to say, most of these so called emergencies come through a simple LACK OF PROPER PREPARATION.

It is also not wrong to find a beautiful or peaceful place to meditate Acts 16:13 and relax, enjoying God's creation, but we must not meet in the buildings - high places - of false religions.

A convocation is ONLY holy if it is God centered! If you go to a service to hear a sermon and then talk ONLY about work and business, the weather, clothes and babies you have PROFANED that convocation and God's Sabbath.

Out of one's mouth come those things that are dearest to one's heart (Mat 12:34). If your heart and mind are not on the things of God, your mouth will reveal this. We should be thinking deeply and discussing the things of God always, especially on the Sabbath. How do you ever expect to begin to UNDERSTAND the things of God, if you do not think and talk about them?

Behold, God will preserve those who think upon His name and make it their pleasure to do God's will (Ezek 9:4-6, Mal 3:16-18).

It is NOT LAWFUL to buy goods and services in restaurants or other establishments. To say that we may buy, because they are going to work anyway, makes a mockery of God's way. For that excuse justifies ALL SIN; because there is NO SIN that men are not going to do ANYWAY! Shall we use the whore because she will do it anyway. Why not have our enemy murdered, for the killer will kill anyway. This is a juvenile and pathetic excuse to justify SIN.

If we say that we are not paying restaurant employees directly, we must admit that we are paying the establishment that hired them. So we are admitting that we are paying the establishment to induce people to sin!

We have CONDEMNED OURSELVES with our own mouths! If we would not work for them on the Sabbath in order to obey God and WE PAY THEM TO HIRE OTHERS ON THE SABBATH, WE ARE HYPOCRITES. There is no other word for it. If we pay others to do what we would not do ourselves, on moral grounds; WE HAVE BECOME HYPOCRITES!

To say that because we have an emergency "ox in our ditch", it somehow justifies painting our house on the Sabbath is ridiculous! Yet some say the very same thing by saying that because they have to cross a toll bridge on the Sabbath to attend a service, it somehow justifies them buying goods and services in restaurants! This excuse is also ridiculous! THE ONE, DOES NOT JUSTIFY THE OTHER!

Some may think that proper Sabbath observance is some kind of burden that God's people should not have to bear. Yet these same people say to the poor man. You must tithe, have FAITH and God will work things out for you.

Where is Our Faith?

If we make an HONEST EFFORT TO PLEASE GOD, don't you think that He WILL HELP us? Most problems involving Sabbath pollution through buying and selling can be resolved simply and easily, with a little forethought, planning and effort. I have avoided this sin for forty years and it has been difficult at times but God has always provided a way.

If we lose a job, God will provide, and if he chooses to test us and does not provide; it is better to die serving the God who is able to raise us up; than to live serving wickedness and be cast into the fire of eternal death!

As for meals, some bread and cheese and fruit, together with each other and our God, would make for an uplifting evening. And probably a healthier one as well! For far too long. the church has been more of a social club then an Ekklesia of GOD! It's time we became more GOD CENTERED and less concerned with social activities. Yes social things are important but the central thing should be OUR GOD. How we impress Him is far more important then how much we impress each other!

Did you think that God created the Sabbath for our hurt? It was made for our benefit, the benefit of all mankind. You should enjoy the Sabbath, but you should not infringe upon the potential enjoyment of this blessing by others. Remember that the burden of Christ is light and His yoke is easy Mat 11:30, it is Satan who comes along and tries to make the burden SEEM HEAVY by persecuting us.

When you can fully understand that Satan is the true source of all our heavy burdens, the true source of SIN, which causes our sufferings and that God's way is really liberating us from that burden, you will have no problem in keeping ALL GOD'S COMMANDMENTS! It is by the doing that we learn! By the proper observance of the Sabbath, we may learn many things and we will show our God how very much we LOVE HIM and HIS WAYS! On the other hand, by not keeping the Sabbath in the commanded manner, are we really keeping it at all, when we do not keep it in a manner acceptable to God?

What can we learn? Why FAITH and TRUST in GOD, as well as all those things that we learn in our studies, meditations and talks. Remember that the Holy Spirit is given to those who obey Him (Acts 5:32) and that it is that Spirit which shall lead you into the truth (Joh 16:13). If you want to know the things of God, you must keep all the commandments of God, in all things, and be pleasing to HIM (1 Joh 3:22).

Because of the complete lack of zeal for the commandments of God, including the Sabbath; God has withdrawn his Spirit from many today. It is those who claim to have the Holy Spirit the most; who have the least; because of their sins against the Word of God.

God's day is a day of rest for all His creation, for all the creation of God. It is a time of rest and it is sanctified to be holy time so that all men could spend time with God. And if all men did observe the Sabbath Day, and did rest on that day, and did seek the Eternal with all their hearts, believe me, they would find the way to peace, which at present time they know not.

Pentecost

Pentecost

The Feast of Pentecost is much more than a picture of the start of the New Testament Ekklesia; it is a prophecy for the future.

Pentecost is also a memorial of the start of the Mosaic Covenant and it is also prophetic; looking forward to the establishment of the New Covenant in its fullness with all flesh after the coming of Jesus Christ with his saints and the establishment of the Kingdom of God over all the earth.

Yes, friends, on the Feast of Pentecost in the wilderness of Sinai; Moses and Israel entered into the Mosaic Covenant of marriage with the Being who later gave up his God-hood to be made flesh as Jesus Christ.

The Mosaic theocratic government of Israel was established at Sinai on the Feast of First fruits, called Pentecost.

This as an allegory that a New Covenant would be initially established on a small way on this very Feast of First Fruits in 31 A.D.; and on a latter Feast of Pentecost, the New Covenant would be expanded to all flesh then living, with the humbling of humanity, repentance and the pouring out of God's Spirit on all flesh (Joel 2:28).

Over a thousand years after the Mosaic Covenant was established, on the Feast of First Fruits called Pentecost; in 31 A.D. the New Covenant of First Fruits was officially confirmed with the public pouring out of God's Spirit upon a few called out to be first fruits of God's New Covenant.

On a soon coming latter day Feast of Pentecost, God's Spirit will be poured out on all flesh living at that time (Joel 2:28) extending the New Covenant to all humanity.

Later on in the fall, the fall festivals picture the resurrection and the bringing in of the main harvest in Palestine, as an allegory of the great main harvest of all who have lived and died never having known or understood anything regarding God.

Then all of humanity who have lived and died in bondage to sin, will be resurrected to flesh and will have their minds opened to godliness. Then most will sincerely repent and be given God's Spirit; and they will also be brought into the Kingdom of God, into the Family of God.

The fall festivals are about the main fall harvest: While the spring festivals are about the early harvest, the first fruits harvest.

There are TWO harvests of humanity, a smaller early harvest pictured by the spring festivals, and the later main harvest represented by the fall festivals!

A small part of the early harvest is resurrected at the end of six thousand years; however those living into or born during the millennium are also first fruits. They do not die and then await a future resurrection to be a part of the main harvest; for they will be repentant and will be given God's Spirit and will qualify for a change to spirit or condemnation at the end of their physical lives.

The completion of the first fruits harvest is at the END of the millennial rest; at the end of the first full seven thousand years.

That is why Pentecost is called the Feast of First Fruits; because the future Feast of Pentecost immediately after the Day of the Lord; continues and expands the early harvest of first fruits right through the Millennium!

On Pentecost:

Leviticus 23:17 Ye shall bring out of your habitations **two wave loaves** of two tenth deals; they shall be of fine flour; they shall be **baken with leaven; they are the firstfruits** unto the LORD.

Notice that while the Wave Offering [and ALL other "meat" offerings] is made without leaven; signifying the sinlessness of Christ, these two loaves are baked with leaven, meaning that sin is present. We therefore know that they cannot refer to Christ, or to the resurrected saints, now perfect in total unity of mind and spirit with God the Father and Jesus Christ.

These two loaves must then represent an INCREASE of the early spring harvest with the multitudes through the millennium who have sincerely repented at the coming of Christ and have had God's Spirit poured out on all flesh, yet still needing to completely overcome all sin (Joel 2:28).

The two loaves representing increase are made with leaven, showing that they are not yet perfected; and that they represent an expansion [an increase] of the early harvest into family of God.

Joel 2:28 And it shall come to pass afterward, that I will pour out my spirit upon all flesh; and your sons and your daughters shall prophesy, your old men shall dream dreams, your young men shall see visions:

We know from John 20:22 that Christ gave the Holy Spirit to his disciples on Wave Sheaf Sunday immediately AFTER his return from God the Father. We also know that many had been given God's Spirit since Abel; in Faith that Christ would complete his mission; however God poured out his Spirit publicly and on many people seeking him at Pentecost in 31 A.D.

Acts 2:14 But Peter, standing up with the [other 11 meaning the whole 12 were present] eleven, lifted up his voice, and said unto them,

Peter's sermon could well be an example of the sermons that will be preached to people all over the earth when God's Spirit is poured out on all flesh and the Kingdom of God is established by Jesus Christ and his bride on a near future Feast of Pentecost.

Ye men of Judaea, and all ye that dwell at Jerusalem, be this known unto you, and hearken to my words: **2:15** For these are not drunken, as ye suppose, seeing it is but the third hour [9 am] of the day.

2:16 But this is that which was spoken by the prophet Joel; **2:17** And it shall come to **pass in the last days, saith God, I will pour out of my Spirit upon all flesh:** and your sons and your daughters shall prophesy, and your young men shall see visions, and your old men shall dream dreams:

2:18 And on my servants and on my handmaidens I will pour out in those days of my Spirit; and they shall prophesy: **2:19 And I will shew wonders**

in heaven above, and signs in the earth beneath; blood, and fire, and vapour of smoke: 2:20 The sun shall be turned into darkness, and the moon into blood, before the great and notable day of the Lord come: **2:21** And it shall come to pass, that whosoever shall call on the name of the Lord shall be saved.

Let me ask: Was 31 A.D. the "last days"? Was God's Spirit poured out on ALL flesh in 31 A.D.? Did the heavenly signs quoted by Peter take place in 31 A.D.? Was the day of the Lord in 31 A.D.?

NO! However Peter by quoting Joel, was revealing that the events of 31 A.D. were a precursor to the events to come on the future day of the Lord and immediately afterwards; when the people would repentantly welcome the coming of Christ with his saints, and God's Spirit would be poured out on all flesh on a future day of Pentecost!

The Feast of Pentecost was the start of the Theocracy of physical Israel: and IT WILL BE the beginning of the Theocracy of the Kingdom of God!

The resurrection will come on the sixth day of Unleavened Bread; to be followed by the marriage supper in heaven while the seven last plagues are poured out! To be capped off by the coming of Christ with his saints to rule the earth in righteousness, and after they have subdued the earth and removed Satan and his angelic followers; God's Spirit will be poured out on a repentant humanity and on all flesh when the very day of Pentecost has come!

Brethren, Peter preached the true Gospel on that first century Feast of Pentecost, as it will be preached to all nations and peoples on a soon coming future Feast of Pentecost!!

We know that all of these things did not happen in their fullness in 31 A.D. and that Christ did not return at that time; therefore Peter was referring to that Pentecost as a symbolic event presaging a later and much bigger fulfillment!

The two loaves waved before God on Pentecost are made with leaven showing the presence of sin; therefore they must be accompanied by a Sin Offering

Leviticus 23:18 And ye shall offer with the bread seven lambs without blemish of the first year, and one young bullock, and two rams: they shall be for a burnt offering unto the LORD, with their meat offering, and their drink offerings, even an offering made by fire, of sweet savour unto the LORD.

The burnt offerings picture the devotion and work of Christ in bringing in the harvest of humanity for God the Father. These offerings being wholly burned, they picture Christ's total devotion in serving God the Father, and the ascending smoke as a sweet smell pictures that the service of Christ is a very sweet and pleasurable thing to the Father.

23:19 Then ye shall sacrifice **one kid of the goats for a sin offering**, and two lambs of the first year for a sacrifice of peace offerings.

The two leaves being covered by a sin offering followed by a peace offering, showing that reconciliation had been made between the people and God the Father and peace had come between man and God.

These were not offerings brought by individuals, but were offerings made by the High Priest on behalf of all the people.

23:20 And the priest shall wave them with the bread of the firstfruits for a wave offering before the LORD, with the two lambs: they shall be holy to the LORD for the priest.

On the Feast of First Fruits [Pentecost] no work of any kind may be done except that which is commanded or specifically allowed by God.

23:21 And ye shall proclaim on the selfsame day, that it may be an holy convocation unto you: ye shall do no servile [no work of any kind] work therein: it shall be a statute for ever in all your dwellings throughout your generations.

> 1) The harvest of first fruits began with Jesus Christ being resurrected and accepted by God the Father on Wave Offering Sunday; as the first of many brethren.
>
> 2) The marriage covenant theocracy of Israel began at Sinai on Pentecost, when the law was written on tables of stone and given to the people.
>
> 3) On Pentecost in 31 A.D. God's Spirit was poured out on some and the law was written on their hearts, as an example of what would happen to all flesh then living on a future Pentecost.

4) After the day of the Lord and the destruction of all resistance with the removal of Satan; the Millennial Theocracy of God will be established with ALL nations grafted into a spiritual Israel and called into the New Covenant (Jer 31:31) and the pouring out of God's Spirit on ALL flesh (Joel 2:28); and the writing of God's law on our hearts on tables of flesh and not stone.

Jeremiah 31:31 Behold, the days come, saith the LORD, that I will make a new covenant with the house of Israel, and with the house of Judah: **31:32** Not according to the covenant that I made with their fathers in the day that I took them by the hand to bring them out of the land of Egypt; which my covenant they brake, although I was an husband unto them, saith the LORD:

The Word of God is the constitution of the Kingdom of God. If we are called and we accept the call into the New Covenant, then we will have the law and Word of God written on our hearts through the Holy Spirit of God and we will be keeping and living by every Word of God (Mat 4:4).

31:33 But this shall be the covenant that I will make with the house of Israel; After those days, saith the LORD, I will put my law in their inward parts, and write it in their hearts; and will be their God, and they shall be my people. 31:34 And they shall teach no more every man his neighbour, and every man his brother, saying, Know the LORD: for they shall all know me [Then all flesh shall be at ONE in spiritual unity with God the Father and Jesus Christ through the zealous keeping of every Word of God.], **from the least of them unto the greatest of them, saith the LORD: for I will forgive their iniquity, and I will remember their sin no more.**

The Mighty One of Jacob declares that the law of God and the whole Word of God are permanent and will last forever. This was quoted by Jesus Christ.

Matthew 5:18 For verily I say unto you, Till heaven and earth pass, one jot or one tittle shall in no wise pass from the law, till all be fulfilled [the word and law of God will be fulfilled (that is KEPT) forever!].

As long as Israel [including spiritual Israel] exists; the whole Word of God will be kept in enthusiastic zeal! All those who depart from any part of the Word of God will be corrected, and if they will not repent, they shall be destroyed forever.

Jeremiah 31:35 Thus saith the LORD, which giveth the sun for a light by day, and the ordinances of the moon and of the stars for a light by night, which divideth the sea when the waves thereof roar; The LORD of hosts is his name: **31:36 If those ordinances depart from before me,** saith the LORD, then the seed of Israel also shall cease from being a nation before me for ever.

31:37 Thus saith the LORD; If heaven above can be measured [by physical man], and the foundations of the earth searched out beneath, I will also cast off all the seed of Israel for all that they have done, saith the LORD.

Pentecost; Hearts of Stone Hearts of Flesh

On the Feast of Pentecost at Sinai, the law was written on tables of stone, and in 31 A.D. the law of God was officially written on the hearts of flesh of the called out!

In a near future Pentecost the law of God will be written on the hearts of all mankind then living. This will begin the New Covenant with all Israel and will be extended to all humanity as all mankind then living is grafted into a kind of spiritual Israel and the spiritual New Covenant.

Jeremiah 31:31 Behold, the days come, saith the LORD, that I will make a new covenant with the house of Israel, and with the house of Judah: **31:32** Not according to the covenant that I made with their fathers in the day that I took them by the hand to bring them out of the land of Egypt; which my covenant they brake, although I was an husband unto them, saith the LORD:

31:33 But this shall be the covenant that I will make with the house of Israel; After those days, saith the LORD, I will put my law in their inward parts, and write it in their hearts; and will be their God, and they shall be my people. **31:34** And they shall teach no more every man his neighbour, and every man his brother, saying, Know the LORD: **for they shall all know me, from the least of them unto the greatest of them, saith the LORD: for I will forgive their iniquity, and I will remember their sin no more.**

Jeremiah was not alone for Ezekiel wrote about this promise of God saying:

Ezekiel 11:17 Therefore say, Thus saith the Lord GOD; I will even gather you from the people, and assemble you out of the countries where ye have been scattered, and I will give you the land of Israel. **11:18** And they shall come thither, and they shall take away all the detestable things thereof and all the abominations thereof from thence.

11:19 And I will give them one heart, and I will put a new spirit within you; and I will take the stony heart out of their flesh, and will give them an heart of flesh: 11:20 That they may walk in my statutes, and keep mine ordinances, and do them: and they shall be my people, and I will be their God.

The Pentecost of 31 A.D. was about the giving of the Holy Spirit to the called out in an official and public manner; writing the Word of God on the hearts of the called out and fulfilling the promise of a New Covenant.

Later at a near future Pentecost the Holy Spirit of the New Covenant will be poured out on all Israel and upon all flesh; extending the calling out to all mankind still living on that future Pentecost, writing the Word of God on the hearts of mankind still living and establishing the Kingdom of God on the earth (Joel 2:27-28).

We have become confused by considering ourselves first fruits and not understanding that those called during the millennium [after the resurrection to spirit] are also first fruits; for the seventh day is still part of the same week of first fruits!

During the millennium, humanity will be called out and will have God's Spirit poured out on them, writing the Word of God on their hearts; and being changed to spirit or destroyed at 100 years old; thus completing the full seven thousand year harvest of first fruits. Then after the millennium comes the main harvest.

Leviticus 23:16 unto the morrow after the seventh Sabbath, you shall number 50 days; and you shall offer a new offering. And you shall bring out of your habitations two wave loaves of two tenth deals; they shall be of fine flour; they shall be baked with leaven.

Leaven is a type or picture of sin.

Leaven in these two Pentecost loaves demonstrates the presence of sin, which requires atonement with a sin offering.

The two loaves picture an increase from the one loaf at Wave Offering, to two loaves at Pentecost. It wasn't necessary to have hundreds or thousands or millions of loaves added to represent everybody. Instead two loaves were to give the picture of increase.

23:21 and you shall proclaim on the selfsame day, [which is the 50th day, a Sunday;] that it may be a holy convocation unto you: you shall do no servile work therein. And the word servile means work of any kind. It shall be a statute forever in all your dwellings throughout your generations.

The offering of these two loaves, the special lifting up and bringing back down of these two loaves, made with the leaven of sin; was to take place on the 50th day after the first unleavened wave loaf representing Christ was raised up.

Two loaves are offered picturing INCREASE; they are to be made with leaven picturing some sin still needing to be overcome, which is in turn covered by a sin offering.

This offering does not picture the resurrection of the first fruits who have been called to God over the past 6,000 years.

This offering and the Feast of Pentecost pictures;

1. The formal establishment of the New Covenant, which happened on Pentecost in the first century as described in the book of Acts, and

2. It pictures the expansion of the first fruits to all of humanity then living with the pouring out of God's Spirit on all flesh (Joel 2:28) on a future Pentecost to begin and fulfill the remaining seventh day [the 7th one thousand year] of the Spring Harvest of First Fruits called out since Abel.

The Feast of Unleavened Bread is not just six days long, it is seven days long. Yes, there is a resurrection to spirit at the end of the sixth day [at the end of 6,000 years], but the remainder of the first fruits harvest continues through the remaining 7th one thousand years.

1. Pentecost pictures the pouring out of God's Spirit on all flesh and at the END of that day the beginning of the Kingdom of God on the earth; The formal beginning of the New Covenant in the first century, and

2. The establishment of the kingdom of God over all the earth after Messiah the Christ comes. and the New Covenant being expanded to include all flesh.

50 is the first day after 49; 49 being seven times seven is a complete, absolutely complete, period of time; with fifty picturing a NEW Beginning.

The 50th day then meant a new beginning for mankind and an increase of the people of God.

Now notice the atoning sin offering sacrifice, which was offered in conjunction with both of these loaves. At this time the people's sin being represented by the leaven, is covered by the sin offering made on behalf of both of the loaves.

This then represents an increase then in the family of God, an increase in the first fruits for it is written in Leviticus 23:17, the last line, "this is the first fruits unto the Lord."

The two loaves represent an increase in the New Covenant calling and writing of the Word of God on the hearts of man; with the leaven within the loaves representing sin; for we must still overcome sin by the power of the Holy Spirit to write God's law on our hearts.

Sin then being covered by the sin offering representing the sacrifice of Jesus Christ; we are then empowered to overcome all sin and to write the word of God on our hearts, if we so desire, and if we follow the Spirit of God to learn and to keep the whole Word of God.

These two loaves represent the physical first fruits called to God during the millennium having some sin left to overcome, but having that sin atoned for and covered through the sacrifice of Jesus Christ.

Therefore the two loaves do not speak of the already resurrected chosen, but represent an increase in the first fruits, when God's Spirit is poured out on a still imperfect humanity at the establishment of the kingdom of God over all humanity at Pentecost beginning the millennial Kingdom of God.

Paul tells us: **Colossians 2:16** let no man therefore judge or condemn you in meat, or in drink, or in respect of a holyday, or of the new moon, or of the Sabbath days: Which are a shadow of things to come.

Paul tells us that Holy Days, New Moons and Sabbaths are shadows of things to come. They are prophetic in nature and there is going to be a fulfillment of these things.

Therefore we know that the wave offering was fulfilled by the ascension to be accepted for us by God the Father and the immediate return for 40 days of Jesus Christ. Therefore on a future literal day of Pentecost, there will be a fulfillment of these things, extending the New Covenant to all humanity (Joel 2:28).

This is to be a New Covenant with all ISRAEL; which has not happened yet! And this writing of God's Word on the hearts of Israel, beings them into a SPIRITUAL New Covenant; and all mankind will be grafted into that Spiritual Israel.

In the first century the Holy Spirit was given to the spiritually called out of both Jew and Gentile; and the Holy Spirit shall be poured out on all flesh (Joel 2:28); after the day of the Lord.

On that Feast of Pentecost, there will be a substantial increase within the potential family of God as God's Spirit of the New Covenant is poured out on all flesh (Joel 2:28); and God's Word is written on the hearts of all humanity.

We can now see how this is coming about, by turning to Acts 2 and when the day of Pentecost was fully come, they were all with one accord or one mind, in one place. And suddenly there came a sound from heaven as of a rushing mighty wind, and it filled all the house where they were sitting. And there appeared unto them cloven tongues like as of fire, and it sat upon each of them. And they were all filled with the Holy Ghost, and began to speak with other tongues, other languages, as the Spirit gave them utterance.

The Spirit of God is a gift from God; the gift of God's very nature, truth and the mind of God; enabling us to keep the law of God which is a spiritual law.

Romans 7:14 For we know that the law is spiritual:

When we have repented and turned away from sin [which is breaking and compromising with God's law], we can then be reconciled to God by the application of the sacrifice of Christ; then God can give his nature to those reconciled to him, so that they may internalize his mind, nature, commandments, spirit and actions; writing them on the hearts of humanity.

This Spirit is NOT a person; and however various people choose to describe it; it is NOT something that we whip up for ourselves. Otherwise the disciples would not have need of it to be given to them, having already been taught the things of God directly by Christ. [Surely, in their zeal for God and Christ, they could have whipped up the Spirit for themselves if that were possible.]

And there were dwelling at Jerusalem Jews, devout men, out of every nation under heaven. Now, when this was noised about, the multitude came together, and were confounded.

They were astonished because every person heard them speaking in his own language. These people were not speaking some gobbledygook or babbling away in some spastic emotional ecstasy. They were speaking in the languages of men, and it was being heard in the languages of all the earth; in the genuine languages of men. People were hearing God's Word preached to them in their own language.

And they were all amazed and marveled, saying one to another, Behold, are not all these which speak Galileans? And how hear we every man in our own tongue, our own language wherein we were born? Parthians, and Medes, and Elamites and the dwellers of Mesopotamia, and in Judaea, and Cappadocia, in Pontus, and Asia, and many others including Cretes and Arabians and Romans.

2:11 we do hear them speak in our [language] tongues the wonderful works and deeds of God. And they were all amazed, and were in doubt, saying one to another: What does this mean? Well, some mocking said, these men are full of new wine.

But Peter, standing up with the 11, [11 apostles, the totaling 12 including Peter], lifted up his voice, and said unto them, You men of Judaea, and all you that dwell at Jerusalem, be this known unto you, and hearken to my words: For these are not drunken, as you suppose, being it is about the third hour of the day, which by the reckoning of the time would be about 9am. But this is that which was spoken by the prophet Joel. And Peter [now quoting Joel 2:23], spoke, and it shall come to pass in the last days, saith God, I will pour out of my Spirit upon all flesh.

Notice at this Feast of Pentecost, in the first century A.D.: Was God's Spirit poured out on all flesh? No it wasn't.

Does all flesh have God's spirit today? No they don't. What is Peter talking about here?

He is quoting Joel 2:28, and the events in Acts, were a down payment, an earnest; a first little bit to demonstrate to everyone that this was still going to happen in future. A little bit then, a lot more in the future.

This prophecy regarding Joel 2:28, that God will pour out his Spirit on all flesh has still to be fulfilled. It was fulfilled only in part on the day of Pentecost in the first century where Peter was speaking. And Peter goes on to quote Joel: and I will show wonders in heaven above and signs in the earth beneath, blood, and fire, and vapor and smoke. The sun shall be turned into darkness, and the moon into blood, before the great and notable day of the Lord come. And it shall come to pass, that whosoever shall call upon the name of the eternal shall be saved.

Did this happen in those days? Were all of these signs and wonders done in Peter's day? No, they weren't.

This is taking about the last days, the end of the age. And at the day of the Lord, when the day of the Lord is over and the Kingdom of God is established; He will pour out his spirit upon all flesh.

Which is why the lion will lie down with the lamb and the child shall play on the hole of the serpent because all flesh, that's not even just human beings but all flesh will be given a spirit of peace and calmness. And the very nature of all creatures including man and also the vicious beast will be changed into a nature, a peaceable nature.

God will pour out his Spirit on all flesh and the Kingdom will be established on the earth, ushering in a period of 1000 years of peace and prosperity unknown to mankind before that time.

A wonderful period; a Sabbath of rest for the people of God: In which all people shall be called out as the Millennial Sabbath First Fruits, and have God's Spirit poured out on them, and the Word of God written on their hearts instead of on tables of stone!

There will be rest from Satan, rest from sin, rest from wickedness and all people will rejoice with their God, and the faithful will be changed to spirit at the age of 100 years.

The Mosaic Covenant was entered into between God and Israel on the Feast of First Fruits, the Feast of Pentecost. In that Covenant, the law of God was written on tables of Stone, and physical Israel having hearts of flint and not of flesh could not keep the Word of God in its spirit and intent or even in the letter.

This was only a fore-type of the spiritual New Covenant of Jeremiah 31 which will also begin on the Feast of Pentecost between God and physical Israel; into which all the Gentiles will be grafted.

Just as those called out to godliness over the past 6,000 years have had to grapple with sin, and humanity in the millennium will have to overcome their own tendencies, which is why the loaves are made with leaven.

Now, we know that people had God's Spirit long before this. That people like Abel and Enoch and Elijah and Moses, all had God's Spirit. And they were given that Spirit by God in faith that Jesus Christ would complete his mission and offer himself as a sacrifice.

The Lamb of God sacrificed from the foundations of the world, would be fulfilled and those people called in faith that Christ would in fact complete the job of atoning for the sins of men. For it is only through repentance and turning away from sin that God's Spirit will be given to men, for God's Spirit is given only to those who obey God.

Acts 5:32 and we are his witnesses of these things; and so is also the Holy Spirit, whom God hath given to those that obey him. **The Holy Spirit is given to those who obey God**.

Spiritual things are spiritually discerned: **1 Corinthians 2:14** the natural, normal, carnal man receiveth not the things of the Spirit of God: for the things of God are foolishness unto them: neither can they know them or understand them, because such things are spiritually discerned.

We must have God's Spirit in order to discern the things of God: And since we know that Moses and Elijah and Abel and Enoch and Noah, understood and discerned many of the things of God. We know that they had God's Spirit.

God's Spirit was given to them in faith that Christ would fulfill this mission of being a sacrifice and of making atonement for the sins of men: By first living the perfect sinless life himself and then allowing himself to be killed for the sins of others.

Afterwards he was raised up by God the Father and then ascended to God the Father to be accepted for us. After which he came down for forty days to demonstrate, and reveal to people that he had indeed been resurrected. After which he ascended back to the Father, where he ministers as our High Priest, our Intercessor and our Mediator; between us and the Father, between us and God: Thus allowing us to have access to God.

Jesus Christ is our High Priest forever, after the order of Melchizedek: This means that he has restored the original pre-Aaron Melchizedek priesthood.

Jesus Christ has become High Priest, and as our High Priest, bringing before God the Father his own self, his own perfect sacrifice; as atonement for our sins and interceding between us and the Father, interceding with the Father on our behalf so that we might be forgiven and made acceptable to God.

No, the ministry today are not some kind of New Covenant Levite, or some advanced, new age kind of Levite, or anything that is a part of the Mosaic covenant; which was a covenant of death, because it offered no spiritual salvation only physical blessings.

We are now under the priesthood of Melchizedek, the priesthood of Jesus Christ. He is our High Priest: Not Aaron.

And he is our sacrifice for sin: Not some physical lambs, bullocks and goats. Jesus Christ was the perfect sacrifice. And having accomplished that perfect sacrifice he was deemed worthy to become our High Priest, interceding and mediating with God the Father on our behalf.

Today, every person who is converted and has God's Spirit, is in the process of having God's Word written on their hearts, and in training to become priests under the High Priest. We are all training to become priests forever after the order of Melchizedek, under our High Priest Jesus Christ.

That is our calling; that is why the Scripture says, you shall become kings and priests of our God. We are going to become kings and priests if we overcome all sin; becoming priests forever after the order of Melchizedek under our High Priest, Jesus Christ.

This is the message of the Apostle Paul throughout the entire book of Hebrews. It is an explanation of a change, or the change, in the priesthood; from the priesthood of Aaron back to the priesthood of Melchizedek.

Yes, there is a New Covenant. It is a Covenant as Paul writes in Hebrews, where God will place his law in our hearts and in our minds.

It is a Covenant where there is an efficacious atonement, an effective sacrifice for sin: Which actually does fulfill the need for a complete and total spiritual redemption and deliverance from sin.

We are then to turn away from our wickedness, to turn toward God, and we are to start living by every Word of God; and in so doing, we can be filled with the Holy Spirit of God.

The Kingdom of God will be set up on the same Feast of Pentecost as the Mosaic theocracy was set up, because God has promised that we shall receive our inheritance over the earth at the end of the days.

Daniel 12:12 Blessed is he that waiteth, and cometh to the thousand three hundred and five and thirty days. **12:13** But go thou thy way till the end be: for thou shalt rest, and stand in thy lot [inheritance] at the end of the days.

This new beginning is pictured by the Feast of Pentecost, the 50th day, being the first day after seven Sabbaths. It is a new beginning on this day, the Feast of First Fruits, the Feast of Pentecost, and there will be a new beginning on this earth for mankind; with God's Spirit poured out on all flesh (Joel 2:28).

Yes, there will be a millennium of peace: and the New Covenant of the writing of God's Word on the hearts of humanity will be expanded to include all mankind then living, on the Feast of Pentecost.

Zechariah 14:16 And it shall come to pass, that every one that is left of all the nations which came against Jerusalem **shall even go up from year to year to worship the King, the LORD of hosts, and** to keep the feast of tabernacles.

Zechariah 8:20 Thus saith the LORD of hosts; It shall yet come to pass, that there shall come people, and the inhabitants of many cities: **8:21** And the inhabitants of one city shall go to another, saying, Let us go speedily to pray before the LORD, and to seek the LORD of hosts: I will go also.

8:22 Yea, **many people and strong nations shall come to seek the LORD of hosts in Jerusalem, and to pray before the LORD.**

8:23 Thus saith the LORD of hosts; In those days it shall come to pass, that ten men shall take hold out of all languages of the nations, even shall take hold of the skirt of him that is a Jew [a converted person], saying, We will go with you: for we have heard that God is with you.

Even as a certain amount of God's Spirit was poured out on a few people on that first century day of Pentecost, it will be poured out in fullness on all people, on that same Feast of Pentecost, the same day of Pentecost in the future, after all evil is stamped out and removed.

The Feast of Pentecost is much more than a picture of the start of the New Testament church:

- Pentecost is a memorial of the start of the Mosaic Covenant of stone,
- It is a memorial of the official beginning of the New Covenant of writing the Word of God on the hearts and circumcising the hearts of a few in 31 A.D., to turn their hearts of stone into hearts of flesh; by the dwelling of Christ in our hearts through his Spirit.
- Finally it is also prophetic, looking forward to the establishment of the New Covenant and the writing of the Word of God on the hearts of all flesh then living, after the coming of Jesus Christ with his saints and at the END of the day, the establishment of the Kingdom of God over all the earth.

Over a thousand years after Sinai, in Jerusalem, on the Feast of First Fruits or Pentecost, the New Covenant of writing the law of God on the hearts of the called out through the gift of the Holy Spirit was officially confirmed; with the public pouring out of God's Spirit upon the called out few in the first century.

Later, in our time at the end of the Great Tribulation, the Spirit will be poured out on all flesh, ushering in and establishing the Kingdom of God over all the earth, bringing in a 1,000 year long Sabbath, or millennium of peace, and extending the New Covenant to all humanity alive at that time.

Yes, friends, on the Feast of First Fruits, in the wilderness of Sinai, the law of God was written on tables of stone; and on a near future Pentecost; the Word of God shall be written on the hearts of humanity!

The end of the Millennial Kingdom will complete the period of the Spring Harvest, or the harvest of First Fruits.

Later on in the fall, the Fall Festivals picture the resurrection and the bringing in of the main harvest, the great harvest of all who have lived and died, never having known or understood anything regarding God. They will be resurrected and have their minds open, they will repent and be given God's Spirit, and will be reaped, or brought into the Kingdom of God, into the family of God.

The fall festivals are about the fall harvest; while the spring festivals are about the spring harvest, the early harvest, the first fruits harvest.

Pentecost is about the establishment of the Kingdom of God over all the earth; and that includes the calling out, repentance and the gift of God's Spirit to all flesh at that time!

The book of Ruth is an allegory, set in the Unleavened Bread to Pentecost period. Ruth being a Gentile or non-Israelite and not a part of the Mosaic Covenant people, is a figure of those who will yet be called to a part in the New Covenant and receive the Holy Spirit which if it is fully followed, will write the Word of God on their hearts

Boaz, was a type of Christ to whom the Gentiles would be married along with Israel.

The book of Ruth shows the Old Covenant being extended to Ruth, a Gentile; by her being grafted in through her marriage to Boaz.

This event in type, foreshadows all mankind being espoused to Jesus Christ (with the potential to overcome and be changed into Spirit, becoming a part of His bride), and grafted into the New Covenant which will be extended to all flesh, at the establishment of the Kingdom of God on Pentecost when God's Spirit is poured out on all flesh (Joel 2:28).

This event at Pentecost brings all who are still alive being spiritually Gentiles, not yet having been called into the New Covenant; into the spiritual New Covenant of espousal to Christ, at the establishment of the Kingdom of God over all the earth.

WARNING

I must add a warning; even the gift of the Holy Spirit can be lost if we harden our hearts, as Israel did in the wilderness.

At this time most of the brethren have by and large, hardened their hearts to do what they think is right, departing from any zeal to live by every Word of God.

If we are zealous to follow the false traditions of men and have no zeal to learn and to keep the Word of God; how can the Holy Spirit then write God's law on our hearts? We must be careful and diligent to love passionately and to keep the whole Word of God; that is how we follow the true Holy Spirit of God!

We must sincerely repent, circumcising our hardened hearts of stone, before the Holy Spirit can begin to write the Word of God on a new heart of flesh.

Peter's Message on the Day of Pentecost

Acts 2 goes directly to the Feast of Pentecost in 31 A.D. All of the disciples had been waiting from Christ's ascension to heaven on the fortieth day after his resurrection, for ten so days; coming to the fiftieth day after Christ's resurrection on Wave Offering Sunday; which is the Feast of Weeks called Pentecost.

The twelve and many hundreds of other disciples and tens of thousands of people had come from across the known world to the Temple for Pentecost.

2:1 And when the day of Pentecost was fully come, they were all with one accord in one place.

The Holy Spirit was poured out on the disciples of Christ as a demonstration of God's approval before all the Jews, and as a partial demonstration of what would take place after the day of the Lord; when God's Spirit will be poured out on ALL flesh (Joel 2:28).

2:2 And suddenly there came a sound from heaven as of a rushing mighty wind, and it filled all the house where they were sitting. **2:3** And there appeared unto them cloven tongues like as of fire, and it sat upon each of them.

2:4 And they were all filled with the Holy Ghost, and began to **speak with other tongues**, as the Spirit gave them utterance.

Glossa: **2)** a tongue **a)** the language or dialect used by a particular people distinct from that of other nations

2:5 And there were dwelling [staying for the Feast] at Jerusalem Jews, **devout men, out of every nation under heaven.**

The tongues were the languages of men from the various nations, and not vain emotionally ecstatic babble.

2:6 Now when this was noised abroad, the multitude came together, and were confounded, because that **every man heard them speak in his own language.**

2:7 And they were all amazed and marvelled, saying one to another, **Behold, are not all these which speak Galilaeans? 2:8 And how hear we every man in our own tongue, wherein we were born**?

The disciples spoke by God's power, languages not native to themselves.

2:9 Parthians, and Medes, and Elamites, and the dwellers in Mesopotamia, and in Judaea, and Cappadocia, in Pontus, and Asia, **2:10** Phrygia, and Pamphylia, in Egypt, and in the parts of Libya about Cyrene, and strangers of Rome, Jews and proselytes, **2:11** Cretes and Arabians, **we do hear them speak in our tongues the wonderful works of God.**

These people were astonished and groping for an answer as to how this could be.

2:12 And they were all amazed, and were in doubt, saying one to another, What meaneth this? **2:13** Others mocking said, These men are full of new wine.

Then Peter stands up and begins to preach

2:14 But Peter, standing up with the [the other 11 plus Peter meaning the whole 12 were present] eleven, lifted up his voice, and said unto them,

Peter's sermon could well be an example of the sermons which will be preached to people all over the earth as God's Spirit is poured out on all flesh and the Kingdom of God is established by Jesus Christ and his bride on a near future Pentecost.

Ye men of Judaea, and all ye that dwell at Jerusalem, be this known unto you, and hearken to my words: **2:15** For these are not drunken, as ye suppose, seeing it is but the third hour [9 am] of the day.

2:16 But this is that which was spoken by the prophet Joel; **2:17** And it shall come to **pass in the last days, saith God, I will pour out of my Spirit upon all flesh:** and your sons and your daughters shall prophesy, and your young men shall see visions, and your old men shall dream dreams:

2:18 And on my servants and on my handmaidens I will pour out in those days of my Spirit; and they shall prophesy: **2:19 And I will shew wonders in heaven above, and signs in the earth beneath; blood, and fire, and vapour of smoke: 2:20** The sun shall be turned into darkness, and the moon into blood, before the great and notable day of the Lord come: **2:21** And it shall come to pass, that whosoever shall call on the name of the Lord shall be saved.

Let me ask: Was 31 A.D. the "last days"? Was God's Spirit poured out on ALL flesh in 31 A.D.? Did the heavenly signs quoted by Peter take place in 31 A.D.? Was the day of the Lord in 31 A.D.?

NO! However Peter by quoting Joel, was inspired to reveal that the events of 31 A.D. were a precursor of the events to come on the future day of the Lord and immediately afterwards; when the people would repentantly welcome the coming of Christ with his saints, and God's Spirit would be poured out on all flesh on a future day of Pentecost!

The Feast of Pentecost was the start of the Theocracy of physical Israel at Sinai: and IT WILL BE the beginning of the Theocracy of the Kingdom of God at Jerusalem!

The resurrection will come on the sixth day of the Feast of Unleavened Bread; to be followed by the marriage feast in heaven while the seven last plagues are poured out on the earth! To be capped off by the coming of Christ with his saints to rule the earth in righteousness, and then the pouring out of God's Spirit on all flesh when the very day of Pentecost comes!

Brethren, Peter preached the true Gospel on that first century Feast of Pentecost, as it will be preached to all nations and peoples on a soon coming future Feast of Pentecost!!

2:22 Ye men of Israel, hear these words; Jesus of Nazareth, a man approved of God among you by miracles and wonders and signs, which God did by him in the midst of you, as ye yourselves also know: **2:23** Him, being delivered by the determinate counsel and foreknowledge of God, ye have taken, and by wicked hands have crucified and slain: **2:24 Whom God hath raised up, having loosed the pains of death: because it was not possible that he should be holden of it.**

2:25 For David speaketh concerning him, [a Davidic prophecy of Jesus Christ] I foresaw the Lord always before my face, for he is on my right hand, that I should not be moved: **2:26** Therefore did my heart rejoice, and my tongue was glad; moreover also my flesh shall rest in hope: **2:27** Because thou wilt not leave my soul in hell, neither wilt thou suffer thine Holy One to see corruption. **2:28** Thou hast made known to me the ways of [eternal] life; thou shalt make me full of joy with thy countenance.

Peter speaks of the resurrection of Christ

2:29 Men and brethren, let me freely speak unto you of the patriarch David, that he is both dead and buried, and his sepulchre is with us unto this day.

2:30 Therefore being a prophet, and knowing that God had sworn with an oath to him, that of the fruit of his loins, according to the flesh, he would raise up Christ to sit on his throne; **2:31** He seeing this before spake of the resurrection of Christ, that his [Christ's] soul was not left in hell, neither his flesh did see corruption.

2:32 This Jesus hath God raised up, whereof we all are witnesses.

Peter proclaims that the things they had seen on that Pentecost were the evidence of the Holy Spirit falling on the sincerely repentant through the death and resurrection of Christ.

2:33 Therefore being by the right hand of God exalted, and having received of the Father the promise of the Holy Ghost, he hath shed forth this, which ye now see and hear. **2:34** For David is not ascended into the heavens: but he saith himself, The Lord said unto my Lord, Sit thou on my right hand, **2:35** Until I make thy foes thy footstool.

2:36 Therefore let all the house of Israel know assuredly, that God hath made the same Jesus [Hebrew: Yeshua], whom ye have crucified, both Lord [Adonai (Lord), the title given to Messiah] and Christ [Messiah, Mashiach: the Anointed One].

The people were taken aback by the flames and signs, and by the preaching of Peter and were moved to repentance; asking what they should do. Even so when Christ comes with his chosen elect and with many signs and wonders, people will be humbled and greatly impressed and ask what they should do to be saved.

2:37 Now when they heard this, they were pricked in their heart, and said unto Peter and to the rest of the apostles, Men and brethren, what shall we do?

Did Peter say: "Don't worry Christ will overlook your sins" as long as you attend some corporate group?

Or did he proclaim: Sincerely REPENT and SIN NO MORE?

The way to salvation is to believe the scriptures, to repent and to make a baptismal commitment to SIN NO MORE, and then the blood of Christ will be applied to you, blotting out sin and bringing the gift of forgiveness and the Holy Spirit!

2:38 Then Peter said unto them, Repent, and be baptized every one of you in the name of Jesus Christ for the remission of sins, and ye shall receive the gift of the Holy Ghost.

2:39 For the promise is unto you, and to your children, and to all that are afar off, even **as many as the LORD our God** [God the Father] **shall call.**

This is only a condensed version of Peter's sermon

2:40 And with many other words did he testify and exhort, saying, Save yourselves from this untoward [perverse, wicked, unfair, surly, forward (stubborn, self-willed)] **generation.**

2:41 Then they that gladly received his word were baptized: and the same day there were added unto them about three thousand souls.

On a future Pentecost these things will be expanded, as all nations repent and welcome the establishment of the millennial Kingdom of God; and God's Spirit will be poured out upon all flesh so that even the wild animals are tamed (Isaiah 11).

2:42 And they [the disciples who remained at Jerusalem after Pentecost] **continued stedfastly in the apostles' doctrine and fellowship, and in breaking of bread, and in prayers.**

2:43 And fear [reverence for God the Father and Jesus Christ] came upon every soul: and many wonders and signs were done by the [power of God in the] apostles.

The coming Kingdom of God is to begin on Pentecost in the very near future, Jesus and his chosen elect who have been resurrected to spirit will do mighty miracles and the whole earth will turn to live by every Word of God.

Revelation 20:1 And I saw an angel come down from heaven, having the key of the bottomless pit and a great chain in his hand. **20:2** And he laid hold on the dragon, that old serpent, which is the Devil, and Satan, and bound him a **thousand years**, **20:3** And cast him into the bottomless pit, and shut him up, and set a seal upon him, that he should deceive the nations no more, till the **thousand years** should be fulfilled:

Then the disciples believing that the end was close at hand, shared all that they had with one another: for the book of Revelation had not yet been given to John, and they thought the Kingdom was at hand.

Acts 2:44 And all that believed [in Jerusalem] were together, and had all things common; **2:45** And sold their possessions and goods, and parted them to all men, as every man had need.

The disciples in Judea gathered to Jerusalem and the Temple, and with James the Lord's brother, were UNITED IN ZEAL for LEARNING and KEEPING the Word of God!

2:46 And they, continuing daily with one accord in the temple, and breaking bread from house to house, did eat their meat [food] with gladness and singleness of heart, **2:47** Praising God, and having favour with all the people. And the Lord added to the church daily such as should be saved.

Repentance

Remember the kind of bride that Christ wants, and always seek him with all your hearts in passionate love for all that he is and does; which is to do God the Father's will!

Run to him like a deer runs upon the mountains; cleave to him with your whole heart, allowing NO willful compromise or sin to defile us; allow NOTHING to separate us from our Beloved!

Would you choose to marry someone who loves another and follows them and not you? Neither will Jesus Christ accept anyone who prefers others to him!

Peter went on to say that he and the other disciples were all witnesses to the fact that this prophecy had been fulfilled.

The crowd had just seen for themselves the evidence of the power of the Holy Spirit because of the miracle of speaking in many different languages by the disciples; people from many lands could hear the message in their own languages and they were astounded.

In Peter's first sermon to the people on Pentecost, we see the hope of the resurrection within the prophecy of David which Peter quoted when he spoke of the death and resurrection of Christ. Peter quoted from Psalm 16:

Psalm 16:8 I have set the Lord always before me: because he is at my right hand, I shall not be moved. **16:9** Therefore my heart is glad, and my glory rejoiceth: my flesh also shall rest in hope. **16:10** For thou wilt not leave my soul in hell; neither wilt thou suffer thine Holy One to see corruption.

Note that Peter's inspired message that day contained the Gospel message of how one can come to God the Father through Christ. This sermon was so powerful that many in the crowd were convicted of their need to do something about their sins and asked what they should do to be saved.

Peter gave them the command of what they should do and three thousand people repented and were baptized that day.

Acts 2:37 Now when they heard this, they were pricked in their heart, and said unto Peter and to the rest of the apostles, Men and brethren, what shall we do?

2:38 Then Peter said unto them, **Repent, and be baptized every one of you in the name of Jesus Christ for the remission of sins, and ye shall receive the gift of the Holy Ghost.**

2:39 For the promise is unto you, and to your children, and to all that are afar off, even as many as the Lord our God shall call. **2:40** And with many other words did he testify and exhort, saying, Save yourselves from this untoward generation.

2:41 Then they that gladly received his word were baptized: and the same day there were added unto them about three thousand souls.

Pentecost and Ruth

When Ezra canonized the Hebrew scriptures the book of Ruth was appointed to be read on the Feast of Pentecost.

After the preamble, the setting of the book in Bethlehem begins in the period of the spring harvest; beginning with the barley harvest at Wave Offering Sunday and continuing through the wheat harvest right up to Pentecost.

Ruth appears to have been written by Samuel. The names used have considerable meaning and may be aliases used for the story.

> Elimelech means "God is King".
>
> Naomi: "Well favored, a delight to God and Man,"
>
> Orpah means "stubborn and stiff necked,"
>
> Chilion: "pining away".
>
> Ruth: "A friend and companion"
>
> Mahlon: "sickly"

Boaz: "In God is Strength;" which is also the name of one of the two pillars beside the entry into the Temple Inner Court.

The first part gives the background to the situation, with the real heart of the story beginning with Ruth accepting the God of Israel and her loyalty to her adopted family.

The book of Ruth shows the Covenant being extended to Ruth, a Gentile; by her being grafted into Israel through her marriage to Boaz.

This is an allegory of and prophesies of the New Covenant calling of both Jew and Gentile, into a kind of spiritual Israel which is to come in its fullness at the coming of Messiah and the pouring out of God's Spirit on all flesh on a future Feast of Pentecost. (Joel 2:28, Acts 2)

Ruth in its ultimate type, prophesies the calling out of all mankind and espousing all people then living to Jesus Christ (with the potential to overcome and be changed into spirit, and being added to His bride), and grafted into the New Covenant; which will be extended to all flesh then living, at the establishment of the Kingdom of God on Pentecost when God's Spirit is poured out on all flesh (Joel 2:28).

The book of Ruth pictures a future Pentecost when all who are still alive including Israelites [today being spiritually Gentiles not yet having been called into the spiritual New Covenant of espousal to Christ] and Gentiles; being called into the New Covenant at the establishment of the Kingdom of God over all the earth.

Ruth is a type of the first fruits of this world; with Boaz as a type of Christ: The book is a type of Christ's love for his bride, and her love and faithfulness to the God she had dedicated herself to.

The harvest gleaning is a type of our diligent personal effort at seeking the Bread of Life, and Christ rewarding us and helping us in that effort just as Boaz helped Ruth.

Ruth 1

Ruth 1:1 Now it came to pass in the days when the judges ruled, that there was a famine in the land. And a certain man of Bethlehemjudah went to sojourn in the country of Moab, he, and his wife, and his two sons. **1:2** And the name of the man was Elimelech, and the name of his wife Naomi, and the name of his two sons Mahlon and Chilion, Ephrathites of Bethlehemjudah. And they came into the country of Moab, and continued there. **1:3** And Elimelech Naomi's husband died; and she was left, and her two sons.

1:4 And they took them wives of the women of Moab; the name of the one was Orpah, and the name of the other Ruth: and they dwelled there about ten years. **1:5** And Mahlon and Chilion died also both of them; and the woman was left of her two sons and her husband.

1:6 Then she arose with her daughters in law, that she might return from the country of Moab: for she had heard in the country of Moab how that the LORD had visited his people in giving them bread. **1:7** Wherefore she went forth out of the place where she was, and her two daughters in law with her; and they went on the way to return unto the land of Judah.

1:8 And Naomi said unto her two daughters in law, Go, return each to her mother's house: the LORD deal kindly with you, as ye have dealt with the dead, and with me. **1:9** The LORD grant you that ye may find rest, each of you in the house of her husband. Then she kissed them; and they lifted up their voice, and wept.

1:10 And they said unto her, Surely we will return with thee unto thy people.

This is a graphic lesson on the difference between mere words and deeds, for Orpah professed loyalty and quickly returned to her own ways and gods; While Ruth professed allegiance to God and her marriage family and she WAS faithful.

That is a lesson for us today.

1:11 And Naomi said, Turn again, my daughters: why will ye go with me? are there yet any more sons in my womb, that they may be your husbands? **1:12** Turn again, my daughters, go your way; for I am too old to have an husband. If I should say, I have hope, if I should have an husband also to night, and should also bear sons;

Now Naomi knew of the levirate law and that the next of kin of her husband or his next of kin should marry the widow yet she was testing her daughters in law; that she would be sure of their loyalty; even as God tests his people to see if they will make a worthy part of the bride of Christ.

1:13 Would ye tarry for them till they were grown? would ye stay for them from having husbands? nay, my daughters; for it grieveth me much for your sakes that the hand of the LORD is gone out against me. **1:14** And they lifted up their voice, and wept again: and Orpah kissed her mother in law; but Ruth clave unto her.

Orpah kissed he mother in law good by, and went back to her family and her gods.

1:15 And she [Naomi] said, Behold, thy sister in law is gone back unto her people, and unto her gods: return thou after thy sister in law.

Ruth however pledged her loyalty to God and to Naomi in the most thorough and loving manner; as we should also pledge our love and loyalty to our God our Father and to our espoused Husband Jesus Christ.

1:16 And Ruth said, Intreat me not to leave thee, or to return from following after thee: for whither thou goest, I will go; and where thou lodgest, I will lodge: thy people shall be my people, and thy God my God: 1:17 Where thou diest, will I die, and there will I be buried: the LORD do so to me, and more also, if ought but death part thee and me.

Thereupon Naomi KNEW her daughter in law was diligently faithful and left off from testing her.

1:18 When she saw that she was stedfastly minded to go with her, then she left speaking unto her.

1:19 So they two went until they came to Bethlehem. And it came to pass, when they were come to Bethlehem, that all the city was moved about them, and they said, Is this Naomi? **1:20** And she said unto them, Call me not Naomi, call me Mara: for the Almighty hath dealt very bitterly with me.

1:21 I went out full and the LORD hath brought me home again empty: why then call ye me Naomi, seeing the LORD hath testified against me, and the Almighty hath afflicted me? **1:22** So Naomi returned, and Ruth the Moabitess, her daughter in law, with her, which returned out of the country of Moab: and they came to Bethlehem in the beginning of barley harvest.

Naomi and Ruth come to Bethlehem where Elimelech owned a field. Elimelech having died, his son Mahlon inherited the field, but he and his brother died childless, now Ruth had control of the field until she bore an heir to her husband Mahlon by his next of kin. If Ruth also died childless the land would then be inherited by the nearest next of kin.

Naomi must have been aware of the natures of the two closest next of kin and she directed Ruth to seek Boaz, rather than to seek out the other. Ruth hearing about Boaz from Naomi then sought him out to glean in his field; for Naomi must have spoken of him as a close kinsman who was of a generous mind.

Ruth 2

Ruth 2:1 And Naomi had a kinsman of her husband's, a mighty man of wealth, of the family of Elimelech; and his name was Boaz. **2:2** And Ruth the Moabitess said unto Naomi, Let me now go to the field, and glean ears of corn [grain, in this case barley] after him in whose sight I shall find grace.

And she said unto her, Go, my daughter. **2:3** And she went, and came, and gleaned in the field after the reapers: and her hap was to light on a part of the field belonging unto Boaz, who was of the kindred of Elimelech.

Boaz coming to his field to visit his laborers, notices Ruth and inquires about her, and then speaks to her.

2:4 And, behold, Boaz came from Bethlehem, and said unto the reapers, The LORD be with you. And they answered him, The LORD bless thee.

2:5 Then said Boaz unto his servant that was set over the reapers, Whose damsel is this? **2:6** And the servant that was set over the reapers answered and said, It is the Moabitish damsel that came back with Naomi out of the country of Moab: **2:7** And she said, I pray you, let me glean and gather after the reapers among the sheaves: so she came, and hath continued even from the morning until now, that she tarried a little in the house.

Ruth later takes a rest in the house [laborers rest shack] and was again inquired about by Boaz, who hearing of her good reputation and her loyalty to God and her adopted family, is willing to give her a blessing.

2:8 Then said Boaz unto Ruth, Hearest thou not, my daughter? Go not to glean in another field, neither go from hence, but abide here fast by my maidens: **2:9** Let thine eyes be on the field that they do reap, and go thou after them: have I not charged the young men that they shall not touch thee? and when thou art athirst, go unto the vessels, and drink of that which the young men have drawn.

2:10 Then she fell on her face, and bowed herself to the ground, and said unto him, Why have I found grace in thine eyes, that thou shouldest take knowledge of me, seeing I am a stranger? **2:11** And Boaz answered and said unto her, It hath fully been shewed me, all that thou hast done unto thy mother in law since the death of thine husband: and how thou hast left thy father and thy mother, and the land of thy nativity, and art come unto a people which thou knewest not heretofore.

2:12 The LORD recompense thy work, and a full reward be given thee of the LORD God of Israel, under whose wings thou art come to trust.

Brethren, this is an allegory of the love of Christ for those that God the Father has called to him; who are faithful and of good reputation; who love God the Father and Jesus Christ to whom they are called to espousal.

This story speaks of how those who are faithful to God and all his ways, finding favor with Christ and finally, will be united in marriage to Christ at the Wedding Feast at the marriage of the Lamb in heaven (Rev 15, Rev 19).

2:13 Then she said, Let me find favour in thy sight, my lord; for that thou hast comforted me, and for that thou hast spoken friendly unto thine handmaid, though I be not like unto one of thine handmaidens.

2:14 And Boaz said unto her, At mealtime come thou hither, and eat of the bread, and dip thy morsel in the vinegar. And she sat beside the reapers: and he reached her parched corn, and she did eat, and was sufficed, and left. **2:15** And when she was risen up to glean, Boaz commanded his young men, saying, Let her glean even among the sheaves, and reproach her not: **2:16** And let fall also some of the handfuls of purpose for her, and leave them, that she may glean them, and rebuke her not.

This gleaning of grain is about our quest for spiritual food from the "Bread of Life" Jesus Christ; and how if we work hard and diligently glean out the words of truth; in his mercy and love our espoused Husband will instruct his angels to give us much increase.

As Ruth worked hard to find food, we are to work hard and diligently, to seek out that spiritual food of the Word of God; diligently seeking to gather into ourselves: the Word, commandments and very nature of God the father and our espoused Husband Jesus Christ.

2:17 So she gleaned in the field until even, and beat out that she had gleaned: and it was about an ephah of barley. **2:18** And she took it up, and went into the city: and her mother in law saw what she had gleaned: and she brought forth, and gave to her that she had reserved after she was sufficed.

2:19 And her mother in law said unto her, Where hast thou gleaned to day? and where wroughtest thou? blessed be he that did take knowledge of thee. And she shewed her mother in law with whom she had wrought, and said, The man's name with whom I wrought to day is Boaz.

Now Naomi when she saw the grain that Ruth brought, knew that the man felt strongly for Ruth to do her such a service, and remarked that he was a near kinsman; this too being part of the analogy, for Jesus Christ is near kinsman to all humans by virtue of being our Creator, and was of Judah and is therefore a near kinsman to physical AND Spiritual Israel, as Boaz was near kinsman through the husband of Ruth..

2:20 And Naomi said unto her daughter in law, Blessed be he of the LORD, who hath not left off his kindness to the living and to the dead. And Naomi said unto her, The man is near of kin unto us, one of our next kinsmen.

2:21 And Ruth the Moabitess said, He said unto me also, Thou shalt keep fast by my young men, until they have ended all my harvest. **2:22** And Naomi said unto Ruth her daughter in law, It is good, my daughter, that thou go out with his maidens, that they meet thee not in any other field.

Boaz entreats Ruth to come to his field only, and Naomi tells Ruth that it would be good for her to go to Boaz only; so that she would not be seen by other potential suitors.

We can see the thoughts of love in the mind of Boaz and that he wanted her for himself, and in the mind of Naomi that she also preferred Boaz over the other near kinsmen.

This is analogous to the love of Christ for those called to him by God the Father; and his jealousy that we should come to him alone.

As Ruth was called by God to come forth from Moab to the field of Boaz; many are called out of this world to come to the field of Christ, there to learn of him by partaking of the Bread of Life the Word of God; which is Jesus Christ in print.

This gleaning period is a period of testing as is our espousal to Christ; Ruth was tested and courted by Boaz; being blessed by him and no doubt conversing with him during the harvest. In the same manner we are to be absolutely faithful through all our testing's and to be in constant communication with God the Father

2:23 So she kept fast by the maidens of Boaz to glean unto the end of barley harvest and of wheat harvest; and dwelt with her mother in law.

In the larger area of Israel, the wheat harvest continued past Pentecost for a few weeks, however in the area by Bethlehem the barley harvest progressed into the wheat harvest which ended by Pentecost.

It is near Pentecost that Naomi advises Ruth to seek marriage with Boaz.

Ruth 3

Ruth 3:1 Then Naomi her mother in law said unto her, My daughter, shall I not seek rest for thee, that it may be well with thee? **3:2** And now is not Boaz of our kindred, with whose maidens thou wast? Behold, he winnoweth barley to night in the threshingfloor.

3:3 Wash thyself therefore, and anoint thee, and put thy raiment upon thee, and get thee down to the floor: but make not thyself known unto the man, until he shall have done eating and drinking. **3:4** And it shall be, when he lieth down, that thou shalt mark the place where he shall lie, and thou shalt go in, and uncover his feet, and lay thee down; and he will tell thee what thou shalt do.

3:5 And she said unto her, All that thou sayest unto me I will do.

Ruth was advised to make herself ready, to cleanse herself and put on her best; and to seek out Boaz asking him to cover her with his garment. This is similar to God's instructions to make ourselves ready for the coming of our Lord husband by cleansing ourselves from all blemishes of uncleanness and sin; so that he might cover us with the garment of His Righteousness.

Boaz had been "winnowing barley" on "the threshing floor." He slept there in order to guard "the heap of grain" which he had been unable to transport into his granary.

At his feet; The Hebrew word is not the usual noun for feet. Outside of this chapter it occurs again in Daniel 10:6 in the phrase translated "arms and legs." The context suggests that Ruth "uncovered the place at his literal feet". She laid down at his feet, which was symbolic of her accepting him as her husband, and accepting him as an authority over her.

Literally your "wings." Boaz had commended Ruth for taking refuge under the "wings" of the Lord, the God of Israel." Now she asked her kinsman to let her find safety under his "wings." However, she implied more. The same noun is used to denote the wings of a garment. The expression "to spread a skirt over" a woman; means to take her in marriage. (Ezekiel 16:8; Deuteronomy 22:30)

3:6 And she went down unto the floor, and did according to all that her mother in law bade her.

3:7 And when Boaz had eaten and drunk, and his heart was merry, he went to lie down at the end of the heap of corn: and she came softly, and uncovered his feet, and laid her down. **3:8** And it came to pass at midnight, that the man was afraid, and turned himself: and, behold, a woman lay at his feet.

3:9 And he said, Who art thou? And she answered, I am Ruth thine handmaid: spread therefore thy skirt over thine handmaid; for thou art a near kinsman. **3:10** And he said, Blessed be thou of the LORD, my daughter: for thou hast shewed more kindness in the latter end than at the beginning, inasmuch as thou followedst not young men, whether poor or rich.

3:11 And now, my daughter, fear not; I will do to thee all that thou requirest: for all the city of my people doth know that thou art a virtuous woman.

Boaz then accepts Ruth to be his wife, but there is another who has first claim on her. It is the very same with us today for sin has its claim on us and that claim must be paid. We must be redeemed from our near kinsman in sin, Satan; by the payment of our debt of sin.

Our Lord loved us so very much that he laid down his life for us in payment of our debt of past sin and redeemed us from our debt:

> **1 Corinthians 6:19** What? know ye not that your body is the temple of the Holy Ghost which is in you, which ye have of God, and ye are not your own? 20 For ye are bought with a price: therefore glorify God in your body, and in your spirit, which are God's.

3:12 And now it is true that I am thy near kinsman: howbeit there is a kinsman nearer than I.

3:13 Tarry this night, and it shall be in the morning, that if he will perform unto thee the part of a kinsman, well; let him do the kinsman's part: but if he will not do the part of a kinsman to thee, then will I do the part of a kinsman to thee, as the LORD liveth: lie down until the morning.

3:14 And she lay at his feet until the morning: and she rose up before one could know another. And he said, Let it not be known that a woman came into the floor.

3:15 Also he said, Bring the vail that thou hast upon thee, and hold it. And when she held it, he measured six measures of barley, and laid it on her: and she went into the city.

3:16 And when she came to her mother in law, she said, Who art thou, my daughter? And she told her all that the man had done to her. **3:17** And she said, These six measures of barley gave he me; for he said to me, Go not empty unto thy mother in law.

3:18 Then said she, Sit still, my daughter, until thou know how the matter will fall: for the man will not be in rest, until he have finished the thing this day.

Boaz acting quickly then goes to the near kinsman before the witnesses of the elders at the city gate, and asks the man about his intentions.

Ruth 4

Ruth 4:1 Then went Boaz up to the gate, and sat him down there: and, behold, the kinsman of whom Boaz spake came by; unto whom he said, Ho, such a one! turn aside, sit down here. And he turned aside, and sat down.

4:2 And he took ten men of the elders of the city, and said, Sit ye down here. And they sat down.

4:3 And he said unto the kinsman, Naomi, that is come again out of the country of Moab, selleth a parcel of land, which was our brother Elimelech's: **4:4** And I thought to advertise thee, saying, Buy it before the inhabitants, and before the elders of my people. If thou wilt redeem it, redeem it: but if thou wilt not redeem it, then tell me, that I may know: for there is none to redeem it beside thee; and I am after thee. And he said, I will redeem it.

4:5 Then said Boaz, What day thou buyest the field of the hand of Naomi, thou must buy it also of Ruth the Moabitess, the wife of the dead, to raise up the name of the dead upon his inheritance. **4:6** And the kinsman said, I cannot redeem it for myself, lest I mar mine own inheritance: redeem thou my right to thyself; for I cannot redeem it.

This man knew that if he produced a child for Ruth, that child would carry on in the name of Mahlon, and not his own name; and would inherit all that was Elimelech's; which if Ruth had no son he would inherit being the nearest kinsman.

4:7 Now this was the manner in former time in Israel concerning redeeming and concerning changing, for to confirm all things; a man plucked off his shoe, and gave it to his neighbour: and this was a testimony in Israel. **4:8** Therefore the kinsman said unto Boaz, Buy it for thee. So he drew off his shoe.

4:9 And Boaz said unto the elders, and unto all the people, Ye are witnesses this day, that I have bought all that was Elimelech's, and all that was Chilion's and Mahlon's, of the hand of Naomi.

4:10 Moreover Ruth the Moabitess, the wife of Mahlon, have I purchased to be my wife, to raise up the name of the dead upon his inheritance, that the name of the dead be not cut off from among his brethren, and from the gate of his place: ye are witnesses this day.

4:11 And all the people that were in the gate, and the elders, said, We are witnesses. The LORD make the woman that is come into thine house like Rachel and like Leah, which two did build the house of Israel: and do thou worthily in Ephratah, and be famous in Bethlehem: **4:12** And let thy house be like the house of Pharez, whom Tamar bare unto Judah, of the seed which the LORD shall give thee of this young woman.

4:13 So Boaz took Ruth, and she was his wife: and when he went in unto her, the LORD gave her conception, and she bare a son.

4:14 And the women said unto Naomi, Blessed be the LORD, which hath not left thee this day without a kinsman, that his name may be famous in Israel.

4:15 And he shall be unto thee a restorer of thy life, and a nourisher of thine old age: for thy daughter in law, which loveth thee, which is better to thee than seven sons, hath born him.

4:16 And Naomi took the child, and laid it in her bosom, and became nurse unto it.

4:17 And the women her neighbours gave it a name, saying, There is a son born to Naomi; and they called his name Obed: he is the father of Jesse, the father of David.

4:18 Now these are the generations of Pharez: Pharez begat Hezron, **4:19** And Hezron begat Ram, and Ram begat Amminadab, **4:20** And Amminadab begat Nahshon, and Nahshon begat Salmon, **4:21** And Salmon begat Boaz, and Boaz begat Obed, **4:22** And Obed begat Jesse, and Jesse begat David.

Now Obed inherited all the land and wealth of Elimelech by the levirate law; and he also inherited all the land and wealth of Boaz. Becoming the head of a very wealthy and powerful family, out of which came David the king and into which family Jesus the Christ the King of kings was born.

The Millennium

The Feast of Pentecost [meaning a fifty count] or Feast of Weeks [referring to the seven Sabbath count] is also called the Feast of First Fruits.

First physical Israel was called out of bondage in Egypt and entered into the Mosaic Covenant at Sinai on Pentecost, as an allegorical type of God calling out an early harvest of first fruits out of bondage to Satan and sin.

The Mosaic Covenant began on Pentecost and the New Covenant of Jeremiah 31 was established on Pentecost for a few called out in the first century; and on a future Feast of Pentecost the Kingdom of God will be established over all the earth and the New Covenant will be extended to all flesh then living!

Satan and his legions will be bound for a thousand years and God's Spirit will be poured out on all flesh (Joel 2:28). This literally means ALL flesh not just humanity, so that even the wild beasts will become tame!

Isaiah 11:1 And there shall come forth a rod out of the stem of Jesse, and a Branch shall grow out of his roots:

11:2 And the spirit of the LORD shall rest upon him, the spirit of wisdom and understanding, the spirit of counsel and might, the spirit of knowledge and of the fear of the LORD [respect and love for the Father in heaven]; **11:3** And shall make him of quick understanding in the fear of the LORD: and he shall not judge after the sight of his eyes, neither reprove after the hearing of his ears: **11:4** But with righteousness shall he judge the poor, and reprove with equity for the meek of the earth: and he shall smite the earth: with the rod of his mouth, and with the breath of his lips shall he slay the wicked. **11:5** And righteousness [commandment keeping] shall be the girdle of his loins, and faithfulness [absolute unshakable loyalty to the Father in heaven] the girdle of his reins.

When the Holy Spirit is poured out on all flesh after the day of the Lord, peace shall reign over all the earth including even the beasts.

11:6 The wolf also shall dwell with the lamb, and the leopard shall lie down with the kid; and the calf and the young lion and the fatling together; and a little child shall lead them. **11:7** And the cow and the bear shall feed; their young ones shall lie down together: and the lion shall eat straw like the ox. **11:8** And the sucking child shall play on the hole of the asp, and the weaned child shall put his hand on the cockatrice' den.

Does this seem too hard a thing? At creation all creatures ate plants and it was only the curse for rebellion against God that brought the bitterness of death and ravaging animals upon this earth. God is the ultimate expert in genetics and with a few genetic tweaks God could change the nature of the beasts [as science is learning today] back to their original created nature.

11:9 They shall not hurt nor destroy in all my holy mountain: for the earth shall be full of the knowledge of the LORD, as the waters cover the sea.

Jesse is likened to the root and stem [trunk] of a tree [think of the common hereditary "family tree"]; and his descendants are likened to the branches.

The God Being who gave up his God-hood to be made flesh and to be surrogated by Miriam [Mary] a descendant of Jesse; was and is The Branch of Jesse, Jesus Christ.

Soon he will come to rule over and save all humanity and the Gentiles shall be grafted into a spiritual Israel; and the millennial Sabbath rest of the Kingdom of God shall be glorious.

Isaiah 65:19 And I will rejoice in Jerusalem, and joy in my people: and **the voice of weeping shall be no more heard in her, nor the voice of crying.**

In the millennium, and likely in the Feast of Tabernacles main judgment which begins AFTER the millennium; human lifespan will be 100 years; and all people during that time will be judged at 100 years old; either translated to spirit or destroyed.

65:20 There shall be no more thence an infant of days, nor an old man that hath not filled his days: for the child shall die an hundred years old; but the sinner being an hundred years old shall be accursed.

There shall be equity, peace and justice and each person will reap the fruits of his own labors.

65:21 And they shall build houses, and inhabit them; and they shall plant vineyards, and eat the fruit of them. **65:22** They shall not build, and another inhabit; they shall not plant, and another eat: for as the days of a tree are the days of my people, and mine elect shall long enjoy the work of their hands. **65:23** They shall not labour in vain, nor bring forth for trouble; for they are the seed of the blessed of the LORD, and their offspring with them.

Most people shall be close to God the Father and Jesus Christ in the millennium and they will live by every Word of God.

No more will anyone say; "I can do this contrary to God's Word because some man or corporate church said so." If any man says "doctrine is not important, do not learn and keep all the doctrine of scripture" and tolerates false doctrine; he will be destroyed as the false teacher he is.

65:24 And it shall come to pass, that before they call, I will answer; and while they are yet speaking, I will hear. **65:25** The wolf and the lamb shall feed together, and the lion shall eat straw like the bullock: and dust shall be the serpent's meat. They shall not hurt nor destroy in all my holy mountain, saith the LORD.

After the correction of tribulation has humbled the whole earth; the Ezekiel Temple will be built and Jerusalem will be exalted in the top of all the world's mountains [governments] and all nations shall be grafted into New Covenant Spiritual Israel in the Kingdom of God.

Isaiah 2:1 The word that Isaiah the son of Amoz saw concerning Judah and Jerusalem. **2:2 And it shall come to pass in the last days,** that the mountain [government] of the LORD's house shall be established in the top of the mountains [governments], and shall be exalted above the hills [local governments]; and all nations shall flow unto it [all people shall bow to the world government of the King of kings].

Then all peoples and nations will learn and keep all the ways and teachings of the Mighty One of spiritual Israel; and will live by Every Word of God!

Great is our God and he is mighty to save all the sincerely repentant who turn away from tolerating sin, false doctrine and lukewarm spiritual laxity, to a consummate zeal for all his ways!

Holy is our Mighty One and glorious in his strength; he is victorious over all his enemies, even death and the grave!

Isaiah 2:3 And many people shall go and say, Come ye, and let us go up to the mountain [government at Jerusalem] of the LORD, **to the house** [the Millennial Temple Ezekiel 40-48] **of the God of Jacob; and he will teach us of his ways, and we will walk in his paths: for out of Zion shall go forth the law, and the word of the LORD from Jerusalem.**

Then Messiah the Christ will judge all people by the whole Word of God and he will bring world peace for a thousand years, and then Satan must be loosed for a very short time.

After the 1,000 year millennium Messiah will destroy Satan and all violence, pain and sorrow forever! He is the Mighty One who parted the Red Sea and made the sun stand still; He and God the Father are the great wisdom which created the universe! What is a man that he should think he can stand on his own ways?

2:4 And he shall judge among the nations, and shall rebuke many people: and they shall beat their swords into plowshares, and their spears into pruninghooks: nation shall not lift up sword against nation, neither shall they learn war any more.

Beloved brethren; come and let us turn in passionate zeal to live by EVERY WORD of GOD! Let us live by the light of the Word of God in all things; always!

2:5 O house of Jacob, **come ye, and let us walk in the light of the LORD.**

A new world will begin with the coming of Messiah the Christ and his deliverance. The Word of the Lord will be opened up to the understanding of all nations and peoples. God's Spirit will be poured out on all flesh on the Feast of Pentecost (Joel 2:28), and all who call on the LORD will be saved

Joel 2:32 And it shall come to pass, that **whosoever shall call on the name of the Lord shall be delivered: for in mount Zion and in Jerusalem shall be deliverance**, as the Lord hath said, and in the remnant [those who survive the tribulation will be called to God] whom the Lord shall call.

Psalm 96

Psalm 96:1 O sing unto the LORD a new song: sing unto the LORD, all the earth. **96:2** Sing unto the LORD, bless his name; shew forth his salvation from day to day.

96:3 Declare his glory among the heathen [all nations], **his wonders among all people.**

96:4 For the LORD is great, and greatly to be praised: he is to be feared above all gods. **96:5** For all the gods of the nations are idols: but the LORD made the heavens. **96:6** Honour and majesty are before him: strength and beauty are in his sanctuary.

All nations and peoples will be called to and they will glorify God the Father and they will live by every Word of God.

96:7 Give unto the LORD, O ye kindreds of the people, give unto the LORD glory and strength. **96:8** Give unto the LORD the glory due unto his name: bring an offering, and come into his courts. **96:9** O worship the LORD in the beauty of holiness: fear before him, all the earth.

96:10 Say among the heathen [nations] that the LORD reigneth [over the earth]: the world [the worldwide Kingdom of God] also shall be established that it shall not be moved: he shall judge the people righteously.

96:11 Let the heavens rejoice, and let the earth be glad; let the sea roar, and the fulness thereof. **96:12** Let the field be joyful, and all that is therein: then shall all the trees of the wood rejoice

96:13 Before the LORD: for he cometh, for he cometh to judge [Rule] the earth: he shall judge the world with righteousness, and the people with his truth [God's Word is truth].

> **John 17:17 Sanctify them through thy truth: thy word is truth**

Psalm 97

The Kingdom of God will be established on a future Feast of Shavuot or Pentecost, and Messiah the Christ will rule all nations as King of kings and Lord of all lords.

Psalm 97:1 The LORD reigneth; let the earth rejoice; let the multitude of isles be glad thereof.

At his coming the earth shall tremble, and when his throne and Kingdom are established on Pentecost, God's Spirit will be poured out on all flesh (Joel 2:28) and all people shall rejoice in his deliverance.

97:2 Clouds and darkness are round about him: righteousness and judgment are the habitation of his throne. **97:3** A fire goeth before him, and burneth up his enemies round about. **97:4** His lightnings enlightened the world: the earth saw, and trembled. **97:5** The hills melted like wax at the presence of the LORD, at the presence of the Lord of the whole earth.

The glory of the Lord

97:6 The heavens declare his righteousness, and all the people see his glory.

Those who trust in their own ways and idols of wood and stone or of men and false traditions of men will be brought to humble contrition; and all people will worship the Eternal.

97:7 Confounded be all they that serve graven images, that boast themselves of idols: worship him, all ye gods.

All physical and spiritual Israel shall rejoice in Messiah the King, and all nations will be humbled.

97:8 Zion heard, and was glad; and the daughters of Judah rejoiced because of thy judgments, O LORD. **97:9** For thou, LORD, art high above all the earth: thou art exalted far above all gods.

A good understanding and God's ultimate deliverance is given to all those who hate and loathe all evil; and love, follow and live by every Word of God.

97:10 Ye that love the LORD, hate evil: he preserveth the souls of his saints; he delivereth them out of the hand of the wicked. **97:11** Light is sown for the righteous, and gladness for the upright in heart.

True godly righteousness is to live by every Word of God

97:12 Rejoice in the LORD, ye righteous; and give thanks at the remembrance of his holiness.

Then all the earth shall worship the Eternal

Isaiah 66:23 And it shall come to pass, that from one new moon to another, and from one sabbath to another, shall all flesh come to worship before me, saith the LORD.

Zechariah 14:6 And it shall come to pass in that day, that the light shall not be clear, nor dark:

14:7 But it shall be one day which shall be known to the LORD, not day, nor night: but it shall come to pass, **that at evening time it shall be light.**

These Living Waters are a picture of the flowing of the Holy Spirit from the throne of God upon all people.

14:8 And it shall be in that day, that **living waters shall go out from** [the temple site] **Jerusalem**; half of them toward the former sea, and half of them toward the hinder sea: in summer and in winter shall it be.

> **Ezekiel 47:1** Afterward he brought me again unto the door of the house [the Ezekiel Temple]; and, behold, waters issued out from under the threshold of the house eastward: for the forefront of the house stood toward the east, and the waters came down from under from the right side of the house, at the south side of the altar. **Read the whole chapter.**

Zechariah 14:9 And **the LORD shall be king over all the earth**: in that day shall there be one LORD [Yahweh], and his name one.

Then ALL nations shall repent and shall know the Eternal (Joel 2:28).

14:16 And it shall come to pass, that **every one that is left of all the nations which came against Jerusalem shall even go up from year to year to worship the King, the LORD of hosts, and to keep the feast of tabernacles.**

And all flesh shall observe the Sabbaths and the New Moons.

> **Isaiah 66:23** And it shall come to pass, that **from one new moon to another, and from one sabbath to another, shall all flesh come to worship before me, saith the Lord.**

Zechariah 14:17 And it shall be, that whoso will not come up of all the families of the earth unto Jerusalem to worship the King, the LORD of hosts, even upon them shall be no rain.

14:18 And if the family of Egypt go not up, and come not, that have no rain; there shall be the plague, wherewith the LORD will smite the heathen that come not up to keep the feast of tabernacles.

Keeping the Sabbath and the New Moons is reckoned with keeping the Feast of Tabernacles! Jesus Christ the King of kings will require all people and nations to keep God's holy [Friday sunset to Saturday sunset] Sabbath and his New Moons and God's Festivals in the millennium and forever after!

Then all people shall:

Psalm 100

Psalm 100:1 Make a joyful noise [Shout for Joy in the Eternal!] unto the LORD, all ye lands [peoples and nations].

100:2 Serve [all peoples and nations shall serve the Eternal willingly] the LORD with gladness: come before his presence with singing.

100:3 Know ye that the LORD he is God [all peoples and nations will know the Eternal and rejoice in Him to serve Him and to live by His Word]: it is he that hath made us, and not we ourselves; we are his people, and the sheep of his pasture.

100:4 Enter into his gates with thanksgiving, and into his courts [the courtyards of God's Temple, symbolic of being grafted into the spiritual Temple [Family] of God] with praise: be thankful unto him, and bless his name.

100:5 For the LORD is good; his mercy [to save the sincerely repentant who turn to live by every Word of God] is everlasting; and his truth endureth to all generations.

Satan and his legions will be imprisoned just before Pentecost and 1,000 years later they will be released just before Pentecost. This period is covered in the next section.

The Memorial of Trumpets

How Lucifer Became Satan and God's Plan for Man

Before the creation of the physical universe God created beings made of spirit which he called angels; then billions of these angels [spirits] were organized and assisted in the creation of the universe.

One of these created spirit beings was a super angel called Lucifer.

In Ezekiel 28 God uses the term "king of Tyrus" to explain the perfection of Lucifer the super angel; the description provided is clearly not the description of any human being.

Ezekiel 28:11 Moreover the word of the LORD came unto me, saying, **28:12** Son of man, take up a lamentation upon the king of Tyrus, and say unto him, Thus saith the Lord GOD; **Thou sealest up the sum, full of wisdom, and perfect in beauty. 28:13 Thou hast been in Eden the garden of God; every precious stone was thy covering, the sardius, topaz, and the diamond, the beryl, the onyx, and the jasper, the sapphire, the emerald, and the carbuncle, and gold: the workmanship of thy tabrets and of thy pipes** [tabrets and pipes referring to musical ability] **was prepared in thee in the day that thou wast created.**

Here we find Lucifer described as one of the anointed Cherub's whose wings covered the very throne of God. The covering Cherubs are represented on the Ark of the Covenant.

When God was creating angels he created archangels or cherubim to have oversight over the others. At least three of these powerful beings are named in scripture: Gabriel, Michael and Lucifer. One of these archangels stood on each side of the throne of the Father in heaven with their wings covering the throne.

Lucifer was one of the covering cherubs over the very throne of God, as close to God as any being at that time.

Yet he became filled with pride and rebelled against God

28:14 Thou art the anointed cherub that covereth; and I have set thee so: **thou wast upon the holy mountain [government] of God; thou hast walked up and down in the midst of the stones of fire** [in heaven].

God said that he had made Lucifer perfect and anointed him to cover the very throne of God the Father.

28:15 Thou wast perfect in thy ways from the day that thou wast created, till iniquity was found in thee.

The greatness of his beauty and the multitude of his riches corrupted Lucifer and filled him with pride. Pride is the foundational cause of all sin!

28:16 By the multitude of thy merchandise they have filled the midst of thee with violence, and thou hast sinned: therefore I will cast thee as profane out of the mountain of God: and I will destroy thee, O covering cherub, from the midst of the stones of fire.

Lucifer was lifted up and filled with pride

28:17 Thine heart was lifted up because of thy beauty, thou hast corrupted thy wisdom by reason of thy brightness: I will cast thee to the ground, I will lay thee before kings, that they may behold thee.

28:18 Thou hast defiled thy sanctuaries by the multitude of thine iniquities, by the iniquity of thy traffick; therefore will I bring forth a fire from the midst of thee, it shall devour thee, and I will bring thee to ashes upon the earth in the sight of all them that behold thee.

28:19 All they that know thee among the people shall be astonished at thee: thou shalt be a terror, and never shalt thou be any more.

Lucifer with his pride in himself began to believe that he should take over from God and rule the universe his own way, thinking that he should be the decider between right and wrong.. Lucifer was the originator of sin which is rebellion against God.

Isaiah 14:12 How art thou fallen from heaven, O Lucifer, son of the morning! how art thou cut down to the ground, which didst weaken the nations!

When Lucifer became corrupted by pride he rebelled against God and sought to rise up against God

14:13 For thou hast said in thine heart, **I will ascend into heaven, I will exalt my throne above the stars** [angels] **of God: I will sit also upon the mount** [as head of government] **of the congregation, in the sides of the north:**

14:14 I will ascend above the heights of the clouds; I will be like the most High.

Lucifer wanted to do things his own way, he wanted to be the decider, the ruler, the boss; instead of following God and living by the Word of God.

Lucifer then rose up against God to overthrow the King of the Universe! But not alone!

First he deceived one third of the angels to follow him. Revelation 12 is a prophecy about the woman [the Ekklesia] and the birth and ascension of Christ, and about the flights of the Ekklesia of God from Satan's persecution through Rome; one in the first century to Pella, and one in the 21st century probably also to Pella.

There is a very revealing statement included in Revelation 12 on the original rebellion of Lucifer.

Revelation 12:4 And his tail drew the third part of the stars [angels] of heaven, and did cast them to the earth:

This reveals that when Lucifer had rebelled, he had also convinced one third of the angels to join with him in rebelling against God. After his rebellion was defeated and Lucifer was cast down to the earth with his angels; his name was changed to Satan the Adversary and his angels were called fallen angels or demons.

God determined to make man to be even closer to him than the angels; but God did not want another Lucifer, God did not want another rebellion on his hands.

Therefore God made man flesh so that humanity could learn that he is not able to decide right and wrong for himself in the crucible of experience without the destroying power of a powerful spirit

Satan was then cast down to the earth and excluded from any authority in the rest of the universe, and is being used by God to teach man lessons that will last for eternity.

From the very beginning God knew that man would go astray and just as Satan did would seek to decide right and wrong for himself. Therefore the Creator set in motion a plan to give his own life for his creation so that when people learn the lesson and sincerely repent of past sin; there would be a way of salvation opened to them.

The plan of the Creator was to impress on humanity how very important it was to live by every Word of God, by giving his own life to atone for the sincerely repented sins of humanity.

Details of these things will be the subject of another book, for now the point is that God had a plan for humanity and salvation from the very foundations of the world.

That plan is revealed in the scriptures and many details are revealed in the Biblical Sabbath, Appointed Times, Holy Days and Festivals.

The bondage of Israel in Egypt is an allegory of humanity's bondage to sin. The calling of Israel out of Egypt is an allegory of God calling humanity out of sin. The Passover lamb was a type of the spiritual Lamb of God dying for the sins of the called out of bondage to sin.

The destruction of the first born in Egypt is an instructional example that all willful sinners who refuse to follow and live by every Word of God, will not have the atoning sacrifice applied to them; while the saving of the first born by the blood on their households, is an example that all those who obey God and follow Him through living by the Word of God will be saved by the application of the atoning sacrifice of the Lamb of God.

The Feast of Unleavened Bread is a seven day period which happened from the time that Israel began their journey out of Egypt until they had crossed the Red Sea. This is a prophetic lesson that God has called certain people out from bondage to sin for the past six thousand years, and at the end of that six thousand years the overcomes will be resurrected from the grave, as Israel passed through the Red Sea to be symbolically resurrected at the end of the sixth day.

The seventh day being a High Holy Day of rejoicing over their deliverance, which represents a thousand year millennial rest and rejoicing of the resurrected first fruits in the Kingdom of God.

> **2 Peter 3:8** But, beloved, be not ignorant of this one thing, that one day is with the Lord as a **thousand years**, and a **thousand years** as one day.

The putting out of all leaven is a lesson that we are to put out all pride in our own selves and are to put out all sin; while the eating of unleavened bread every day of the seven day Feast, represents eating [internalizing] and living by every Word of God

None of these things which happened in Egypt needed to happen, in the sense that God could have prevented Israel's bondage in Egypt with a wave of his hand. They happened as lessons for our instruction.

God prophesied of these events to Abraham and then brought them to pass as evidence of his foreknowledge and his power to fulfill his plan and perform his will.

Genesis 15:13 And he said unto Abram, Know of a surety that thy seed shall be a stranger in a land that is not theirs, and shall serve them; and **they shall afflict them four hundred years;**

Israel went down into Egypt where they were well treated for thirty years, and then a new pharaoh arose and they were afflicted for four hundred years, just as God had foretold to Abraham. Almighty God fulfilling his Word to the very day!

Exodus 12:40 Now the sojourning of the children of Israel, who dwelt in Egypt, was four hundred and thirty years.

12:41 And it came to pass at the end of the four hundred and thirty years, **even the selfsame day** it came to pass, that all the hosts of the LORD went out from the land of Egypt.

The Transition from Pentecost to the Feast of Trumpets

The scriptures teach us about a very definite period between Pentecost and the Fall Festivals

Satan Restrained

When Messiah the Christ comes to the earth with his faithful, all resistance will be crushed, and Satan with his spirit followers, who have deceived the nations for millennia, will then be taken into custody and restrained in prison for one thousand years.

Then on the Feast of Pentecost God will pour out His Spirit on ALL flesh and the Kingdom of God will be formally established over all the earth (Joel 2:28).

Just before the Kingdom of God is established on the Feast of Pentecost, Satan the Adversary and his spirit followers are to be bound up for one thousand years; and humanity will have a millennial Sabbath of rest from his deceptions and rebellions!

Revelation 20:1 And I saw an angel come down from heaven, having the key of the bottomless pit and a great chain in his hand.

20:2 And he laid hold on the dragon, that old serpent, which is the Devil, and Satan, and **bound him a thousand years,**

20:3 And cast him into the bottomless pit, and shut him up, and set a seal [locking up his detention] upon him, that **he should deceive the nations no more, till the thousand years should be fulfilled: and after that he must be loosed a little season.**

Just before the Feast of Pentecost, Satan and his demons will be bound for one thousand years and during that time all the earth will be at peace and all humanity will exalt the Eternal and serve Him, with every person living by every Word of God!

Since Satan is bound just before the Feast of Pentecost and his imprisonment is to last for exactly one thousand years; Satan must then be released on the same day on which he was imprisoned, one thousand years before.

Therefore Satan will be released just before the Feast of Pentecost one thousand years after his initial imprisonment!

The Two New Year's

The ancients began the year in the autumn near what we would call the Feast of Trumpets today, and it was commonly understood that the creation was in the fall, but when God called Israel out of Egypt he declared that the year was to begin in the spring for the called out ones.

We can see that the new year began in the fall for the bulk of humanity, and the spring new year was about the early harvest.

God began his main creation in the fall and God began his Calling Out of a kind of first fruits or early harvest in the spring.

Now if Satan were bound at or just before Pentecost then he would not have received his full six thousand years from the fall creation of man; therefore it is to give Satan his full six thousand years, that Satan must be released at the same date that he was first bound on, one thousand later; and he must be given the remainder of his six thousand years which would then be completed in the fall.

Satan uses his remaining few months to deceive again

When Satan is released around the Feast of Pentecost he will then go back to his old habits and will again go forth to deceive people to rebel against God.

Satan will be released after the thousand year millennial Sabbath of rest, and will have one last chance to repent. Instead he will again deceive many, many millions into following him away from God.

20:7 And when the thousand years are expired, Satan shall be loosed out of his prison,

The prophecy of Ezekiel 38-39 is a dual prophecy which will be partially fulfilled when the nations of Asia come up against Jerusalem the first time, just at the coming of Messiah the Christ; and then after one thousand years of peace Ezekiel 38 - 39 will be fulfilled in its fullness.

Revelation 20:8 And shall go out to deceive the nations which are in the four quarters of the earth, Gog, and Magog [the nations of Asia], to gather them together to battle: the number of whom is as the sand of the sea.

20:9 And they went up on the breadth of the earth, and compassed the camp of the saints about, and the beloved city: and fire came down from God out of heaven, and devoured them.

Satan will deceive the nations of the East from a point just before the Feast of Pentecost when he is released, and the deceived multitudes will then come up against Jerusalem, from where Messiah the Christ is ruling over all the earth, and will come against the people of God who are dwelling in peace.

Ezekiel 38 - 39 is a DUAL prophecy: First fulfilled only in part, as the smallest fore-type at the end of the tribulation; and then later fulfilled in all its overwhelming fullness AFTER the millennium.

Ezekiel 38:1 And the word of the LORD came unto me, saying, **38:2** Son of man, set thy face against Gog, [and against] the land of Magog, [Gog being the chief ruler (leader) of the nations of Asia] the chief prince of Meshech [Moscow] and Tubal [Tobolsk, Siberia], and prophesy against him,

Ezekiel 38-39

The Biblical account of the tribulation, the Asian armies and the FIRST fulfillment of Ezekiel 38-39

Keep this biblical account of Asia during the tribulation in mind, and compare it to the prophecy of Ezekiel 38-39 as we study it out. Doing this will help you to separate the two fulfillments.

The New Europe will first conquer Jerusalem and Judea at the beginning of the tribulation and later in the third year the New Federal Europe will attack Asia (Dan 11:42).

The ruler of the soon coming New Europe will attack Asia in the third year of the rising New Europe.

Asia will endure the European attack and will respond, striking and devastating Europe and then pouring through the Middle East to attack the final false prophet and the political ruler who have fled to Jerusalem.

In doing this the Asian armies will destroy the New Europe and all her Mideast allies. Finally the Asian armies will attack Jerusalem (Zech 14), and then Messiah the Christ will come to destroy all the enemies of the righteousness of zeal to learn and live by Word of God; and the Kingdom of God will be established on the Feast of Pentecost. For details and much more see our "Tribulation and Deliverance" book on bible prophecy.

This prophecy is Dual with the tribulation fulfillment being only a fore-type fulfillment of a much larger even coming after the millennium. The tribulation will be a period of great tribulation and bloody war; while the final fulfillment of the Ezekiel 38-39 prophecy takes place AFTER all Israel has come back to the land and is living in peaceful abundance.

This event will happen only in part during the tribulation! Later it will be fulfilled in its fullness after the end of the one thousand year millennium!

The Ezekiel prophecy; The bloody tribulation is only a precursor to a different and even larger fulfillment when all are at peace and living in abundant safety; AFTER the millennium.

Ezekiel 38:3 And say, Thus saith the Lord GOD; Behold, I am against thee, O Gog, the chief prince of Meshech [Moscow] and Tubal [Tobolsk, Siberia]: 38:4 And I will turn thee back, and put hooks into thy jaws, and I will bring thee forth, and all thine army, horses and

horsemen, all of them clothed with all sorts of armour, even a great company with bucklers and shields, all of them handling swords:

With Russia will come the Iranians, the Mongolians of the north; and Ethiopia and Libya will be with them; while in the tribulation Libya and Ethiopia will be subject to the New Europe, the king of the North! (Dan 11:43) which is the enemy of Asia!

38:5 Persia, Ethiopia, and Libya with them; all of them with shield and helmet: **38:6** Gomer, and all his bands; the house of Togarmah of the north quarters, and all his bands: and many people with thee.

38:7 Be thou prepared, and prepare for thyself, thou, and all thy company that are assembled unto thee, and be thou a guard unto them.

Here the term **"latter years"** refers to the period AFTER the one thousand year millennium, and not to the **"latter days'** which is pre- millennial.

38:8 After many days thou shalt be visited: in the latter years [after the millennium] thou shalt come into the land that is brought back from the sword, and is gathered out of many people, against the mountains of Israel, which have been always waste: but it is brought forth out of the nations, and they shall dwell safely all of them.

Revelation 20:7 is the key to understanding the duality of Ezekiel 38-39

> **Revelation 20:7** And **when the thousand years are expired, Satan shall be loosed out of his prison,**
>
> **20:8** And shall go out to deceive the nations which are in the four quarters of the earth, Gog, and Magog, to gather them together to battle: the number of whom is as the sand of the sea.
>
> **20:9** And they went up on the breadth of the earth, and compassed the camp of the saints about, and the beloved city: and fire came down from God out of heaven, and devoured them.

Ezekiel 38:9 Thou shalt ascend and come like a storm, thou shalt be like a cloud to cover the land, thou, and all thy bands, and many people with thee.

38:10 Thus saith the Lord GOD; It shall also come to pass, that at the same time shall things come into thy mind, and thou shalt think an evil thought:

- Late in the tribulation the New Federal Europe will attack Asia and they will counterattack flooding down into the Middle East.
- It is after the end of his one thousand years of imprisonment that Satan tempts the nations to follow Gog [deceived by Satan] to try to despoil and seize the great riches of Israel once again!

Notice the time period of **the second and final fulfillment**: all Israel has returned to the promised land and is living is total security and abundance because of their zeal to live by every Word of God. Nothing here about the bloodshed of great tribulation!

38:11 And thou shalt say, I will go up to **the land of unwalled [undefended land] villages; I will go to them that are at rest, that dwell safely, all of them dwelling without walls, and having neither bars nor gates, 38:12** To take a spoil, and to take a prey; to turn thine hand upon **the desolate places that are now inhabited, and upon the people that are gathered out of the nations, which have gotten cattle and goods, that dwell in the midst of the land.**

38:13 Sheba, and Dedan [India], and the merchants of Tarshish, with all the young lions thereof, shall say unto thee, Art thou come to take a spoil? hast thou gathered thy company to take a prey? to carry away silver and gold, to take away cattle and goods, to take a great spoil?

Jesus Christ will allow Satan to deceive the nations of Asia, because after one thousand years of peaceful prosperity humanity has become complacent, proud and self-satisfied and is losing its zeal for godliness; so Christ will demonstrate his sovereignty and power one more time!

38:14 Therefore, son of man, prophesy and say unto Gog [The ruler of the nations of Magog and a type of Satan.], Thus saith the Lord GOD; **In that day when my people of Israel dwelleth safely, shalt thou not know it? 38:15** And thou shalt come from thy place out of the north parts, thou, and many people with thee, all of them riding upon horses, a great company, and a mighty army: **38:16** And thou shalt come up against my people of Israel, as a cloud to cover the land; it shall be in the latter days, and **I will bring thee against my land, that the heathen may know me, when I shall be sanctified in thee, O Gog, before their eyes.**

Then Jesus Christ the Messiah, ruling as King of kings shall destroy these deceived armies [which will later be resurrected and given another chance during the Feast of Tabernacles Ingathering of tehr main harvest of humanity].

38:17 Thus saith the Lord GOD; Art thou he of whom I have spoken in old time by my servants the prophets of Israel, which prophesied in those days many years that I would bring thee against them? **38:18** And it shall come to pass at the same time when Gog shall come against the land of Israel, saith the Lord GOD, that my fury shall come up in my face.

Then the King of kings will thunder and shake the earth in his wrath and he shall cause the invaders to turn upon and kill one another.

38:19 For in my jealousy and in the fire of my wrath have I spoken, Surely in that day there shall be a great shaking in the land of Israel; **38:20** So that the fishes of the sea, and the fowls of the heaven, and the beasts of the field, and all creeping things that creep upon the earth, and all the men that are upon the face of the earth, shall shake at my presence, and the mountains shall be thrown down, and the steep places shall fall, and every wall shall fall to the ground. **38:21 And I will call for a sword against him throughout all my mountains, saith the Lord GOD: every man's sword shall be against his brother.**

Then the real Jesus Christ will rain hail and fire upon the invaders.

38:22 And I will plead against him with pestilence and with blood; and I will rain upon him, and upon his bands, and upon the many people that are with him, **an overflowing rain, and great hailstones, fire, and brimstone. 38:23** Thus will I magnify myself, and sanctify myself; and I will be known in the eyes of many nations, and they shall know that I am the LORD.

Ezekiel 39

Does Israel dwell in safety in an undefended land today? Obviously there will be a great fulfillment AFTER the millennium!

Only one sixth of the invaders will survive.

Ezekiel 39:1 Therefore, thou son of man, prophesy against Gog, and say, Thus saith the Lord GOD; Behold, I am against thee, O Gog, the chief prince of Meshech and Tubal: **39:2** And I will turn thee back, and leave but the sixth part of thee, and will cause thee to come up from the north parts, and will bring thee upon the mountains of Israel: **39:3** And I will smite thy bow out of thy left hand, and will cause thine arrows to fall out of thy right hand.

This prophecy is dual and concerns the period late in the tribulation as a very minor fore-type of a later post millennium event.

39:4 Thou shalt fall upon the mountains of Israel, thou, and all thy bands, and the people that is with thee: I will give thee unto the ravenous birds of every sort, and to the beasts of the field to be devoured. **39:5** Thou shalt fall upon the open field: for I have spoken it, saith the Lord GOD. **39:6** And I will send a fire on Magog, and among them that dwell carelessly [without any concerns or fears] in the isles: and they shall know that I am the LORD.

The coming of Messiah and the deliverance of Israel will turn them to true godliness! They will not again rebel at the keeping of every Word of God as physical and spiritual Israel does today.

Then AFTER the millennium; Satan will be released and will deceive and bring his deceived armies up against God at Jerusalem.

39:7 So will I **make my holy name known in the midst of my people Israel; and I will not let them pollute my holy name any more: and the heathen shall know that I am the LORD, the Holy One in Israel. 39:8** Behold, it is come, and it is done, saith the Lord GOD; this is the day whereof I have spoken.

39:9 And they that dwell in the cities of Israel shall go forth, and shall set on fire and burn the weapons, both the shields and the bucklers, the bows and the arrows, and the handstaves, and the spears, and they shall burn them with fire seven years: **39:10** So that they shall take no wood out of the field, neither cut down any out of the forests; for they shall burn the weapons with fire: and they shall spoil those that spoiled them, and rob those that robbed them, saith the Lord GOD.

The graves of Gog in Israel

39:11 And it shall come to pass in that day, that I will give unto Gog a place there of graves in Israel, the valley of the passengers on the east of the sea: and it shall stop the noses of the passengers: and there shall they bury Gog and all his multitude: and they shall call it The valley of Hamongog.

39:12 And seven months shall the house of Israel be burying of them, that they may cleanse the land. **39:13** Yea, all the people of the land shall bury them; and it shall be to them a renown the day that I shall be glorified, saith the Lord GOD. **39:14** And they shall sever out men of continual employment, passing through the land to bury with the passengers those that remain upon the face of the earth, to cleanse it: after the end of seven months shall they search.

39:15 And the passengers [travelers] that pass through the land, when any seeth a man's bone, then shall he set up a sign by it, till the buriers have buried it in the valley of Hamongog. **39:16** And also the name of the city shall be Hamonah. Thus shall they cleanse the land.

39:17 And, thou son of man, thus saith the Lord GOD; Speak unto every feathered fowl, and to every beast of the field, Assemble yourselves, and come; gather yourselves on every side to my sacrifice that I do sacrifice for you, even a great sacrifice upon the mountains of Israel, that ye may eat flesh, and drink blood. **39:18** Ye shall eat the flesh of the mighty, and drink the blood of the princes of the earth, of rams, of lambs, and of goats, of bullocks, all of them fatlings of Bashan. **39:19** And ye shall eat fat till ye be full, and drink blood till ye be drunken, of my sacrifice which I have sacrificed for you. **39:20** Thus ye shall be filled at my table with horses and chariots, with mighty men, and with all men of war, saith the Lord GOD.

The First Fulfillment

> **Revelation 19:17** And I saw an angel standing in the sun; and he cried with a loud voice, saying to all the fowls that fly in the midst of heaven, Come and gather yourselves together unto the supper of the great God;
>
> **19:18** That ye may eat the flesh of kings, and the flesh of captains, and the flesh of mighty men, and the flesh of horses, and of them that sit on them, and the flesh of all men, both free and bond, both small and great.
>
> The kings of the east along with the remaining forces of the new Europe will turn and fight Christ at his coming.

> **19:19** And I saw the beast, and the kings of the earth, and their armies, gathered together to make war against him that sat on the horse, and against his army.

But first all the earth will see the power and glory of Messiah the Christ when he does this thing and defeats the massive armies gathered to fight against him at his coming!

When Christ comes all the earth shall repent and turn to live by every Word of God.

Ezekiel 39:21 And I will set my glory among the heathen, and all the heathen shall see my judgment that I have executed, and my hand that I have laid upon them.

39:22 So the house of Israel shall know that I am the LORD their God from that day and forward. **39:23** And the heathen shall know that the house of Israel went into captivity for their iniquity: because they trespassed against me, therefore hid I my face from them, and gave them into the hand of their enemies: so fell they all by the sword.

It is because of our wickedness that we are corrected.

39:24 According to their uncleanness and according to their transgressions have I done unto them, and hid my face from them.

39:25 Therefore thus saith the Lord GOD; Now will I bring again the captivity of Jacob, and have mercy upon the whole house of Israel, and will be jealous for my holy name; **39:26** After that they have borne their shame, [been corrected for their sin] and all their trespasses whereby they have trespassed against me, when they dwelt safely in their land, and none made them afraid.

39:27 When I have brought them again from the people, and gathered them out of their enemies' lands, and am sanctified in them in the sight of many nations; **39:28** Then shall they know that I am the LORD their God, which caused them to be led into captivity among the heathen [for all our abominations]: but I have gathered them unto their own land, and have left none of them any more there.

Then God will pour out his Spirit on all Israel (Jer 31:31) and on all flesh (Joel 2:28).

39:29 Neither will I hide my face any more from them: for I have poured out my spirit upon the house of Israel, saith the Lord GOD.

The prophecy is DUAL; referring to BOTH the coming of Christ and to the final rebellion immediately AFTER the end of the millennium!

When the New Europe rises they will strike out at Asia in their third year and the Asian armies will come up against Europe, finally chasing down the political and religious leaders at Jerusalem. Then Christ will come WITH his resurrected chosen and will destroy these Asian armies as well as the residue of the New Europe and will restrain Satan for one thousand years.

The Second Fulfillment after the Millennium

Then AFTER the one thousand year millennium ends, near the Feast of Pentecost, Satan and his demon spirits will be released and will again deceive the peoples of Asia who will come up against Jerusalem only to be destroyed a few months later, very near the Feast of Trumpets.

Remember that the millennium had ENDED at Pentecost, after which Satan is released for a few months only to be defeated one final time.

To Recap

Satan is imprisoned with his spirit followers just before or at the Feast of Pentecost, and he is released with his spirit followers one thousand years later, at or just before the Feast of Pentecost. After his release Satan deceives many nations which would involve hundreds of millions if not billions of people.

This would be a final chance for Satan and his followers to repent which they will spurn; at the same time this will be a lesson for the masses of humanity including Israel who have gotten complacent after one thousand years of peace.

Just look about today at the lack of zeal to live by every Word of God in the called out Ekklesia - who have the example of a very wicked world all around them - and who are supposed to have the Holy Spirit; and it should be clear that people could easily become complacent and lacking in zeal after one thousand years of peace and prosperity without the presence of any evil.

The Feast of Trumpets begins the events of the Seventh Month containing the final main fall harvest of mankind; by celebrating the final defeat of

Satan and a general waking up and returning to a zeal to live by every Word of God by mankind [those who are killed will later be resurrected and given a chance in the final harvest of mankind]; who [Satan and his spirit followers] will then be held and judged and removed and destroyed on the Day of Atonement, so that the Feast of Tabernacles main harvest of lives can proceed.

The Memorial of Trumpets

The Feast of Trumpets is a memorial; memorials have the purpose of causing something to be remembered. To remember to sound trumpets is rather pointless; the point is that trumpets are to be sounded to bring something else to remembrance.

The memorial [called a Feast by some] of Trumpets and the sounding of trumpets looks forward to God's complete and final victory over Satan, and once that event happens all future Feasts of Trumpets will be memorials of that final and complete victory of God over Satan which took place at that time.

The Feast of Trumpets and the sounding of trumpets is to remember and rejoice over God's deliverance, to remember the mighty power and absolute sovereignty of God over his creation, and to remember the vast multitudes of dead and God's promises to resurrect to a great main fall harvest of lives.

The Feast of Trumpets being the HEAD or beginning of the seventh month, pictures the overall events of the seventh month and calls on God to remember the vast main harvest of humanity still dead and still waiting to be raised up and brought into the family of God; and it calls on the people of the main fall harvest to come to God.

As the Head of the seventh month, the Feast of Trumpets is representative of all that takes place in the main fall harvest of humanity.

The sounding of the shofars throughout the land pictures the tremendous rejoicing that the seventh month brings.

The Festivals during the seventh month picture deliverance and the absolute final victory over Satan and a Great Resurrection of all those who have lived and died not having known God, opening an opportunity for them to learn godliness and opening the way to the removal of Satan forever on the Fast Day of Atonement!

The Feast of Trumpets itself is about introducing the events of the seventh month main harvest of humanity; it is about remembering and rejoicing over deliverance from and final victory over the Adversary of God and man; Satan and his spirit followers.

After one thousand years of imprisonment Satan will be released close to Pentecost and he will deceive many peoples who have lost their zeal and become lukewarm and complacent. Just like many in the Ekklesia have grown lukewarm and complacent today and lacking a zeal to live by every Word of God have become deceived into following corporate idols contrary to God and the Word of God.

Then after the millennium and after Satan is released and deceives the nations, the armies of the people deceived by Satan will gather at Jerusalem to attack the King of kings.

Then, close to the Feast of Trumpets, Messiah the King of kings, ruling the whole earth from Jerusalem; will show forth his sovereign glory and mighty power by destroying these vast armies without building any physical army of his own.

Just as he slew the first born of man and beast at midnight in Egypt, the Mighty One will destroy the forces deceived by Satan and arrayed against him at the city of Jerusalem with a wave of his hand.

> When Christ comes to begin the millennium and he destroys the wicked, and then quickly restrains Satan just before Pentecost, for one thousand years; all humanity will see his might and glory and will turn to live by every Word of God.

Then after one thousand years of peace, many then living will have forgotten the pain of sin and how easily men can drift away from God and into evil, and Satan will still have the few months left from Pentecost to the Feast of Trumpets to fill his allotted six thousand years.

Even today many very sincere folks, who have been called to God, have become proud and grown self-satisfied and spiritually complacent; and have drifted very far from God without even realizing it.

In our day, proud self-justifying people will be corrected in great tribulation and then saved by the coming of Christ. The whole earth will then acknowledge His power and authority after Satan is restrained and the nations see his mighty deeds.

Then after one thousand years of peace and prosperity, many will again become proud and spiritually complacent; and one final demonstration of how easily man is deceived, and the glory, greatness and power of our Mighty One will be provided.

This final battle against Satan will happen just before the Feast of Trumpets, AFTER the end of the millennium. At that battle the final victory over Satan will be completed; and then on the first day of the Seventh Month; trumpets and great rejoicing will sound throughout the land!

The Hebrew language calls the Feast of Trumpets; the Yom [day] of Teruah [the blasting of trumpets and shouts of great rejoicing].

The first day of the Seventh Month, called the Feast of Trumpets; is a High Holy Day on which no work of any kind may be done: except those things commanded by God for the observance of the day, and acts of mercy.

The Feast of Trumpets is; first of all the New Moon of the seventh month. Scripturally every Biblical Month begins with the sighting of the first visible light of the new moon from Jerusalem.

Near the end of the sixth biblical month, at the end of the millennium, Satan will be defeated one last time. The armies of the deceived people will be totally destroyed, and on the spiritual plane Satan and his angelic host will be thoroughly defeated and taken into custody ending the sixth month of the biblical year [which is analogous to ending Satan's six thousand year rule over humanity].

Then as the sun sets on the sixth biblical month the two silver trumpets will blast loud and long in the Ezekiel Temple at Jerusalem announcing the beginning of the seventh biblical Month of Deliverance, the New Moon and High Holy Day!

The two silver trumpets will blast loudly and continually from the Temple throughout the day in celebration of the final victory over Satan, and Shofars will be sounded in great rejoicing throughout the whole night and all the day until the next sunset; throughout all the land!

The Feast of Trumpets is a Day of Great Rejoicing over the defeat of the attacking armies of those deceived by Satan - delivered by Almighty God with no human defenders involved - a day of Great Rejoicing over the final defeat of Satan himself, the ultimate source of all suffering and death for humanity - and Great Rejoicing over the seventh month events still to come.

The Feast of Trumpets acknowledges the absolute sovereignty and glory of God and the removal of Satan once and for all. Later on the Fast of Atonement on the tenth day of the seventh month, Satan will be judged and removed forever and the sacrifice of Messiah will be made available to all who have died not knowing God who will be raised up in the main harvest of humanity called the Feast of Tabernacles.

This High Holy Day New Moon is the first day of the seventh biblical month, and as the first day of that month is the Head of the Seventh Month, sanctifying that month and all that it contains, including all of the seventh month Holy Days.

God could have chosen any day for this day of rejoicing, yet he chose a new moon and understanding the new moons is an essential part of this Feast of Rejoicing.

The New Moon is the Head of the Month

The Head of the month, determined by the first visible light of the new moon and is a New Beginning, and a special time to remember the Headship of God over his Creation.

We are to observe the first light of every new moon with Bible Studies and worship, as a day to remember and acknowledge that the Creator is the true HEAD of the Ekklesia [under God the Father] and that it is the spiritual LIGHT of God's Word which drives away the darkness of ignorance.

The Moon being new, pictures a New Beginning and a monthly Reminder to dedicate ourselves to godliness, to particularly repent of sin; and to acknowledge the Authority of God as our Sovereign King and Sovereign Head.

God in his wisdom has given us the weekly Sabbath to worship Him, and he has given us a monthly New Moon time to worship Him, and he has given us His annual Festivals: All for our good, as a help to keep our hearts and minds always on Him!

The Sounding of Trumpets on the Seventh New Moon

In the law of God the blasting of the Silver Trumpets is enjoined: to call the people to God. The two silver trumpets were also to be sounded over all Sabbath, New Moon and Festival sacrifices offered by the high priest on behalf of the whole people; to call on God to accept the sacrifices offered by the high priest on behalf of all the people.

Every sacrifice is an allegory of a type of the sacrifice of the Lamb of God for his creation; and the physical blasting of the Silver Trumpets in its spiritual aspect, calls on God the Father to accept the sacrifice of the Lamb of God for the people and to remember, deliver and accept the people on whose behalf the sacrifice was made.

Numbers 10:10 Also in the day of your gladness, and **in your solemn days** [Sabbaths, Appointed Times and Festivals] , and **in the beginnings of your months** [New Moons], ye shall blow with the [the two silver] trumpets over your burnt offerings, and over the sacrifices of your peace offerings [the special offerings of those days; not the personal offerings made at other times]; that they may be to you for a memorial before your God [To call you to remember and come to God]: I am the LORD your God.

Physically and spiritually the sounding of the silver trumpets calls on God to remember, deliver and accept the people and to accept the sacrifices made by the high priest for the whole people!

The Two Silver Trumpets and the Shofar

On the Feast of Trumpets we have two different kinds of trumpets:

The Shofar

The sounding of the shofars throughout the land pictures the tremendous rejoicing that the seventh month brings, beginning with the final and total victory over Satan.

Imagine the outpouring of rejoicing as a vast army bent on killing, pillage and destruction, an army so large as to be humanly impossible to resist; is completely destroyed by God Himself right before their eyes, and Satan and his millions of spirit followers are defeated and taken into charge for their final judgment and punishment!

The two silver trumpets call God to remember, deliver and accept the people and calling the people to God [reconciling the two] at the place that God has placed his name; and second, the shofar of rejoicing in every community throughout the land.

The Two Silver Trumpets

Leviticus 23:23 And the LORD spake unto Moses, saying, 23:24 Speak unto the children of Israel, saying, In the seventh month, in the first day of the month, shall ye have a sabbath, a memorial of blowing of trumpets [Strong's 8643 Shout for joy, hence the rejoicing of sounding the shofar being added to the silver trumpets], **an holy convocation. 23:25 Ye shall do no servile work therein: but ye shall offer an offering made by fire unto the LORD.**

Numbers 29:1 And in the seventh month, on the first day of the month, ye shall have an holy convocation; ye shall do no servile work: it is a day of blowing the trumpets [8643 Shout for joy, hence the rejoicing of sounding the shofar being added to the silver trumpets] **unto you.**

When the temple was destroyed and the two silver trumpets lost; the sounding of the two silver trumpets was lost for a time, but the blasting of the shofars through every congregation may continue.

The Command Concerning the Silver Trumpets

The first part is about the journey in the wilderness, during which the trumpets were used to call the people to meet with Moses [the mediator of the Mosaic Covenant]. This is a type of the calling of those in the spiritual wilderness to come to God the Father trough Jesus Christ the Mediator of the New Covenant.

Numbers 10:1-10 And the LORD spake unto Moses, saying, **10:2 Make thee two trumpets of silver;** of a whole piece shalt thou make them: that thou mayest use them for the calling of the assembly, and for the journeying of the camps.

10:3 And **when they shall blow with them** [both]**, all the assembly shall assemble themselves to thee at the door of the tabernacle of the congregation** [to assemble before God].

10:4 And if they blow but with one trumpet, then the princes, which are heads of the thousands of Israel, shall gather themselves unto thee.

10:5 When ye blow an alarm [a special call], then the camps that lie on the east parts shall go forward. **10:6** When ye blow an alarm the second time, then the camps that lie on the south side shall take their journey: they shall blow an alarm for their journeys.

10:7 But when the congregation is to be gathered together, ye shall blow, but ye shall not sound an alarm [a special call to battle].

10:8 And **the sons of Aaron, the priests, shall blow with the** [silver] **trumpets**; and they shall be to you for an ordinance for ever throughout your generations.

The spiritually called out first fruits are called into the priesthood of Jesus Christ and in the spiritual sense they are to be like silver trumpets calling the nations to God. Which is the task given to today's Ekklesia (Isaiah 58:1).

Matthew 28:18 And Jesus came and spake unto them, saying, All power is given unto me in heaven and in earth.

28:19 Go ye therefore, and teach all nations, baptizing them in the name of the Father, and of the Son, and of the Holy Ghost: **28:20** Teaching them to observe all things whatsoever I have commanded you: and, lo, I am with you always, even unto the end of the world. Amen.

In this section of Numbers the silver trumpets are sounded to call God to remember the people

10:9 And if ye go to war in your land against the enemy that oppresseth you, then **ye shall blow an alarm with the trumpets; and ye shall be remembered before the LORD your God, and ye shall be saved from your enemies.**

10:10 Also **in the day of your gladness, and in your solemn days, and in the beginnings of your months,** ye shall blow with the trumpets over your burnt offerings, and over the sacrifices of your peace offerings; **that they may be to you for a memorial before your God: I am the LORD your God.**

The blasting of trumpets on this Holy Day of the Feast of Trumpets is to remember and rejoice that God has remembered his creation and delivered them from Satan the Adversary in an absolutely complete and total victory over Satan; and to remember the mighty power and absolute sovereignty of God over his creation.

The sounding of shofars throughout the land pictures the tremendous rejoicing that the seventh month brings; beginning with the final and total victory over Satan.

The Festivals during the seventh month picture deliverance and victory over Satan beginning with the Feast of Trumpets, and the removal of Satan forever on the Fast of Atonement; followed by the saving of all those who were dead and will now be brought to life in the Feast of Ingathering [Tabernacles], as per Ezekiel 37.

The Command to Keep the Feast of Trumpets

Leviticus 23:23 And the LORD spake unto Moses, saying, **23:24** Speak unto the children of Israel, saying, **In the seventh month, in the first day of the month, shall ye have a sabbath, a memorial of blowing of trumpets**

The two silver trumpets were blasted all day long at the tabernacle or later at the temple to call on God to remember the people and to accept the sacrifice made on behalf of the whole people; and calling the people to come to God.

The prescribed offerings for the Memorial of Trumpets

The Holy Day offerings consisted of the ordinary morning and evening sacrifices first, and then the regular New Moon offerings of the burnt-offerings.

After that came the extra Feast of Trumpets burnt-offering of **one young bullock** [picturing the strong patient service of Christ, producing much fruit], **one ram** [signifying Christ as the Head or king of the Covenant people]**, and seven lambs** [picturing Christ as totally innocent and pure from all sin], with their appropriate **meat** [unleavened bread] **and drink offerings** [Symbolic of Jesus Christ the Bread of Life and the shed blood of Christ], together with 'one kid of the goats for a sin-offering, to make an atonement for you.'

The sounding of the silver trumpets called on God to remember the people and to accept the sacrifices made by the high priest for the whole people; this being a physical type of God remembering the people and and delivering them from bondage to Satan and sin.

Psalm 81 uses the delivering of Israel out from the bondage of Egypt as an allegory of being delivered from bondage to Satan and sin.

Psalm 81

81:1 Sing aloud unto God our strength: make a joyful noise unto the God of Jacob. **81:2** Take a psalm, and bring hither the timbrel, the pleasant harp with the psaltery.

81:3 Blow up the trumpet in the new moon, in the time appointed, on our solemn feast day [the Feast of Trumpets]. **81:4** For this was a statute for Israel, and a law of the God of Jacob.

81:5 This he ordained in Joseph for a testimony, when he [God commanded and ordained this at Sinai, the time that Israel went out of Egypt] went out through [from] the land of Egypt: where I heard a language that I understood not.

God delivered them from the burden of Pharaoh and Egypt and God has delivered us from the burden of Satan - spiritual pharaoh and Egypt - and God will yet call all humanity to himself in the main fall harvest of mankind!

81:6 I removed his shoulder from the burden [a type of our spiritual bondage of sin] his [the hands of the called out] hands were delivered from the pots [of slime and making bricks in Egypt].

As physical Israel called out for deliverance, let us also call out for deliverance from spiritual bondage.

81:7 Thou calledst in trouble, and I delivered thee; I answered thee in the secret place of thunder: I proved thee at the waters of Meribah. Selah.

What does God require of us?

81:8 Hear, O my people, and I will testify unto thee: O Israel, if thou wilt hearken unto me;

81:9 There shall no strange god be in thee; neither shalt thou worship [obey] any strange [false doctrine] god.

Seek out the Eternal thy God hungering and thirsting after his righteousness and you shall be filled.

81:10 I am the Lord thy God, which brought thee out of the land of Egypt: open thy mouth wide, and I will fill it.

At their appointed time all humanity will be called out of sin and delivered from bondage to sin; called to come to God!

81:11 But my people would not hearken to my voice; and Israel would none of me. **81:12** So I gave them up unto their own hearts' lust: and they walked in their own counsels.

And we know the history of Physical Israel; the conditions are similar in today's Ekklesia [where everyone trusts in their own counsels instead of the Word of God] and we are at the point where we will be rejected by Christ and given over to the affliction of the flesh in the hope that God may perchance save the spirit and bring us to sincere repentance.

81:13 Oh that my people had hearkened unto me, and Israel had walked in my ways! **81:14** I should soon have subdued their enemies, and turned my hand against their adversaries.

Most of resurrected to physical life humanity who have never known God, will eventually repent in the fall main harvest and then they will run to the Mighty One of Abraham!

81:15 The haters of the LORD should have submitted themselves unto him: but their time should have endured for ever. **81:16** He should have fed them also with the finest of the wheat: and with honey out of the rock should I have satisfied thee.

God wants to save all humanity and God will do so, at their proper appointed times.

The Great Ezra Revival

The Ezra Revival of the Seventh Month foretells a future when all people will come to God, sincerely repentant and hungering and thirsting to learn an d live by the whole Word and Will of God, embracing true godliness with great rejoicing; and receiving God's gift of eternal life!

The great Ezra revival in Judah on the Feast of Trumpets was a prophetic allegory of a future great turning to God!

Visualize the palpable fear as vast armies millions come up and surround Jerusalem, a city which has known only peace and prosperity for a thousand years, a city with no defenses: and then picture the tremendous rejoicing over the final and absolute victory of God over Satan!

Visualize that awesome final victory opening the way for the final judgement and destruction of Satan on the Fast of Atonement, and the people remembering the Glory of God and turning back to him with a newfound Awe and Enthusiastic Zeal which will last for all eternity!

Then visualize the Great Revival of the nations and peoples who have become lax and complacent, as our spiritual High Priest, Jesus Christ himself teaches the Word of Life to people; now sincerely repentant of their lack of zeal.

Reading out the Word of God by Jesus Christ and expounding and explaining that Word by the spirit priests of the spiritual High Priesthood of Jesus Christ, first when he comes at the end of the tribulation and later during the main harvest of humanity!

Brethren, that is what we are in training for! To teach all people about God and the way to reconciliation with God the Father to eternal salvation!

To teach the whole Word and Will of God to a humbled, teachable and sincerely repentant humanity! Throughout the millennium and after the millennium, and yes going on and teaching a passionate zeal for godliness through the Tabernacles harvest of humanity and then going onward to lead and focus all living beings on God the Father for all eternity!

Consider that within that multitude could be our wives, husbands, parents or children or our dear friends, and know that our enemies will seek us out to be reconciled to us, and to learn of God from us!

On the Feast of Trumpets let us cry out to our Mighty Deliverer that his will be done and that his plan bear much fruit; for God's glory and the good of all people! Let us cry out to God to remember his plan and his creation to save humanity! And during the High Holy Days of the seventh month, let us greatly rejoice and glorify our truly Awesome God!

From Scripture we know how the first day of the seventh month, The Feast of Trumpets, was observed at the restoration of Ezra, and how deeply moved the people were by the public reading and explanation of the law.

Nehemiah 8:1-12 And all the people gathered themselves together as one man into the street that was before the water gate; and they spake unto Ezra the scribe to bring the book of the law of Moses, which the LORD had commanded to Israel.

8:2 And **Ezra the priest brought the law before the congregation both of men and women, and all that could hear with understanding, upon the first day of the seventh month.**

8:3 And he read therein before the street that was before the water gate from the morning until midday, before the men and the women, and those that could understand; and the ears of all the people were attentive unto the book of the law.

8:4 And Ezra the scribe stood upon a pulpit of wood, which they had made for the purpose; and beside him stood Mattithiah, and Shema, and Anaiah, and Urijah, and Hilkiah, and Maaseiah, on his right hand; and on his left hand, Pedaiah, and Mishael, and Malchiah, and Hashum, and Hashbadana, Zechariah, and Meshullam.

8:5 And Ezra opened the book in the sight of all the people; (for he was [on a speaking platform above the people] above all the people;) and when he opened it, all the people stood up: **8:6** And Ezra blessed the LORD, the great God. And all the people answered, Amen, Amen, with lifting up their hands: and they bowed their heads, and worshipped the LORD with their faces to the ground.

8:7 Also Jeshua, and Bani, and Sherebiah, Jamin, Akkub, Shabbethai, Hodijah, Maaseiah, Kelita, Azariah, Jozabad, Hanan, Pelaiah, and the Levites, caused the people to understand the law: and the people stood in their place.

8:8 So **they read in the book in the law of God distinctly, and gave the sense, and caused them to understand the reading.**

8:9 And Nehemiah, which is the Tirshatha, and Ezra the priest the scribe, and the Levites that taught the people, said unto all the people, This day is holy unto the LORD your God; mourn not, nor weep. For all the people wept, when they heard the words of the law.

8:10 Then he said unto them, Go your way, eat the fat, and drink the sweet, and send portions unto them for whom nothing is prepared: for this day is holy unto our LORD: neither be ye sorry; for the joy of the LORD is your strength.

8:11 So the Levites stilled all the people, saying, Hold your peace, for the day is holy; neither be ye grieved.

8:12 And all the people went their way to eat, and to drink, and to send portions, and to make great mirth [Joy], **because they had understood the words that were declared unto them.**

In the Scriptures this day is known as Yom Teruah, the day of Shofar sounding in great joy: or the Memorial of Trumpets.

Welcome the Feast of Trumpets with the Shofar.

The Fast of Atonement

Introduction

Just before the millennial Kingdom of God begins on the Feast of Pentecost, Messiah will come and put down all rebellion, placing Satan under restraint for one thousand years.

Then just before the Feast of Pentecost one thousand years later, Satan will be released and will deceive many into rebellion once again. They will go up against the King of kings at Jerusalem and the armies will be destroyed, with Satan and his angels being taken and restrained.

Then after the humbling of humanity there will be great rejoicing over God's deliverance on the Feast of Trumpets.

Then on the tenth day after the Feast of Trumpets, Satan will be judged and condemned and finally completely destroyed; while the atoning sacrifice of the Lamb of God made on Passover for the first fruits who have been called to God during the first seven thousand years; will be extended to all those having died not yet having been called to God in the main harvest of humanity.

The fast of Atonement is about the final judgment and end of Satan, the general repentance of humanity and the extension of the Atoning Sacrifice of the Lamb of God to the main harvest of humanity, and the Feast of Tabernacles is about the resurrection to physical life of the as yet uncalled; and their ingathering into the family of God in the main harvest of humanity.

Godly Fasting

The Day of Atonement is a day of fasting in which nothing is taken into the body for a full night and day. Fasting is often called "afflicting the soul [body]" and is meant to teach us to hunger and thirst after godliness in sincere repentance from all sin.

AN ALLEGORY: We ARE called to become the Bride of Christ

When we are in deep passionate love with our physical mates or spiritual espoused Husband as yesterday's post described, we want to please our Lover, and our spiritual LORD with all our being.

Now if we have a spat or something comes that offends the one we truly love with all our hearts; what do we do? Why we stop at nothing to repair the relationship and reconcile to the one we love!

When we are separated by offenses from our lover we are heart sick, miserable; often we cannot eat or sleep, overcome by anxiety and severe pain of our mind and spirit, often we will set aside everything else to work out a reconciliation. In terms of our relationship with our spiritual

Husband Jesus Christ; He is the perfect Husband and only our own sins can separate us from his profound love.

Romans 8:38 For I am persuaded, that neither death, nor life, nor angels, nor principalities, nor powers, nor things present, nor things to come, **8:39** Nor height, nor depth, nor any other creature, shall be able to separate us from the love of God, which is in Christ Jesus our Lord.

It is our own sins that separate us from our beloved Husband!

Isaiah 59:1 Behold, the Lord's hand is not shortened, that it cannot save; neither his ear heavy, that it cannot hear: **59:2** But your iniquities have separated between you and your God, and your sins have hid his face from you, that he will not hear.

Speaking of a woman as the spiritual Bride of Christ here [in physical relationships BOTH mates should seek reconciliation wholeheartedly]: If a person who is called out as a part of the collective spiritual bride of Jesus Christ, a loving husband; should suddenly fall to a temptation follow another away from Him, committing spiritual adultery: What must be done?

When we come to our reason and realize that we are in error and sin on ANY point, thereby separating ourselves from our Beloved. Is it not incumbent on us to acknowledge the sin that separates us from our beloved and quickly and sincerely repent?

If we truly loved our spiritual Husband, if we truly loved Christ in deed and not just words: we would throw ourselves at the feet of her husband and beg for his mercy; his understanding, his forgiveness.

The same is true of our spiritual relationship with our spiritual Husband Jesus Christ. When we go astray and act contrary to his Word, when we follow others instead of him in spiritual adultery, when we set up men and false teachings as idols in our hearts and obey them instead of our Husband: When we see that we have sinned: Then we are to throw ourselves on his mercy and seek his tender mercies in sincere repentance with all our hearts.

When there is much true love and one's foot slips and the other is offended; does it not immediately become our sole mission in life to effect a reconciliation? Do we not focus all of our efforts and attention on the one goal of repairing the relationship?

You who have loving and sound marriages understand what I am talking about and others will just have to imagine this; but when anything at all threatens a good loving marriage: both sides will not rest until the threat is past. I am talking about real genuine love here; something that is badly lacking in the Church and in our society at large.

Let us understand that the Covenant we have with Jesus Christ is a MARRIAGE COVENANT!

We are espoused to our Lord as a wife undergoing a period of testing to see if we will make a good wife for him. If our love for him should endure and we allow nothing to jeopardize our relationship: If we always put our espoused Husband first; before any other man or god: if we remain faithful to him alone: then we shall be chosen at the resurrection to spirit and become fully at one in spirit with our Lord!

Like a loving husband and wife; if we let absolutely nothing threaten that relationship. And if something does; if some sin enters in. We must quickly repent, throwing ourselves on the mercy of our Lord; seeking reconciliation and a renewing of the relationship. We must diligently seek his forgiveness until it is given: allowing absolutely NOTHING to interfere with our goal until the relationship is restored. We must throw ourselves at his feet in the same way that an erring spouse would repent and beg for mercy.

That is what fasting is all about!

When there is a marital fight; a true lover feels literally sick; he or she cannot eat; they cannot sleep, or think about anything else: Only about repairing the breach between them. That is what fasting is all about!

Fasting is about turning from sin [which separates us from our Lord]; it is about repenting from emotional and spiritual adultery: as we for a small moment were deceived to follow someone else. As we for a moment followed some leader away from him.

Brethren; to follow men instead of our Lord; is spiritual Adultery. As soon as it is recognized it MUST be repented of; and we MUST seek out our Lord and seek to repair the breach with ALL our hearts. That is what fasting is all about! Fasting is sincere repentance and the seeking of our God with all our hearts; to the exclusion of all else including eating and drinking.

The purpose of fasting is to humble ourselves and destroy our personal pride, to sincerely repent of sin; which comes between us and God, separating us from our spiritual Husband.

Fasting is to turn from our own ways and turn back to God. It is to seek God with all our beings to the exclusion of all else.

We should NEVER fast to try to get something until we have FIRST repaired our relationship with God and repented of our sin, reconciling to him. Once we have sincerely repented of being selfishly zealous for our own ways and neglecting zeal for the whole word of God; then we can make our petition to God and he will hear us.

1 John 3:21 Beloved, if our heart condemn us not, then have we confidence toward God. **3:22** And **whatsoever we ask, we receive of him, because we keep his commandments, and do those things that are pleasing in his sight.**

Let each person fast in sincere repentance to seek forgiveness and reconciliation with God will all their hearts; then the sin which is the fundamental cause of the problem will be rooted out and forgiven.

Only when each person has turned to our Lord with all his strength and heart will God correct the problem. It may well be as in the case of Job that God allowed the problem in the beginning to cause us to turn to him in repentance.

Fasting accomplishes nothing if we then continue in sin! It serves NO purpose; we are to fast in repentance from sin, committing to "Go and sin no more!" We are not to fast so that we may feel righteous about ourselves as we continue in sin.

Fasting should never become a matter of routine or self justification, after which we go on our way as before.

The job of any godly person who has the means, is to tell God's people their sins and call them to repentance. That job begins with the Ekklesia and then spreads out to others. It is when the elders refuse to do this job and become lax themselves that others must step up and be counted.

Isaiah 58

Isaiah 58:1 Cry aloud, spare not, lift up thy voice like a trumpet, and shew my people their transgression, and the house of Jacob their sins.

Today the brethren take delight in going to services and giving the appearance of seeking of godliness and of being righteous; but it is all appearance with no substance.

58:2 Yet they seek me daily, and delight to know my ways, as a nation that did righteousness, and forsook not the ordinance of their God: they ask of me the ordinances of justice; they take delight in approaching to God.

They fast and then ask why God does not see and help them; when they were fasting to get what they wanted and to have their own ways; instead of repenting and humbling themselves to abandon their false ways and turn to all the teachings and commandments of God.

Behold while many fast, you continue in your own false ways, taking pleasure in your worldliness and many abuse others.

58:3 Wherefore have we fasted, say they, and thou seest not? wherefore have we afflicted our soul, and thou takest no knowledge? Behold, **in the day of your fast ye find pleasure, and exact all your labours.**

Often we fast for our own advantage over others; and continue to smite out neighbor. We are NOT to fast to feel righteous in our own eyes and to seek advantage over others, or to continue on our own ways contrary to the word of God.

58:4 Behold, ye fast for strife and debate, and to smite with the fist of wickedness: ye shall not fast as ye do this day, to make your voice to be heard on high. **58:5** Is it such a fast that I have chosen? a day for a man to afflict his soul? is it to bow down his head as a bulrush, and to spread sackcloth and ashes under him? wilt thou call this a fast, and an acceptable day to the LORD?

The godly acceptable fast is the fast of repentance of standing on our own ways and humbling ourselves before God.

58:6 Is not this the fast that I have chosen? to loose the bands of wickedness [to turn from our evil doings and humble ourselves before God to DO his will], to undo the heavy burdens [to repent of oppressing others, like Pack, Flurry, Meredith and other elders and brethren do], and to let the oppressed go free, and that ye break every yoke [to repent and break the bondage and yoke of sin]?

We are to fast and repent and learn of the mercy of God, to begin to help others; and to bring our pride down to contrition and start eating and internalizing the whole bread of life, the whole Word of God.

It is a disgrace that some even turn away from their own flesh and reject them, simply because they attend a different corporate church within the Ekklesia.

58:7 Is it not to deal thy bread to the hungry, and that thou bring the poor that are cast out to thy house? when thou seest the naked, that thou cover him; and that thou hide not thyself from thine own flesh?

When our pride is removed and we are repentant of following men, corporations and our own false traditions; when we follow the whole word of God: Then the light of our example will shine forth and we shall become like Christ. Our spiritual health shall become as a Mighty Man of Strength through the word and spirit of God that we follow and our reward will be to become like-minded and in total Spiritual Unity with the Father and Jesus Christ.

58:8 Then shall thy light break forth as the morning, and thine health shall spring forth speedily: and thy righteousness shall go before thee; the glory of the LORD shall be thy rereward.

God will answer us if we fast the fast of repentance to learn of his ways to DO them; casting aside our pride and the ways of our own imagination.

58:9 Then shalt thou call, and the LORD shall answer; thou shalt cry, and he shall say, Here I am. If thou take away from the midst of thee the yoke [burden of sin], the putting forth of the finger [falsely accusing], and speaking [the emptiness of false teachings] vanity;

If we preach the truth of the bread of life to the spiritually hungry and deliver the afflicted to the gospel of Jesus Christ; which is the whole word of God; and if we set the example of the mercy and righteousness of Christ: We shall shine forth the light of godliness and the righteousness of the whole word of God.

58:10 And if thou draw out thy soul to the hungry, and satisfy the afflicted soul; then shall thy light rise in obscurity, and thy darkness be as the noon day:

The following is true SPIRITUALLY in this dispensation as it was physically in the Mosaic Covenant.

To make fat is a reference to the opposite of famine; it means to make strong and healthy; this is also a New Covenant reference to making spiritually healthy and full of the good things of the spirit, as it was to the physical blessings of keeping the Mosaic Covenant.

58:11 And the LORD shall guide thee continually, and satisfy thy soul in drought, and make fat [healthy] thy bones: and thou shalt be like a watered garden, and like a spring of water, whose waters fail not.

The person who takes a stand for the whole Word of God, in its complete physical and spiritual sense; to learn it and to do it; is standing in the breach between God and the people, and shall build up those places that have fallen waste through sin and the correction of our Maker.

58:12 And they that shall be of thee shall build the old waste places: thou shalt raise up the foundations of many generations; and thou shalt be called, The repairer of the breach, The restorer of paths to dwell in.

Those who make the seventh day Sabbath [Fri sunset to Sat sunset] their delight and are zealous to keep it in its full sanctity; who reject doing their own pleasure like participating in sin by buying food and service in restaurants, cooking and doing any work or paying others to work [except for doing what God has commanded to be done on Sabbath, and acts of mercy to care for man and beast], are honoring their Father in heaven according to the commandments and shall reap a blessing for doing so.

Brethren we pollute the Sabbath by even speaking of business! We are to speak of the scriptures and holy things and we are NOT to speak of worldliness and our own words; and yes, we are not to gossip about family things either. Save your own words for other times, and use God's time to speak of him.

58:13 If thou turn away thy foot from the sabbath, from doing thy pleasure on my holy day; and call the sabbath a delight, the holy of the LORD, honourable; and shalt honour him, not doing thine own ways, nor finding thine own pleasure, nor speaking thine own words:

Deuteronomy 5:16 Honour thy father and thy mother, as the Lord thy God hath commanded thee; that thy days may be prolonged, and that it may go well with thee, in the land which the Lord thy God giveth thee.

When we think about, and hear, and speak of the whole word of God; we learn of the wondrous perfection of all his ways; and by following the Father and Christ and longing to be with them, learning of them both and keeping all the ways of God, doing all we can to please God and become like our Father and espoused Husband, on HIS Sabbath Day; they will bless for learning and keeping the whole Word of God.

To go to a service and then do our own thing, and speak our own words the remainder of the day; is to pollute the Sabbath and is SIN! It is dishonoring our Father and it is STEALING God's time, which is NOT our time, to do as we want with!

To do our own thing and to speak our own words on Sabbath; is to demonstrate to Christ and the Father that we are only attending for social purposes and to experience an emotional feeling of righteousness, of thinking of ourselves as pretty good godly people!

That is SELF- righteousness and NOT godly righteousness; for godly righteousness would be focusing on the whole word of God and not on our own pleasures on GOD'S DAY!

Isaiah 58:14 Then shalt thou delight thyself in the LORD; and I will cause thee to ride upon the high places of the earth, and feed thee with the heritage of Jacob thy father: for the mouth of the LORD hath spoken it.

Isaiah 59

When we are rejected by Christ and cast into great tribulation, it is not that he cannot save us; it is that we have first rejected his ways for our own ways, toleration of false teachings and rejection of the knowledge of the whole word of God.

The truth is; We have rejected him and his ways for our own ways and he is just tired of pleading with us to learn and keep the way of life.

Isaiah 59:1 Behold, the LORD's hand is not shortened, that it cannot save; neither his ear heavy, that it cannot hear: **59:2 But your iniquities have separated between you and your God, and your sins have hid his face from you, that he will not hear.**

Again telling a partial truth for the purpose of deceiving about the whole truth is lying. This form of lying has become an art on the church of God groups. We are defiled with the blood of those we have not warned to repent and to zealously embrace the whole Word of God. We are full of sin and we have spoken to turn people away from any zeal for all the teachings and commandments of Christ.

59:3 For your hands are defiled with blood, and your fingers with iniquity; your lips have spoken lies, your tongue hath muttered perverseness.

There is no justice in the church of God and we persecute the zealous and speak false teachings instead of the truth of God's word.

59:4 None calleth for justice, nor any pleadeth for truth: they trust in vanity, and speak lies; they conceive mischief, and bring forth iniquity.

Many hide themselves behind a cloak of an appearance of worldly goodness, to strike out at those passing by and take them unawares into their deceptions.

59:5 They hatch cockatrice' eggs, and weave the spider's web: he that eateth of their eggs dieth, and that which is crushed breaketh out into a viper.

We are spiritually naked, bereft of the garments of righteousness, as we try to hide ourselves behind a cloak of our own ways.

59:6 Their webs shall not become garments, neither shall they cover themselves with their works: their works are works of iniquity, and the act of violence is in their hands.

Many religious leaders and elders are full of sin and run to teach their own evil ways to others, not being zealous not live by every Word of God

59:7 Their feet run to evil, and they make haste to shed innocent blood: their thoughts are thoughts of iniquity; wasting and destruction are in their paths.

These men do not know the way to peace with the Father, or even peace among themselves; they each do what is right in our own eyes and seek personal exultation and advantage against the other.

59:8 The way of peace they know not; and there is no judgment in their goings: they have made them crooked paths: whosoever goeth therein shall not know peace.

The lukewarm for the whole Word of God in the Ekklesia; lack the light of God's Spirit because they have quenched that Spirit; rejecting the Word of God and teaching for doctrines the commandments of men. We are spiritually blind and know it not (Rev 3:16).

59:9 Therefore is judgment far from us, neither doth justice overtake us: we wait for light, but behold obscurity; for brightness, but we walk in darkness. **59:10** We grope for the wall like the blind, and we grope as if we had no eyes: we stumble at noon day as in the night; we are in desolate places as dead men.

We have strayed from the whole Word of God and are filled with sorrows caused by our wickedness, and yet we count ourselves righteous.

59:11 We roar all like bears, and mourn sore like doves: we look for judgment, but there is none; for salvation, but it is far off from us.

The scripture is written, first; for those who are expected to understand it. This is about US personally, about those who call themselves by the name of God! Jesus Christ is about to reject us from his body for standing on our own false traditions and rejecting him and any zeal to live by every Word of God.

59:12 For our transgressions are multiplied before thee, and our sins testify against us: for our transgressions are with us; and as for our iniquities, we know them;

We pollute the Sabbath and High Days, we idolize men and organizations, committing spiritual adultery against our espoused Husband by exalting our idols of men, organizations and false traditions above the word of God and then we dare to call ourselves by the name of God.

We lie against Christ by saying that we can do whatever we want and he will overlook it; when we are to live by every Word of God.

59:13 In transgressing and lying against the LORD, and departing away from our God, speaking oppression and revolt [against the teachings and commandments of Christ], conceiving and uttering from the heart words of falsehood [to deceive people away for Christ to gain a personal following].

59:14 And judgment is turned away backward, and justice standeth afar off: for truth is fallen in the street, and equity cannot enter.

59:15 Yea, truth [sound doctrine] faileth; and he that departeth from evil maketh himself a prey [the faithful to God have become victims of the wicked in the corporate Ekklesia] : and the LORD saw it, and it displeased him that there was no [godly] judgment.

Jesus Christ will repay us for all our many sins against him; he WILL reject us for we have rejected him; and he will correct us in the furnace of affliction that by the destruction of the flesh we may be humbled and spiritually saved.

59:16 And he saw that there was no man, and wondered that there was no intercessor: therefore his arm brought salvation unto him; and his righteousness, it sustained him. **59:17** For he put on righteousness as a breastplate, and an helmet of salvation upon his head; and he put on the garments of vengeance for clothing, and was clad with zeal as a cloak.

Christ will humble spiritual and physical Israel and every nation, and will bring them to contrite repentance before him.

59:18 According to their deeds, accordingly he will repay, fury to his adversaries, recompence to his enemies; to the islands he will repay recompence.

Then Christ and all his teachings and commandments will be respected, learned and kept in the earth and when the enemy comes pouring into Jerusalem he will come and set his Banner in Jerusalem and save Jacob and all repentant persons.

59:19 So shall they fear the name of the LORD from the west, and his glory from the rising of the sun. When the enemy shall come in like a flood, the Spirit of the LORD shall lift up a standard against him. **59:20** And the Redeemer shall come to Zion, and unto them that turn from transgression in Jacob, saith the LORD.

Christ makes a personal covenant with all the sincerely repentant who are wholeheartedly dedicated to live in passionate Christ-like zeal by EVERY WORD of GOD!

59:21 As for me, this is my covenant with them, saith the LORD; **My spirit that is upon thee, and my words which I have put in thy mouth, shall not depart out of thy mouth, nor out of the mouth of** thy seed, nor out of the mouth of thy seed's seed, saith the LORD, from henceforth and for ever.

Psalms of Repentance for Passover and Atonement

Physical Israel in bondage to pharaoh in Egypt and being called out of Egypt, was an instructional illustration or allegory of a Spiritual Israel being called out of worldliness and bondage to Satan and sin.

The sacrifice of the Passover lamb or kid covering physical Israel and saving them from the destroyer in Egypt was a type of the sacrifice of the spiritual Lamb of God covering and saving Spiritual Israel from bondage to Satan and sin.

What about the latter main harvest of humanity? The day of Atonement is the latter main harvest of humanity counterpart of the Passover, with the sacrifice of the goat.

Spiritually Passover is about the spiritual Sacrifice of Christ; but before the sacrifice of Christ the Lamb of God may be applied to us, we must first be called out of sin by God and then we must sincerely repent and commit ourselves to go forward to live by every Word of God.

The future main harvest will be resurrected to physical life and will also be called to repentance. The fast of Atonement pictures the repentance of that main harvest and also pictures the removal of Satan and the application of the sacrifice of Christ [by the sacrifice of the Atonement goat].

These are Psalms of sincere repentance traditionally read before Passover and Atonement.

Psalm 6

A prayer for deliverance

Psalm 6:1 O LORD, rebuke me not in thine anger, neither chasten me in thy hot displeasure. **6:2** Have mercy upon me, O LORD; for I am weak: O LORD, heal me [deliver us from the Adversary for we cannot deliver ourselves]; for my bones are vexed [by the enemies of righteousness]. **6:3** My soul [breath, life] is also sore vexed: but thou, O LORD, how long?

How long must I wait for your merciful deliverance?

6:4 Return, O LORD, deliver my soul [breath, life]: oh save me for thy mercies' sake.

David is faithful to God but feels overwhelmed by the adversaries of godliness; who refuse to live by God's Word and who persecute those who do.

The dead are like a machine with the power switch shut off, unable to do anything

6:5 For in death there is no remembrance of thee: in the grave who shall give thee thanks?

This is a call to be saved from physical death, as an allegory of being saved from the grave in the resurrection to spirit.

6:6 I am weary with my groaning; all the night make I my bed to swim [with my tears of sorrow]; I water my couch with my tears. **6:7** Mine eye is consumed because of grief; it waxeth old because of all mine enemies.

God will deliver all those who exalt and put their trust in him to live by God's Word, and all those who condemn them for their Christ-like zeal for God will be ashamed.

6:8 Depart from me, all ye workers of iniquity; for the LORD hath heard the voice of my weeping. 6:9 The LORD hath heard my supplication; the LORD will receive my prayer. 6:10 Let all mine

enemies be ashamed and sore vexed: let them return and be ashamed suddenly.

Psalm 32

A Psalm about the blessing of forgiveness for the sincerely repentant

Psalm 32:1 Blessed is he whose transgression is forgiven, whose sin is covered. **32:2** Blessed is the man unto whom the LORD imputeth not iniquity, and in whose spirit there is no guile.

To be forgiven one must sincerely repent from all past sin and STOP sinning [stop transgressing the Word of God] in future, committing to go forward and sin no more. Only then will the sinner be forgiven and justified by the application of the sacrifice of Jesus Christ. the Atoning sacrifice.

Romans 2:13 (For not the hearers of the law are just before God, but **the doers of the law shall be justified.**

When we keep silent and fail to sincerely repent of our past sins and we refuse to commit to STOP sinning, we begin to die spiritually and such people will not be forgiven nor raised up from the grave to eternal life.

Psalm 32:3 When I kept silence [did not sincerely repent], my bones waxed old [all hope of lasting life failed and my body judged for destruction] through my roaring [proud self-will] all the day long. **32:4** For day and night thy hand [chastening and rebuke] was heavy upon me: my moisture [my life strength dried up as moisture in a drought] is turned into the drought of summer. Selah.

Because we will surely die in our sin, let us quickly acknowledge our iniquity and sincerely repent to turn to live by every Word of God; so that we might be saved from eternal death.

If we confess our sins against God and we sincerely repent, committing ourselves to go forward and live by every Word of God; we shall be forgiven, justified by the application of the sacrifice of the Lamb of God and saved from damnation.

32:5 I acknowledge my sin unto thee, and mine iniquity have I not hid. I said, I will confess my transgressions unto the LORD; and thou forgavest the iniquity of my sin. Selah.

Every godly person prays for forgiveness from sins and the godly strength to live by every Word of God.

32:6 For this shall every one that is godly pray unto thee in a time when thou mayest be found: surely in the floods of great waters [the godly shall be delivered from the grave as pictured by Israel being delivered from the waters of the Red Sea] they shall not come nigh unto him.

The godly put their trust in God and live by every Word of God, quickly repenting when any sin or error is discovered.

32:7 Thou art my hiding place; thou shalt preserve me from trouble [God's Word teaches us the way to peace and life]; thou shalt compass me about [God will ultimately surround those who are zealous to follow him with eternal blessings] with songs of deliverance. Selah.

God's Word instructs his faithful in the ways of peace and eternal life.

32:8 I will instruct thee and teach thee in the way which thou shalt go: I will guide thee with mine eye.

Let us not be self-willed so that we must be forced to obey God's Word, but let us obey willingly and enthusiastically because God's Word is for our good.

32:9 Be ye not as the horse, or as the mule, which have no understanding: whose mouth must be held in with bit and bridle, lest they [if we are self-willed like the stubborn mule, we shall be corrected] come near unto thee.

The unrepentant refuse to live by God's Word to their own hurt; while those who are zealous to live by every Word of God are greatly blessed in learning the way to peace, blessings and eternal life.

32:10 Many sorrows shall be to the wicked: but he that trusteth in the LORD, mercy shall compass him about.

Those who sincerely repent of their failure to live by every Word of God and who dedicate themselves to live by every Word of God in Christ-like zeal; shall surely Greatly Rejoice and Shout for Joy at their resurrection and change to eternal spirit.

32:11 Be glad in the LORD, and rejoice, ye righteous [true righteousness is to live by EVERY WORD of GOD]: and shout for joy, all ye that are upright in heart.

Psalm 38

God will correct all those he loves when the go astray, so that by afflicting the flesh the spirit may be saved

Psalm 38:1 O lord, rebuke me not in thy wrath: neither chasten me in thy hot displeasure. **38:2** For thine arrows stick fast in me, and thy hand presseth me sore. **38:3** There is no soundness in my flesh because of thine anger; neither is there any rest in my bones because of my sin.

Own stubborn self-will and insistence on living by our own ways instead of living by the Word of God will bring our eternal destruction. When we fall into such pride, a loving God corrects us afflicting the flesh to bring us to repentance and save the spirit.

38:4 For mine iniquities are gone over mine head: as an heavy burden they are too heavy for me. **38:5** My wounds [which have come as the result of sins] stink and are corrupt because of my foolishness.

38:6 I am troubled; I am bowed down greatly [greatly afflicted]; I go mourning [over the evils in the land, and repenting over my sins] all the day long. **38:7** For my loins are filled with a loathsome disease: and there is no soundness in my flesh. **38:8** I am feeble and sore broken: I have roared [cried out in anguish] by reason of the disquietness of my heart.

The godly are full of sorrow over the wickedness overspreading the earth.

If our desire is to live by every Word of God, God will correct us when we go astray and he will deliver us when we learn our lesson and turn back to him. Nothing can be hidden from God.

38:9 Lord, all my desire is before thee; and my groaning is not hid from thee.

Even though all the earth is against us because we live by every Word of God, the godly will be steadfast and will put their trust in the Eternal. Even if we must suffer many sorrows in this physical life our Mighty One will deliver us from the grave into an eternal life of blessings and rejoicing.

38:10 My heart panteth, my strength faileth me: as for the light of mine eyes, it also is gone from me. **38:11** My lovers and my friends stand aloof from my sore; and my kinsmen stand afar off. **38:12** They also that seek after my life lay snares for me: and they that seek my hurt speak mischievous things, and imagine deceits all the day long.

The righteous put their trust in God and the Word of God; and not in men.

8:13 But I, as a deaf man, heard not; and I was as a dumb man that openeth not his mouth. **38:14** Thus I was as a man that heareth not, and in whose mouth are no reproofs. **38:15** For in thee, O LORD, do I hope: thou wilt hear, O Lord my God.

God will deliver his faithful and the enemy will not continue in rejoicing over the fall of the godly, but will be corrected.

38:16 For I said, Hear me, lest otherwise they should rejoice over me: when my foot slippeth, they magnify themselves against me. **38:17** For I am ready to halt [ready to perish] sorrow is continually before me.

When we are afflicted, let us sincerely repent and RUN to the Eternal our Deliverer.

38:19 But mine enemies [spiritually our enemies are Satan and sin] they that hate me wrongfully are multiplied. **38:20** They also that render evil for good are mine adversaries; because I follow the thing that good is.

When we do well, the wicked hate us and attack us for living by God's Word.

38:21 Forsake me not, O LORD: O my God, be not far from me. **38:22** Make haste to help me, O Lord my salvation.

Ultimately God delivers those who live by every Word of God: May God's deliverance come quickly

Psalm 51

An Psalm of repentance and prayer for mercy

Psalm 51:1 Have mercy upon me, O God, according to thy lovingkindness: according unto the multitude of thy tender mercies blot out my transgressions. **51:2** Wash me throughly from mine iniquity, and cleanse me from my sin.

Only sincere repentance and a wholehearted commitment to live by every Word of God will bring cleansing from sin by the application of the sacrifice of Christ the Lamb of God (Rom 2:13).

51:3 For I acknowledge my transgressions: and my sin is ever before me [we are to be always alert to seek out and expunge our sins]. **51:4** Against thee, thee only, have I sinned, and done this evil in thy sight: [let us accept that our own ways and stubborn self-will are wrong, and that God's Word is right and the right way to live] that thou mightest be justified when thou speakest, and be clear when thou judgest. **51:5** Behold, I was shapen in iniquity; and in sin did my mother conceive me. **51:6** Behold, thou desirest truth in the inward parts: and in the hidden part thou shalt make me to know wisdom.

John 17:17 Sanctify them through thy truth: **thy word is truth.**

Psalm 51:7 Purge me with hyssop [Hyssop was used to sprinkle the blood of the lamb, this reference meaning: please purge my sins by the blood of the Lamb of God.], and I shall be clean [from all sin]: wash me, [with the water of the Word and Spirit of God (Eph 5:26)] and I shall be whiter than snow. **51:8** Make me to hear joy and gladness [when God tells us that we are forgiven we will delight in God's salvation]; that the bones which thou hast broken may rejoice. **51:9** Hide thy face from my sins, and blot out all mine iniquities.

51:10 Create in me a clean heart [God will purify the sincerely repentant from all sin and all proud self-will, to follow God] O God; and renew a right spirit [give us a proper godly attitude of love for God and loving zeal to live by every Word of God] within me. **51:11** Cast me not away from thy presence; and take not thy holy spirit from me. **51:12** Restore unto me the joy of thy salvation [deliver the repentant by thy tender mercies, for we abhor our sins against the Word of God]; and uphold me with thy free spirit.

When we live by every Word of God, we set an example for all who see us; and we learn by doing the ways of God so that we may teach others to do the same.

51:13 Then will I teach transgressors thy ways; and sinners shall be converted unto thee. **51:14** Deliver me from bloodguiltiness, O God, thou God of my salvation: and my tongue shall sing aloud of thy righteousness.

51:15 O Lord, open thou my lips; and my mouth shall shew forth thy praise. **51:16** For thou desirest not sacrifice; else would I give it: thou delightest not in burnt offering.

51:17 The sacrifices of God are a broken spirit [submissive humility before God, with all stubborn self-will and pride crushed to powder]: a broken and a contrite heart [the pride of sin crushed to powder], O God, thou wilt not despise.

51:18 Do good in thy good pleasure unto Zion [Messiah, come to Jerusalem and build the Kingdom of God]: build thou the walls of Jerusalem. **51:19 Then shalt thou be pleased with the sacrifices of righteousness, with burnt offering and whole burnt offering** [When Christ comes God will convert Israel and Jerusalem to sincere repentance, and then their repentance (now sincere) and their sacrifices both physical and spiritual will be accepted.]: **then shall they offer bullocks upon thine altar.**

Sin and Trespass Offerings represent sin repented of, and Burnt Offerings represent the righteousness of wholehearted obedience, dedication and Christ-like zeal to live by every WORD of God.

Psalm 102

Correction of the flesh brings sorrow over sin unto sincere repentance, which brings deliverance to the spirit.

Psalm 102:1 Hear my prayer, O LORD, and let my cry come unto thee. **102:2** Hide not thy face from me in the day when I am in trouble; incline thine ear unto me: in the day when I call answer me speedily. **102:3** For my days are consumed [dissipate] like smoke, and my bones are burned as [in the fire] an hearth.

102:4 My heart is smitten [our pride must be broken to contrition], and withered like grass; so that I forget to eat my bread [we are to fast for sorrow and heaviness of spirit in sincere repentance over our sins]. **102:5** By reason of the voice of my groaning my bones cleave to my skin.

Those separated from God by their sins, are alone and wondering like a bird in the wilderness.

102:6 I am like a pelican of the wilderness: I am like an owl of the desert. **102:7** I watch, and am as a sparrow alone upon the house top.

Our enemies mock us because we are afflicted for our sins.

102:8 Mine enemies reproach me all the day; and they that are mad against me are sworn against me. **102:9** For I have eaten ashes [the sinful will partake of affliction like daily eating until they sincerely repent] like bread, and mingled my drink with weeping.

God called us and lifted us up from bondage to sin, and God casts us back down and afflicts us when we turn away from him to sin against His Word.

102:10 Because of thine indignation and thy wrath: for thou hast lifted me up, and cast me down.

102:11 My days are like a shadow that declineth [my life is fading and withering away because of my sins]; and I am withered like grass.

David learns that man is but flesh which is temporary and passing; while God and the Word of God are forever and forever.

102:12 But thou, O LORD, shall endure for ever; and thy remembrance unto all generations.

God will have mercy on the sincerely repentant who turn to live by every Word of God.

102:13 Thou shalt arise, and have mercy upon Zion [the Temple is a type of the people of God who seek to sincerely repent and live by every Word of God]: for the time [for the coming of Christ is at hand] to favour her [Jerusalem and the people of God], yea, the set time, is come.

The true servants of God love his presence among them; they will love Jerusalem because the Temple of God the Father will be there and Messiah the Christ will rule all nations from Jerusalem.

102:14 For thy servants take pleasure in her stones, and favour the dust thereof.

When Christ comes all nations will sincerely repent, to serve and live by every Word of God.

102:15 So the heathen shall fear the name of the LORD, and all the kings of the earth thy glory.

When Christ comes as King of kings with his chosen, he will be glorified in all the earth.

102:16 When the LORD shall build up Zion, he shall appear in his glory.

Then God will regard the prayers of the sincerely repentant who acknowledge that they are spiritually destitute and in need of God.

102:17 He will regard the prayer of the destitute [poor in the spirit of pride and self-will], and not despise their prayer.

When Christ comes in his glory the story will be told from generation to generation.

102:18 This shall be written for the generation to come: and the people which shall be created shall praise the LORD.

Our Mighty One will hear the groaning of his afflicted and he will see their sincere repentance; and he will deliver them.

102:19 For he hath looked down from the height of his sanctuary; from heaven did the LORD behold the earth; **102:20** To hear the groaning of the prisoner; to loose those that are appointed to death;

Messiah will teach the Word of God the Father to all people when he comes, and they will worship God and live by every Word of God.

102:21 To declare the name of the LORD in Zion, and his praise in Jerusalem; **102:22** When the people are gathered together, and the kingdoms, to serve the LORD.

For a short time we will be afflicted because of our sins, so that by afflicting the flesh the spirit might repent and be saved.

102:23 He weakened my strength in the way; he shortened my days.

In our affliction we will acknowledge the transitory and meaningless nature of the flesh and our own ways, then we will sincerely repent turning to the things that last forever.

102:24 I said, O my God, take me not away in the midst of my days: thy years are throughout all generations. **102:25** Of old hast thou laid the foundation of the earth: and the heavens are the work of thy hands.

102:26 They shall perish, but thou shalt endure: yea, all of them shall wax old like a garment; as a vesture shalt thou change them, and they shall be changed:

102:27 But thou art the same, and thy years shall have no end.

Even if the earth itself should perish, God and every Word of God will last forever: What is man when God has power to change the very planets.

Men can also live forever if they are founded and established on the Word of God.

102:28 The children of thy servants shall continue, and their seed shall be established before thee.

Psalm 130

A Psalm of Repentance; read on the Day of Atonement by the early Ekklesia

Psalm 130:1 Out of the depths have I cried unto thee, O LORD.

David cries out in repentance out of the depth of his despair over sin, as an example for us that we should also sincerely repent and wholeheartedly turn to the Eternal.

130:2 Lord, hear my voice: let thine ears be attentive to the voice of my supplications. **130:3** If thou, LORD, shouldest mark iniquities, O Lord, who shall stand? **130:4** But there is forgiveness with thee, that thou mayest be feared.

Let us all sincerely repent and seek our God with all of our hearts, let us all beg our merciful LORD to remember our sins no more and to forgive us so that we may serve him and live by his every Word from henceforth and forever more!

130:5 I wait for the LORD, my soul doth wait, and in his word do I hope. **130:6** My soul waiteth [longs] for the Lord more than they that watch for the morning: I say, more than they that watch for the morning.

Let us sincerely repent and long for the Eternal's merciful redemption; so that we may serve him with wholehearted diligence, now and forever more!

130:7 Let Israel hope in the LORD: for with the LORD there is mercy, and with him is plenteous redemption. **130:8** And he shall redeem Israel from all his iniquities.

Messiah has paid the penalty for our iniquity with his own life as the Lamb of God; redeeming the sincerely repentant who fully commit to: "Go and sin no more" (John 8:11, and "To live by every Word of God" (Matthew 4:4).

Psalm 143

When we find ourselves in times of trouble and we wonder what to do and where we should go; there is only one answer. We must turn to God and immerse ourselves in the Word of God. We must humble ourselves before God and diligently seek Him with a whole heart.

We must sincerely repent of trusting in any unscriptural false words of men, to turn to and to live by every Word of God. Only then can we expectantly call on God for His mercy and deliverance; and the Eternal Deliverer will hear us and accept us as His own.

Psalm 143:1 Hear my prayer, O LORD, give ear to my supplications: in thy faithfulness answer me, and in thy righteousness. **143:2** And enter not into judgment with thy servant: for in thy sight shall no man living be justified.

If the godly fall away becoming proud and self- justifying, full of our own ways and our own high opinions of our own righteousness; God will correct us, crushing our arrogance to contrition and humbling us before Him.

143:3 For the enemy hath persecuted my soul; he hath smitten my life down to the ground; he hath made me to dwell in darkness, as those that have been long dead. **143:4** Therefore is my spirit overwhelmed within me; my heart within me is desolate.

When our pride has been purged and turned to humility before God, then we will turn in sincere repentance to remember and to study the Word of God to learn it, and internalize it and to live by every Word of God.

143:5 I remember the days of old; I meditate on all thy works; I muse on the work of thy hands. **143:6** I stretch forth my hands unto thee: my soul thirsteth after thee, as a thirsty land. Selah.

Then with our wholehearted turning to the Eternal, He will deliver his people from bondage to Satan, sin and the grave in the resurrection.

143:7 Hear me speedily, O LORD: my spirit faileth: hide not thy face from me, lest I be like unto them that go down into the pit. **143:8** Cause me to hear thy lovingkindness in the morning; for in thee do I trust: cause me to know the way wherein I should walk; for I lift up my soul unto thee.

143:9 Deliver me, O LORD, from mine enemies [our true enemies are spiritual; Satan, sin and the grave]: I flee unto thee to hide me. **143:10** Teach me to do thy will; for thou art my God: thy spirit is good; lead me into the land of uprightness [the upright live by every Word of God].

143:11 Quicken [make alive, give life, resurrect] me, O LORD, for thy name's sake: for thy righteousness' sake bring my soul out of trouble.

A faithful servant obeys his master; therefore we are the servants of those we obey. Either doing what we want - which is sin - to our own destruction; or obeying and living by every Word of God, and receiving God's Gift of Eternal Life.

143:12 And of thy mercy cut off mine enemies, and destroy all them that afflict my soul [our enemies are spiritual; Satan, sin and the grave]: for I am thy servant.

Satan's Final End

Peter wrote that no scripture can be interpreted privately, meaning that all scriptures on any subject must fit together and support one another and that no single scripture can stand alone, or contrary to other scriptures.

2 Peter 1:20 Knowing this first, that no prophecy of the scripture is of any private interpretation.

All scriptures on a given subject must fit together, and in studying any subject we must put all the scriptures on a subject together. In that way God protects us from translation faults, and the truth of his Word is revealed.

This is the process by which we must apply in resolving the enigma of having several scriptures refer to the end of Satan as death, while Revelation 20:10 seems to refer to his end being eternal torment.

Revelation 20:10 And the devil that deceived them was cast into the lake of fire and brimstone, where the beast and the false prophet are, and shall be tormented day and night for ever and ever.

Romans 6:23 For the wages of sin is death; but the gift of God is eternal life through Jesus Christ our Lord.

The wages of sin is DEATH!

Ezekiel 18:4 Behold, all souls are mine; as the soul of the father, so also the soul of the son is mine: **the soul that sinneth, it shall die.**

Romans 6:23 For **the wages of sin is death**; but the gift of God is eternal life through Jesus Christ our Lord.

Who must pay those wages?

ALL unrepentant sinners! and that includes angels who are unrepentant sinners!

God will pass judgment on Satan and those angels who follow him on a future Day of Atonement.

Can angels die?

Did the very Creator God die for us? If the Creator God himself could give up his God-ship to die for his creation; then the sinful angels can also be destroyed by God for their wickedness.

Show me where in the scriptures it says that angels cannot die if God should choose to destroy the wicked among them?

Satan's Fate

Isaiah said it this way:

Isaiah 27:1 "In that day the LORD with his sore and great and strong sword shall punish leviathan [Satan and his Babylonian Mysteries system] the piercing [criminal] serpent, even leviathan that crooked serpent [the evil system of the criminal 1281]; and **he shall slay the dragon** [winged serpent, Satan] **that is in the** (Rev 13:1) **sea** [among many peoples]."

The Sea is a type of the many peoples that follow Satan's system. Satan deceives and leads the nations and peoples.

Revelation 20:15 And he saith unto me, The waters which thou sawest, where **the whore sitteth, are peoples, and multitudes, and nations, and tongues.**

Because Lucifer sought to steal the throne of God the Father in heaven; he is cast down and called the Adversary [Satan].

Satan is to be restrained for one thousand years and soon after that will be cast into death

Isaiah 14:12 How art thou fallen from heaven, O Lucifer, son of the morning! how art thou cut down to the ground, which didst weaken the nations! **14:13** For thou hast said in thine heart, I will ascend into heaven, I will exalt my throne above the stars of God: I will sit also upon the mount of the congregation, in the sides of the north: **14:14** I will ascend above the heights of the clouds; I will be like the most High. **14:15** Yet thou shalt be brought down to hell, to the sides of the pit.

The king of Babylon and the spiritual king of Babylon [Satan] will be brought down to destruction.

14:16 They that see thee shall narrowly look upon thee, and consider thee, saying, Is this the man that made the earth to tremble, that did shake kingdoms; **14:17** That made the world as a wilderness, and destroyed the cities thereof; that opened not the house of his prisoners? **14:18** All the kings of the nations, even all of them, lie in glory, every one in his own house.

The beast and the final false prophet shall be thrown alive into the fire of Gehenna; as an example of the final fate of the ultimate spiritual king of spiritual Babylon and rebellion against the will and commandments of God, Satan.

14:19 But thou art cast out of thy grave like an abominable branch, and as the raiment of those that are slain, thrust through with a sword, that go down to the stones of the pit; as a carcase trodden under feet. **14:20** Thou shalt not be joined with them in burial, because thou hast destroyed thy land, and slain thy people: the seed of evildoers shall never be renowned.

Ezekiel said it this way:

Ezekiel's prophecy of the physical prince as a type of the spiritual king of Tyre; Lucifer/Satan himself

28:11 Moreover the word of the LORD came unto me, saying, **28:12** Son of man, take up a lamentation upon **the king of Tyrus**, and say unto him,

The king of Tyre is quickly identified by the description. In the beginning Lucifer was full of godly wisdom and spiritual beauty as God's people should be.

. . . Thus saith the Lord GOD; **Thou sealest up the sum, full of wisdom, and perfect in beauty**.

28:13 Thou hast been in Eden the garden of God; every precious stone was thy covering, the sardius, topaz, and the diamond, the beryl, the onyx, and the jasper, the sapphire, the emerald, and the carbuncle, and gold: the workmanship of thy tabrets and of thy pipes was prepared in thee in the day that thou wast created.

Here Lucifer is undeniable identified.

28:14 Thou art the anointed cherub that covereth [the throne of God with his wings]; and I have set thee so: thou wast upon the holy mountain of God; thou hast walked up and down in the midst of the stones of fire.

28:15 Thou wast perfect in thy ways from the day that thou wast created, till iniquity was found in thee.

Lucifer was corrupted by his beauty, wisdom and wealth and his position, into an overwhelming pride; just as the church of God has been corrupted into great pride in their assumed righteousness and imagined spiritual riches.

28:16 By the multitude of thy merchandise [riches] they have filled the midst of thee with violence, and thou hast sinned: therefore I will cast thee as profane out of the mountain of God: and I will destroy thee, O covering cherub, from the midst of the stones of fire.

28:17 Thine heart was lifted up [PRIDE] because of thy beauty, thou hast corrupted thy wisdom by reason of thy brightness [you and we became filled with pride because we think of ourselves as having all spiritual knowledge and needing nothing Rev 3:16]: I will cast thee to the ground, I will lay thee before kings, that they may behold thee.

Like Lucifer, today's Spiritual Ekklesia is full of iniquities and is blind to their condition because of our pride. Because we will not listen to the Word of God and exalt ourselves above God and his Word to do as we think best, because of PRIDE: we are rejected by Jesus Christ and by God the Father!

Revelation 3:16 So then because thou art lukewarm [hot for our own ways and cold regarding any zeal for God; equals lukewarm], and neither cold nor hot, I will spue thee out of my mouth. **3:17** Because thou sayest, I am rich [spiritually], and increased with goods, and have need of nothing; and knowest not that thou art wretched, and miserable, and poor, and blind, and naked:

Ezekiel 28:18 Thou hast defiled thy sanctuaries by the multitude of thine iniquities, by the iniquity of thy traffick;

Satan's end and the end of all the unrepentant proud who have no zeal to learn and to keep the whole Word of God: is eternal death!

. . . therefore will I bring forth a fire from the midst of thee, it shall devour thee, and I will bring thee to ashes upon the earth in the sight of all them that behold thee. **28:19** All they that know thee among the people shall be astonished at thee: thou shalt be a terror, and never shalt thou be any more.

The Wages of Sin

Ezekiel 18:4 Behold, all souls are mine; as the soul of the father, so also the soul of the son is mine: **the soul that sinneth, it shall die.**

Romans 6:23 For **the wages of sin is death**; but the gift of God is eternal life through Jesus Christ our Lord.

Who must pay those wages? ALL unrepentant sinners; and that includes angels who are unrepentant sinners!

God has already passed judgment on Satan and those angels who follow him; their judgment is to be cast into utter eternal darkness **Jude 1:13** Raging waves of the sea, foaming out their own shame; **wandering stars**, to whom is reserved the blackness of darkness [oblivion] for ever.

And what is utter eternal darkness but the oblivion of death?

It is mere assumption that no spirit can die.

God is eternal and exists as long as he wants to exist, and can voluntarily give up eternal life, if he so chooses, the Being who became Jesus Christ being an express example of a God giving up his Godhood to be made flesh and die!

All lesser spirits are subject to the commandments, judgment, authority and power of God!

Angels are NOT God the Father! They are subject to God the Father, and HE can judge the wicked among them, and apply to the wicked spirits the wages of their sins! Those who do not rebel and sin have life; and those who rebel and sin will reap the wages of that rebellion and sin; just like unrepentant human beings.

To say that the Father cannot destroy the wicked spirits; is to LIMIT the POWER of ALMIGHTY GOD!

Let us consider **Revelation 20:10** And the devil that deceived them was cast into the lake of fire and brimstone, where the beast and the false prophet are, and shall be tormented day and night for ever and ever.

The key to understanding this; is that the word "torment" in 1611 English the word "torment" is synonymous with "judged" or "condemned".

Tormented and judged meant the same thing in 1611, because the condemned were tormented by torture. Since that time various translators have maintained this wording because of their Roman Catholic doctrinal bias of an eternal tormenting hell fire. A better wording of Rev 20:10 is that Satan would be judged and condemned forever and would never again exist day or night forever.

Can a resurrected child of God who has been given eternal life ever die?

Finally, if once given the gift of eternal life; can any human having been elevated to God spirit status; rebel and sin and then still be condemned to death?

God has taken great pains to prevent that from ever happening and it is not likely to ever happen.

Man has been allowed to taste Satan's ways to the full and will then be allowed to taste of God's ways; after which we will make a well informed choice.

It is unthinkable that after tasting BOTH ways to the full, any one person would choose to rebel and sin against God in future eternity: Yet if that were to ever happen, the wicked rebel would lose his eternal life and be destroyed.

Nevertheless, just like the possession of the physical promised land is ABSOLUTELY CONDITIONAL on faithfully living by every Word of God: A place in the spiritual Promised Land of eternal life, is ABSOLUTELY CONDITIONAL on faithful, without compromise; OBEDIENCE to God our Father and to the Husband of our baptismal Covenant!

The book of Deuteronomy teaches us, that possession of the Promised Land is totally conditional on diligent obedience to ALL of God's commandments. This is why Judah and Israel shall soon go into another captivity for the many sins and abominations they do in their land.

That lesson is also for us; the Called Out of the New Covenant.

Any person who is not diligently, zealously, faithful to all of God's commandments today; WILL be rejected by Messiah: just as surely as Israel was rejected and thrust out of the land for their rebellion, disobedience and for their Sabbath breaking.

Our peaceful relationship with God the Father and our Husband: UTTERLY DEPENDS on our faithfulness and zeal for them! FOREVER! and EVER! and EVER!

When I say that if a person, after being changed to spirit, begins to sin deliberately and willfully and rejects God like Satan has would have his eternal life withdrawn; I was not implying that such a thing would happen, only stating that IF this happened, the person would reap the wages of sin. Of course even Almighty God finds that situation unthinkable since we have his promise that death itself will end (Rev 21:4).

If we make an honest mistake, and repent of that when it is brought to our attention, that is one thing; but God will not tolerate any willful deliberate rebellion against him and his ways.

God is working very hard to demonstrate to every person the ways of Satan and God's own ways, so that an informed choice can be made. **I do sincerely doubt that any person after being changed to spirit would ever turn against God**. However: if they did, they would have to face the price for doing so.

Revelation 21:4 And God shall wipe away all tears from their eyes; and **there shall be no more death**, neither sorrow, nor crying, neither shall there be any more pain: for the former things are passed away.

We need to realize that the drying of every tear cannot be accomplished without putting away the cause of our tears, which is Satan and sin itself. Yes, God will dry every tear and will put all sin OUT of his people, and we shall go on into eternity in harmony with the Father, our Husband and their teachings and commandments.

We must root out the attitude that we can compromise with God's ways and have no tears; for it is disobedience to God and his ways, by ourselves or others, that is the source of our tears.

God will not tolerate willful sin among his people, and is eradicating it from physical persons today; so that it will not exist in eternity.

Those who say that Jesus is love and will understand and wink at or tolerate our sins: ARE LIARS and Antichrists!

The Day of Atonement

What does it mean to be "cut off from your people"? It means that if we do not fast on this day we shall be rejected from being a part of the Covenant people; rejected from being a part of the bride - the Spiritual Ekklesia of the faithful!

The tabernacle and later the temple were to be made according to the pattern provided by God. The scriptures even give us detailed instructions on the plan of the millennial temple to be built by Christ.

All scripture was given for our instruction, and the tabernacle, priesthood and the Holy Days are no exception.

2 Timothy 3:16 All scripture is given by inspiration of God, and is profitable for doctrine, for reproof, for correction, for instruction in righteousness: **3:17** That the man of God may be perfect, thoroughly furnished unto all good works.

Inside the tabernacle in the far west was the Most Holy Place, which represents the throne room of God the Father. All those coming to the

Father had to turn their backs on the east [the sun as the symbol of Lucifer [Satan] for sun worshippers] and seek God the Father in the west.

Between the Most Holy Place and the priesthood and people, was a heavy curtain [drapery] that represented the barrier of sin that separates the people from God the Father.

The High Priest was an allegory of Jesus Christ who became the High Priest between the Father and the people forever on Wave Offering Sunday in 31 A.D. It is Jesus Christ who intercedes for us with the Father and applies his reconciling sacrifice to the sincerely repentant.

At the death of Christ on Passover as the sacrifice for the repentant, the veil representing the sin that separates us form the Father was torn in two opening the way for access by people to the Father through repentance and the application of the sacrifice of Christ.

Jesus Christ died ONCE, yet the Passover [in the first month] represents the atoning sacrifice of Jesus Christ applied to the sins of the repentant Called Out of physical and spiritual Egypt; and the Day of Atonement [in the seventh month] represents the atoning sacrifice being applied to the repentant of the main harvest of humanity.

These things are explained in detail in the Hebrews studies, which I highly recommend reviewing in the context of this Day of Atonement:

Instructions for the Day of Atonement

The physical High Priest may not enter the Most Holy Place when or as he wished; lest he die. This means that anyone tainted by sin cannot enter into the presence of God the Father

Leviticus 16:1 And the LORD spake unto Moses after the death of the two sons of Aaron, when they offered before the LORD, and died; **16:2** And the LORD said unto Moses, Speak unto Aaron thy brother, that he come not at all times into the holy place within the vail before the mercy seat, which is upon the ark; that he die not: for I will appear in the cloud upon the mercy seat.

To enter the Most Holy Place, and that only once a year; the physical high priest must present a sin offering and a burnt offering for himself. The sin offering covered his own sins and the burnt offering pictured wholehearted dedication to God the Father and his Word.

16:3 Thus shall Aaron come into the holy place: with a young bullock for a sin offering, and a ram for a burnt offering.

To enter the Most Holy Place the physical high priest must wash himself, picturing the washing away of all sin and being washed clean from all sin by sincere repentance and the application of the sacrifice of Christ; followed by baptism and going forward to live by every Word of God in future.

The Word of God teaches us to discern between good and evil, and to reject the evil and accept the good thereby keeping us from future sins.

Ephesians 5:25 Husbands, love your wives, even **as Christ also loved the church, and gave himself for it; 5:26 That he might sanctify and cleanse it with the washing of water by the word, 5:27 That he might present it to himself a glorious church, not having spot, or wrinkle, or any such thing; but that it should be holy and without blemish.**

The high priest is then to put on pure priestly linen garments, linen being a type of purity and righteousness of keeping the Word of God.

Revelation 19:7 Let us be glad and rejoice, and give honour to him: for the marriage of the Lamb is come, and his wife hath made herself ready. **19:8** And to her was granted that she should be arrayed in fine linen, clean and white: for **the fine linen is the righteousness of saints.**

Leviticus 16:4 He shall put on the holy linen coat, and he shall have the linen breeches upon his flesh, and shall be girded with a linen girdle, and with the linen mitre shall he be attired: these are holy garments; therefore shall he wash his flesh in water, and so put them on.

The physical high priest must offer the sin offering and the burnt offering for himself; and also take two kids of goats for a sin offering, and a ram for a burnt offering for the assembly of people.

16:5 And he shall take of the congregation of the children of Israel **two kids of the goats for a sin offering, and one ram for a burnt offering.**

Verse six is only an explanation of what the bullock was for; the order of offering is laid out further on.

16:6 And Aaron shall offer his bullock of the sin offering, which is for himself, and make an atonement for himself, and for his house.

Instructions for The Two Goats.

Both goats are to be presented at the door of the tabernacle where the lots were to be cast.

16:7 And he shall take the two goats for the sin offering, and present them before the LORD at the door of the tabernacle of the congregation.

One lot was cast for sacrifice representing Christ, and another lot for the scapegoat. It is God who decides the fall of the lot, to demonstrate that God decides between good and evil as the ultimate judge of humanity

"Azazel" is translated as "scapegoat" in the KJV. This is misleading, since the word scapegoat has connotations of wrongful accusation in modern English. "Azazel" actually means "appointed for complete removal" and refers to this goat representing Satan the original source of sin being entirely removed.

16:8 And Aaron shall cast lots upon the two goats; one lot for the LORD, and the other lot for the scapegoat.

The lot of Christ identifies the goat to be sacrificed as representative of the sacrifice of Jesus Christ to atone for sin.

The sacrificial lamb or goat of Passover represented the application of the sacrifice of Christ to the early harvest of the Called Out; and the sacrificial goat of the Day of Atonement represents the sacrifice of Christ being applied to the rest of humanity in the fall main harvest.

16:9 And Aaron shall bring the goat upon which the LORD's lot fell, and offer him for a sin offering.

The scapegoat was to carry uncleanness and sin away from the main fall harvest of humanity. This represents the removal of all uncleanness and sin so that the repentant of the main harvest can be reconciled to God the Father. The scapegoat represents Satan being removed from influencing humanity forever more.

16:10 But the goat, on which the lot fell to be the scapegoat, shall be presented alive before the LORD, to make an atonement with him, and to let him go for a scapegoat [To be completely removed from among the people forever.] into the wilderness.

The Sin Offering

Then the Sin Offering was made [after the lots, but before the two goats ceremony] for the physical high priest. Please bear in mind that the physical high priest was a physical man who must have his own sins atoned for, before he could enter the Most Holy Place [The Hebrews study is key here.].

Yet we now have a High Priest who has entered the Most Holy Place in heaven without any sacrifice for his own sins, because he was free from all sin and perfect before God the Father, being the sacrifice and sin bearer for both the Called Out of the early harvest [and once these things happen in their full fulfillment] for main fall harvest of humanity.

16:11 And Aaron shall bring the bullock of the sin offering, which is for himself, and shall make an atonement for himself, and for his house, and shall kill the bullock of the sin offering which is for himself:

After sacrificing the bullock for himself, the physical high priest entered the Most Holy Place on the Day of Atonement, with the censor filled with the holy fire and the incense of the prayers and praise of the repentant faithful.

The incense was to be be placed before the Mercy Seat which is the name of the throne of God the Father, figurative that God's throne is covered in the prayers and praise of those who come to him in sincere repentance, petitioning him for reconciliation through the blood of the Sin Offering [Jesus Christ].

The fire that came from heaven and burned perpetually on the altar in the temple was a symbol of the Shekinah [glory of the presence of God, which came down from heaven in the form of fire] or Holy Spirit.

The sweet incense represented the rising of prayers and praise, offered to God the Father in heaven.

The glory of God the Father is so great that a cloud of incense picturing prayers of sincere repentance from sin; must come between the Father and the petitioner; demonstrating that the Father will not tolerate any sin at all, not even the appearance of sin, to pollute His Holy presence.

Just as God will not tolerate sin, neither should we. Those who compromise with God's Word will NEVER be reconciled to God; for the sacrifice of Christ is ONLY applied to the sincerely repentant!

Romans 2:13 (For not the hearers of the law are just before God, **but the doers of the law shall be justified.**

The incense pictures the prayers of repentance of those seeking to be reconciled to God the Father in heaven; and without that complete wholehearted repentance, we CANNOT be reconciled to God the Father and we DO NOT have access to God.

Any organization that teaches tolerance for sin and compromise with any part of God's Word is cut off from God!

On this Day of Atonement, let us fast the fast of true repentance and renew our zeal to live by every Word of God!

16:12 And he shall take a censer full of burning coals of fire from off the altar before the LORD, and his hands full of sweet incense beaten small, and bring it within the vail: **16:13** And he shall put the incense upon the fire before the LORD, that the cloud of the incense may cover the mercy seat that is upon the testimony, that he die not: **16:14** And he shall take of the blood of the bullock, and sprinkle it with his finger upon the mercy seat eastward; and before the mercy seat shall he sprinkle of the blood with his finger seven times.

The seven times sprinkling pictures the complete acceptance by God the Father of the atoning sacrifice of Christ [who is the spirit High Priest being illustrated by the Aaronic high priest] for all of humanity; first for the early harvest and now on Atonement for the main harvest of humanity.

Now the goat of the Sin Offering for the multitude is sacrificed, and its blood is also brought into the Most Holy Place and sprinkled on and before the throne of God the Father. This offering atones for the people of the fall main harvest of humanity..

Then the First Goat Representing Christ is Sacrificed [Like the Passover Lamb] **For The Sins of the Main Harvest**

16:15 Then shall he kill the goat of the sin offering, that is for the people, and bring his blood within the vail, and do with that blood as he did with the blood of the bullock, and sprinkle it upon the mercy seat, and before the mercy seat: **16:16** And he shall make an atonement for the holy place, because of the uncleanness of the children of Israel, and because of their transgressions in all their sins: and so shall he do for the tabernacle of the congregation, that remaineth among them in the midst of their uncleanness.

No person may enter the tabernacle/temple during the entire ceremony while the physical high priest is moving between the Most Holy Place and the altar of sacrifice.

16:17 And there shall be no man in the tabernacle of the congregation when he goeth in to make an atonement in the holy place, until he [the high priest] come out [of the tabernacle / temple after completing the ceremony], and have made an atonement for himself, and for his household, and for all the congregation of Israel.

16:18 And he [the high priest] shall go out [of the Most Holy Place] unto the altar that is before the LORD, and make an atonement for it [an atonement to cleanse the altar]; and shall take of the blood of the bullock, and of the blood of the goat, and put it upon the horns of the altar round about. **16:19** And he shall sprinkle of the blood upon it with his finger seven times, and cleanse it, and hallow it from the uncleanness of the children of Israel.

After this ceremony of entry into the Most Holy Place and the reconciliation of the people to the Father; the sins of the nations were be laid on the head of the ScapeGoat.

The Live Azazel Goat

After the sacrificial goat is killed as a Sin Offering for all the people; the scapegoat is removed from among the people. This was an instructional allegory that all humanity of the latter main harvest could only enter the presence of God the Father only after the removal of sin [by the removal of Satan and sincere repentance] and the application of the sacrifice of Christ the Lamb of God.

16:20 And when he hath made an end of reconciling the holy place, and the tabernacle of the congregation, and the altar, he shall bring the live goat: [outside the Most Holy Place]

16:21 And Aaron shall lay both his hands upon the head of the live goat, and confess over him all the iniquities of the children of Israel [In future all nations shall be grafted into Israel], and all their transgressions in all their sins, putting them upon the head of the goat, and shall send him away by the hand of a fit man into the wilderness: **16:22** And the goat shall bear upon him all their iniquities unto a land not inhabited: and he shall let go the goat in the wilderness.

The "Azazel" goat [representing Satan] does not bear the sins of the people like Christ bears and atones for sin; rather the goat representing Satan bears **responsibility** for the sins of the whole main harvest of humanity who had died in their sins. The removal of this goat symbolizes the removal of Satan the source of the sins of the people, freeing the people of the main fall harvest from their bondage to Satan, sin and death.

Then with the Fast of Atonement removal of Satan, the ultimate fountainhead of sin, and the people repenting with fasting; the sacrifice of Christ can be expanded from the Passover sacrifice for a few, to redeem the entire [repentant] main harvest of humanity from all sin.

The high priest must leave the tabernacle after having touched the goat of sin, and he must remove the holy garments and wash himself from his contact with the Satan goat.

Then the holy garments must be washed after contact with sin because they picture the total purity from sin and the complete righteousness of Jesus Christ the High Priest of the New Covenant.

16:23 And Aaron [and subsequent high priests] shall come into the tabernacle of the congregation, and shall put off the linen garments, which he put on when he went into the holy place, and shall leave them there: **16:24** And he shall wash his flesh with water in the holy place, and put on his garments, and come forth,

Once the Satan goat is removed, the people have sincerely repented and sin having been atoned for by the Sin Offerings [which represent the application of Christ's sacrifice], the main fall harvest of humanity can be reconciled to God the Father as they are resurrected in their courses through the seven thousand year main harvest of the Feast of the Ingathering of Nations [Tabernacles].

The burnt offerings representing a reconciled people serving the Father in wholehearted completeness, just as Jesus Christ also serves God the Father in total passionate wholehearted loving faithful obedience and zeal to do the whole will of God the Father!

. . . and offer his burnt offering, and the burnt offering of the people, and make an atonement for himself, and for the people. **16:25** And the fat of the sin offering shall he burn upon the altar.

The fit [strong] man who took the goat into the wilderness, must wash himself and his clothes before coming back among the people. This to cleanse even the uncleanness incurred by touching the goat, which was bearing the sins out from among the people.

16:26 And he that let go the goat for the scapegoat shall wash his clothes, and bathe his flesh in water, and afterward come into the camp.

Then the bodies of the goat and bull sin offerings, are to be removed from the camp and burned outside the congregation, according to the law of the Sin Offerings.

16:27 And the bullock for the sin offering, and the goat for the sin offering, whose blood was brought in to make atonement in the holy place, shall one carry forth without the camp; and they shall burn in the fire their skins, and their flesh, and their dung.

The men who carried the bodies of the Sin Offerings outside the camp must also wash themselves and their clothes from the uncleanness of being associated with the sin being borne by the sacrifices.

16:28 And he that burneth them shall wash his clothes, and bathe his flesh in water, and afterward he shall come into the camp.

The Command for a Complete Fast on the Tenth Day of the Seventh Month

This is not just some ritual fast; it is to be a fast of repentance from all sin, and a commitment to go forward and sin no more; so that the sin offering of Jesus Christ may be applied to us personally.

16:29 And this shall be a statute for ever unto you: that **in the seventh month, on the tenth day of the month, ye shall afflict your souls, and do no work at all**, whether it be one of your own country, **or a stranger that sojourneth among you**: **16:30** For on that day shall the priest make an atonement for you, to cleanse you, that ye may be clean from all your sins before the LORD. **16:31** It shall be a sabbath of rest unto you, and ye shall afflict your souls, by a statute for ever.

The ceremony began with Aaron, and was to be carried on by his successors in the high priesthood. Jesus Christ has now replaced the high priesthood of Aaron as the spiritual High Priest of the New Covenant, removing our sins and reconciling us to God the Father in heaven.

16:32 And the priest, whom he shall anoint, and whom he shall consecrate to minister in the priest's office in his father's stead, shall make the atonement, and shall put on the linen clothes, even the holy garments: **16:33** And he shall make an atonement for the holy sanctuary, and he shall make an atonement for the tabernacle of the congregation, and for the altar, and he shall make an atonement for the priests, and for all the people of the congregation.

All humanity is to be grafted into spiritual Israel in the millennial kingdom of God; after which all humanity that has ever lived and died and not had a part in the resurrection to spirit, will be resurrected in their courses and also grafted into spiritual Israel.

The spring Holy Days picture the early spiritual harvest, and the fall Holy Days of the Seventh Month, picture the main harvest of humanity.

The Passover lamb pictures the sacrifice for the early spiritual harvest of the Called Out, and the goat Atonement Sin Offering pictures the sacrifice of Christ as applied to the main fall harvest.

Israel, called out of Egypt, is a type of the spiritual called out from sin for the first six thousand years, and a type of the early harvest!

Israel in the main fall harvest festivals is a type of the main harvest of all humanity to be reconciled to the Father and brought into the family of God.

16:34 And this shall be an everlasting statute unto you, to make an atonement for the children of Israel for all their sins once a year. And he did as the LORD commanded Moses.

Atonement

The word "Atonement" means:

1) to cover, purge, make an atonement, make reconciliation by sincere repentance and to redeem by paying for the offenses of another.

Therefore the word "Atonement" means to purge out sin, by STOPPING the offending sin and turning AWAY from sin and "covering" past sin, paying for sins with the blood of the sacrifice of Christ.

There are several aspects to the Day of Atonement.

One is the judgment and removal of Satan forever as the primary source of rebellion and sin against God.

Another is the restoration of all things to their original created state at the first Sabbath and the ruler-ship of God.

A third is the application of the sacrifice of Jesus Christ for the main body of humanity, who will then be brought up in their courses for the seven thousand years of the main harvest of humanity, known as: The Feast of the Ingathering of Nations [Tabernacles].

The word "Atonement" means: Redemption or Atonement: It refers to buying back from another that which had fallen into the care of another.

This is a "redeeming" as one would redeem something that was given over to another as collateral for a loan, and is redeemed by the sum agreed in repayment.

In this sense, the Day of Atonement refers to the buying back of those lost to Satan and sin, through the paying of the cost and price of sin [which is death] by Jesus Christ the Redeemer of mankind; and the application of that payment to those who afflict their souls, fasting in sincere repentance on this day.

To afflict one's soul, means to fast the fast of sincere repentance, and to STOP and turn away from the sins which necessitated such redemption.

The sacrifice of Christ is ONLY applied to the sincerely repentant who reject sin and turn away from any hint of sin in their lives, to zealously learn and keep the whole word of God and "Go and sin no more!"

Since this Day of Atonement is in the seventh month, it refers to the fall main harvest of humanity; and is a kind of expansion of the Passover sacrifice which was made on behalf of the "Called Out' of Egypt, as a symbolic analogy of the Sacrifice of Christ being applied ONLY to the "Called Out" first fruits of the early harvest.

All of us need to be reminded of the human propensity to sin and we need to humble ourselves before God by afflicting the flesh with repentant fasting, to save the spirit.

All those in BOTH the early and main harvests, must repent and turn away from all sin, with a sincere and passionate abhorring of the sin which causes so much sorrow, suffering and death; before the atoning redeeming sacrifice of Christ can be applied to us, reconciling us with God and bringing us into his family.

Leviticus 23:26 And the Lord spake unto Moses, saying, **23:27** Also on the tenth day of this seventh month there shall be a day of atonement: it shall be an holy convocation unto you; and ye shall afflict your souls, and offer an offering made by fire unto the Lord.

23:28 And ye shall do no work in that same day: for it is a day of atonement [Redemption], to make an atonement [to redeem those in bondage to Satan and sin] for you before the Lord your God.

No work at all may be done as we fast and wholeheartedly repent and reject all sin; seeking out our God, single-mindedly wholeheartedly and without any other distraction. Turning to the Great God with all our hearts; seeking that Christ's redeeming sacrifice be applied to us..

If we refuse to humble ourselves in true repentance before God and if we refuse to fast in sincere repentance on this day in obedience to God's direct command; we shall be cut off from the Father and Jesus Christ by our sins.

23:29 For whatsoever soul it be that shall not be afflicted in that same day, he shall be cut off from among his people. **23:30** And whatsoever soul it be that doeth any work in that same day, the same soul will I destroy from among his people.

23:31 Ye shall do no manner of work: it shall be a statute for ever throughout your generations in all your dwellings.

Although the weekly Sabbath is NOT a fast day; in the context of doing work, the Day of Atonement is like the seventh day weekly Sabbath, during which no work of any kind may be done; except that work which God specifically commands to be done on that day.

23:32 It shall be unto you a sabbath of rest, and ye shall afflict your souls: in the ninth day of the month at even, from even unto even, shall ye celebrate your sabbath.

The statement that this is a Sabbath of Rest, clearly reveals that the weekly Sabbath and the Fast of Atonement are BOTH to have a complete rest from normal physical activities; and if we pay others to work for or serve us on the Sabbath or any High Day; we are suborning their rebellion against God and leading them to destruction; which violates the second great commandment that we are to love our neighbor as we love ourselves.

The Sacrifices of the Day of Atonement

Here we see the Burnt Offering of Leviticus 16 explained more fully.

Numbers 29:7 And ye shall have on the tenth day of this seventh month an holy convocation; and ye shall afflict your souls: ye shall not do any work therein:

26:8 But ye shall offer **a burnt offering** unto the Lord for a sweet savour; **one young bullock, one ram, and seven lambs of the first year** [in their first year]; they shall be unto you without blemish [representing the perfection of Christ (which we are to emulate) and his tireless work to serve the Father in his office as redeemer and Advocate as our High Priest with the Father]:

26:9 And their meat [Unleavened Bread picturing the Lamb of God as the Bread of Life] offering shall be of **flour mingled with oil** [picturing the Holy Spirit], three tenth deals to a bullock, and two tenth deals to one ram,

26:10 A several tenth deal for one lamb, throughout the seven lambs:

26:11 One kid of the goats for a sin offering [representing Christ's Passover sacrifice for the Called out now being opened to the masses]; beside the [bull for the physical high priest to enter the Most Holy Place representing access to the Father] sin offering of atonement, and the continual burnt offering, and the meat offering of it, and their drink offerings.

The Role of the High Priest

It is important to understand that the physical High Priest of Aaron was a symbol of the spirit High Priest of the order of Melchizedek, Jesus Christ; who replaced the High Priest of Aaron when the Mosaic Covenant ended with the death of the Husband of Israel, Jesus Christ.

Christ was then resurrected by God the Father and ascended to the Father to be accepted for us as our ONLY Mediator and Intercessory High Priest.

1 Timothy 2:5 For there is one God [the Father], and one mediator between God [the Father] and men, the man Christ Jesus [The one who became Jesus Christ gave up his Godhood, and was made flesh giving his life for us, after which he was resurrected back to spirit and returned to God-hood as the ONLY Intercessor between men and God the Father.]; **2:6** Who gave himself a ransom for all, to be testified in due time.

The Mercy Seat represents the throne of God the Father, WHO IS ABSENT FROM THE EARTH until the plan for humanity is completed.

The High Priest entering the Throne Room of God the Father once a year, pictured the fact that the way to reconciliation with the Father was not known or opened to humanity, until the sacrifice of Christ had come and Christ had ascended to the Father on Wave Sheaf Sunday to be accepted for us.

It was for this reason that the curtain [heavy drape] separating the Most Holy Place from the Temple was torn in two at the death of Christ; to demonstrate that the way to atonement, redemption and reconciliation, had now been opened to the Father by the sacrifice of the son of God.

The physical high priest must be absolutely pure and free from even the hint of sin, to enter the Throne Room of the Father to make atonement for all the people.

Our High Priest, Jesus Christ was absolutely sinless and therefore had no need to atone for any sin of his own; being sinless he could offer himself as an atonement for the sins of others.

Now, we have access to the Father through the perfection of the sinless one; who stands as the ONLY High Priest, Intercessor and Mediator between men and God the Father. See the Hebrews study.

Our High Priest intercedes for all those that the Father has called at this time as pictured by the Passover lamb covering the sins of the Called Out during the seven thousand years of Unleavened Bread!

On the Day of Atonement the sacrifice of Christ will be opened to the main harvest of the main mass of humanity! so that they too can have access to the Father and be reaped into the Family of God in the post millennial Feast of Tabernacles!

Christ's sacrifice will then atone for all of repentant humanity, as the Father will then call all mankind to reconciliation to himself; bringing them into the Family of God.

The Rite of the Azazel Goat in Temple History

The goat upon whom all sin was to be placed, was to be taken out into the wilderness and let go. Since Azazel means "for absolute removal" or "absolute outcast". The removal of the goat from the society of men into a wilderness represented the removal of sin from among the people.

In the temple period which began with the restoration of these things by Ezra, who was sent by God for that purpose; this goat was taken into the wilderness and cast off a high cliff and destroyed; for the goat represented sin and the scripture says: The soul that sinneth, it shall die.

The wages of sin is death. Should Satan the ultimate sinner escape his wages?

We are commanded to put all scriptures on a particular subject to establish a doctrine, and in this case all scriptures except Revelation 20:10 consistently say that Satan will die for his many sins.

The word tormented in Revelation 20:10 also means judgment, and is translated as tormented because that was a synonym of judgment in the old English of the KJV.

The more accurate translation consistent with all other scriptures would be: And the devil that deceived them was cast into the lake of fire and brimstone, where the beast and the false prophet [were cast, and shall receive eternal judgment].

The Wages of Sin

Ezekiel 18:4 Behold, all souls are mine; as the soul of the father, so also the soul of the son is mine: **the soul that sinneth, it shall die.**

Romans 6:23 For **the wages of sin is death**; but the gift of God is eternal life through Jesus Christ our Lord.

Who must pay those wages? ALL unrepentant sinners! and that includes angels who are unrepentant sinners!

God has already passed judgment on Satan and those angels who follow him; there judgment is to be cast into utter eternal darkness **Jude 1:13** Raging waves of the sea, foaming out their own shame; **wandering stars**, to whom is reserved the blackness of darkness [oblivion] for ever.

And what is utter eternal darkness but the oblivion of death?

But can an angel die?

Did the very Creator God die for us? If the Creator God himself could give up his God-ship to die for his creation; then the sinful angels can also be destroyed for their wickedness.

Show me, where in the scriptures does it say that angels cannot die, if God should choose to destroy the wicked among them?

The killing of the sin goat prevented it from wondering back and symbolically bringing sin back into society, for the Azazel goat represents sin and Satan; both of which are to be removed from humanity forever.

The Mishnah (Yoma 39a) explains the ritual which followed the Hebrew Bible text; two goats were procured, similar in respect of appearance, height, cost, and time of selection.

Having one of these on his right and the other on his left, the high priest, who was assisted in this rite by two subordinates, put both his hands into a wooden case, and took out two labels, one inscribed "for Yahweh" and the other "for absolute removal" (or "for Azazel").

The high priest then laid his hands with the labels upon the two goats and said, "A sin-offering to Yahweh" and the two men accompanying him replied, "Blessed be the name of His glorious kingdom for ever and ever."

He then fastened a scarlet woolen thread to the head of the goat "for Azazel"; and laying his hands upon it again, recited a confession of sin and prayer for forgiveness:

A man was then selected, preferably a priest, to take the goat to the precipice in the wilderness; and he was accompanied part of the way by the most eminent men of Jerusalem.

Ten booths had been constructed at intervals along the road leading from Jerusalem to the steep mountain. At each one of these the man leading the goat was formally offered food and drink, which he, however, refused. When he reached the tenth booth those who accompanied him proceeded no further, but watched the ceremony from a distance.

When he came to the precipice he divided the scarlet thread into two parts, one of which he tied to the rock and the other to the goat's horns, and then pushed the goat down (Yoma vi. 1–8). The cliff was so high and rugged that before the goat had traversed half the distance to the plain below, it was utterly shattered and dead.

Men were stationed at intervals along the way; and then as soon as the goat was thrown down the precipice, they signaled to one another by means of kerchiefs or flags, until the information reached the high priest, whereat he proceeded with the other parts of the ritual.

The Final Removal of Satan

This fast pictures the removal of Satan and the opening of the way for the application of the sacrifice of Christ to be expended from the Passover sacrifice for the called out first fruits, to include the main fall harvest of mankind.

Just at the Feast of Pentecost immediately after the millennium pictured by the seventh day of the spring Feast of Unleavened Bread, Satan will be released from his 1,000 year imprisonment; and will once again lead much of humanity in rebellion against God (Rev 20:1-5); after which he will be judged and removed forever on a future Fast Day of Atonement.

Then after the final removal of Satan the main fall harvest of humanity called the Feast of the Ingathering of Nations [Tabernacles] will bring the vast majority of humanity into the family of God.

The Feast of Tabernacles

Introduction

The fall harvest Feast called the Feast of Tabernacles represents the reaping of the fall harvest of humanity into the family of God. For this reason Tabernacles is also called the "Feast of Harvest" and the "Feast of Ingathering."

Exodus 23:16 And **the feast of harvest**, the firstfruits of thy labours, which thou hast sown in the field: and **the feast of ingathering**, which is in the end of the year, when thou hast gathered in thy labours out of the field.

Exodus 34:2 And thou shalt observe the feast of weeks, of the firstfruits of wheat harvest, and **the feast of ingathering** at the [agricultural year's end] year's end.

The Feast of Tabernacles is seven days long and Peter tells us that one day is as one thousand years, therefore this Feast represents a seven thousand year main harvest of humanity as they are resurrected in their courses; and this Feast could not possibly represent any 1,000 year millennium.

2 Peter 3:8 But, beloved, be not ignorant of this one thing, that **one day is with the Lord as a thousand years, and a thousand years as one day.**

The Feast of Ingathering Symbols

- Living in tents pictures the temporary nature of physical life and the need to become spiritual,

- Rejoicing with the branches represents bringing in the branches [people] into the Temple [Family] of God (john 15)

- The sacrifice of the seventy bullocks over the seven days, pictures the work of Christ on behalf of the seventy families of mankind.

In addition the spring harvest must be reaped in the spring and not in the fall; the fall festivals picturing the latter main harvest and having nothing to do with the spring early harvest of first fruits.

- Satan is to be held in prison for one thousand years during the millennium and will then be released to deceive humanity AFTER the millennium!

- Therefore the Atonement removal of Satan forever, cannot take place until AFTER the millennium: and the Atonement removal of Satan forever, comes BEFORE the Feast of Tabernacles.

- The Feast of Tabernacles coming AFTER atonement must therefore also come AFTER the millennium.

- Because the Feast of Tabernacles comes AFTER the millennium that Festival cannot possibly represent the millennium itself.

Revelation 20:1 And I saw an angel come down from heaven, having the key of the bottomless pit and a great chain in his hand.

20:2 And he laid hold on the dragon, that old serpent, which is the Devil, and Satan, and bound him a thousand years, **20:3** And cast him into the bottomless pit, and shut him up, and set a seal upon him, that he should deceive the nations no more, till the thousand years should be fulfilled: and after that he must be loosed a little season.

Brethren, we are called out to be trained to be labourers [priests of Jesus Christ, teachers, role models and guides]; to first bring in the millennial harvest represented by the seventh day of the Feast of Unleavened Bread [which is the day that DOES represent the millennial Sabbath of rest for humanity]; and then together with those changed in the millennial [still the early spring] harvest; we are to work as labourers to bring in the main fall harvest of humanity!

Branches and Booths

God commands that a fall Feast be kept in the Seventh Biblical month which answers to the September October time frame.

A Harvest Festival called the Feast of Ingathering or the Feast of Tabernacles and is to be kept from the 15th day through the 21st day of the seventh biblical month with rejoicing over the main harvest in Israel.

Exodus 34:22 And thou shalt observe the feast of weeks, of the firstfruits of wheat harvest, and the feast of ingathering at the year's end.

The main harvest in Israel is used as an allegory of a main spiritual harvest of humanity and the symbols of the Feast of Tabernacles apply directly to a resurrection to flesh followed by their sincere repentance and conversion and then a change to spirit in a final main harvest of all humanity into the family of God.

During this main harvest festival we are to reside in temporary dwellings to indicate the temporary nature of the flesh and all things physical, which is why it is called the Feast of Tabernacles and why the book of Ecclesiastes was appointed since Ezra to be read during this Festival.

At this Fall Harvest Feast we are also commanded to cut branches and to rejoice with them, the branches picturing the main harvest of people being resurrected to flesh and being brought into the family of God with great rejoicing.

Leviticus 23:39 Also in the **fifteenth day of the seventh month,** when ye have gathered in the fruit of the land,

This Feast is to be held when the main fall harvest in the Judea and the Israel area is nearing completion, as an analogy of bringing in the main spiritual harvest of humanity into the family of God.

. . . 23:39 ye shall keep a feast unto the Lord **seven days**: on the first day shall be a sabbath, and on the eighth day shall be a sabbath. **23:40** And ye shall **take you on the first day the boughs of goodly trees, branches of palm trees, and the boughs of thick trees, and willows of the brook: and ye shall rejoice before the Lord your God seven days.**

We are commanded to rejoice with the branches for each and every day of the Feast of Ingathering, beginning on the first day.

23:41 And you shall keep it a feast unto the Lord seven days in the year. [seven days each year, in the Seventh Month]. It shall be a statute for ever in your generations: ye shall celebrate it in the seventh month.

We are also commanded to reside in temporary dwellings each and every day of the seven day Feast.

23:42 Ye shall dwell in booths seven days; all that are Israelites born shall dwell in booths: **23:43 That your generations may know that I made the children of Israel to dwell in booths** [temporary dwellings in the wilderness], **when I brought them out of the land of Egypt: I am the Lord your God.**

The command to reside in temporary dwellings for the seven days of this Feast is specifically stated as having the purpose of reminding the people that when they were called out of Egypt, Israel was made to dwell in temporary circumstances in the wilderness before and until they entered the physical promised land.

This was an allegory that when called out of sin and grafted into the spiritual New Covenant, people will no longer belong to Satan's world of bondage to sin, and will have become travelers and strangers, seeking the spiritual Promised Land of eternal life.

Dwelling in temporary structures in the midst of the plenty and rejoicing of the Feast is also a reminder that physical things are transitory and that the only really permanent things are spiritual and the spiritual New Covenant Promised Land of eternal life; which is the lesson of the book of Ecclesiastes.

A good many people attending the Feast, often for many years; still don't understand the meaning of the Festival, because they do not keep the Feast as God commands it to be kept.

Notice that God said **on the first day**; cut some branches and rejoice before God, and later on He says, build booths.

They are two separate instructions. NOWHERE does God say to build the booths out of the branches which we are to cut. And Israel did not go out and live for 40 years in the wilderness in shacks made of branches. They had tents in the wilderness when they came out of Egypt! Yet God says **"I made the children of Israel to dwell in booths, when I brought them out of the land of Egypt"**

We are to reside in temporary structures [any structure that is not permanently our own] to learn and understand that when we come out of this world [spiritual Egypt] of bondage to sin, we are no longer of that world of sin, but are only travelers journeying towards and seeking another and far, far better, permanent New Covenant (Jer 31:31); which brings entry into the Promised Land of eternal life.

The word "booths" simply means: a hut or lair:--booth, cottage, covert, pavilion, tabernacle, tent (H5520); which indicates any structure that is temporary and not our own permanent dwelling place.

The idea here, is that we are to live in tents or temporary dwellings which are not our regular permanent dwellings during the Feast of Tabernacles, beginning in the evening starting the first day; which means that the booths had to be ready by sunset before beginning the first day, while the branches were to be cut ON the first day.

These are two separate commands, the first being:

1. We are to move into temporary quarters before the first day begins so that we spend the first night in those temporary structures,

And

2. That ON the first day we are to cut branches and rejoice WITH the branches through the seven days of the Feast!

Why? Cutting and bringing the branches into the temple and rejoicing with them, is acting out the bringing in of the main harvest of people to God and into the family of God!

Again what are the two commands?

1. To build booths before the first day so that we can spend the full seven nights in them beginning on the first evening beginning the Feast, to remember that this flesh and all physical things are only temporary; and

2. To cut branches ON the first day and bring them into the temple, rejoicing with them every day of the Feast, acting out the bringing in of the families of humanity into the family of God.

The commands to build booths and to cut branches are TWO SEPARATE commands, not related to each other!

Booths are tents or temporary dwellings to live in, and can be made of branches if one desires; but there is also a specific command to cut branches and bring them before God rejoicing with them, which second command is quite distinct and separate from building booths!

Boughs or branches of goodly or healthy, beautiful, strong trees, are to be cut on the very first day, the high holy day, and we are **to rejoice with them before God for seven days**.

The palm, myrtle and willow are specifically mentioned because the willow represents vigorous growth, the myrtle represents beauty and the palm represents regal dignity. However, we are not told that these are the only branches that can be cut: The command also states, goodly trees.

Nehemiah and the people built booths out of branches. But they would also have rejoiced before God with branches, for Ezra and Nehemiah set the Temple service and included the rejoicing with branches in the temple Feast of Tabernacles services.

Today we have the added advantage of the spiritual teachings of Jesus Christ who revealed the spirit and intent of this commandment.

Besides making booths with branches, Ezra and Nehemiah had the people cut bundles of branches to rejoice in the temple with! We know this because they restored and established the temple Feast of Tabernacles services which prevailed from then on.

We are to rejoice with these branches. Why is that? It is because of what they represent.

It is now the time to restore to the Ekklesia the spiritual meaning of this rejoicing with branches as revealed by Jesus Christ.

In the temple celebration, on each day of the Feast of Tabernacles, the people in the temple courtyard would hold their clusters of branches, waving them before the Lord and making a procession around the altar.

The first six days they would circle the altar once, and on the seventh day they would circle the altar seven times to increase the joy. During the procession on the seventh day, they would recite a prayer which became known as the Hoshana (Psalms 118:25).

118:25 Save now, I beseech thee, O LORD: O LORD, I beseech thee, send now prosperity.

Hebrew

אָנָּא יְהוָה הוֹשִׁיעָה נָּא אָנָּא יְהוָה הַצְלִיחָה נָּא׃

O LORD, deliver us! O LORD, let us prosper!

For this reason the **last and seventh day of the Feast of Tabernacles,** [NOT the Feast of The Eighth Day] became known as Hoshana Rabbah, meaning the [Last] **Day of the Great Salvation**, or the Last Great Day of the Feast of Tabernacles.

They marched around the altar once each day, holding their branches and saying "save us, give salvation". And on the seventh day they marched around seven times repeating the same words.

This process is a duplicate of the seven day march around Jericho with the city being marched about seven times on the seventh day and total victory over the city representing total victory over sin.

The seven times march around the altar on the seventh day of the Feast; represented a total and final victory over all sin being granted by God to the main harvest of all repentant humanity!

The Feast of Tabernacles then pictures, the main harvest in Israel, and a celebration of rejoicing for that harvest; but raised to a spiritual level, it pictures the main harvest of humanity!

The bringing in of the branches pictures the bringing in of the main harvest of mankind right up to the altar where the sacrifices were made, and the sacrifices of the blood dashed at the foot of the altar represented Christ's sacrifice. So bringing the branches right up to the altar represented leading humanity in the main harvest right up to the sacrifice of Jesus Christ the Lamb of God!

We can understand this through the words of Jesus in **John 15:1 I am the true vine, and my Father is the husbandman. 15:2 Every branch** [that abides] **in me that beareth not fruit he** [the Father] **taketh away: and every branch that** [abides in Christ and] **beareth fruit, he purgeth it, that it may bring forth more fruit.**

God the Father and Jesus Christ are the foundation of the Word of God and we are to abide in Him—not in some other guy, not in some group; but in God the Father in heaven and Jesus Christ the Lamb of God. And if we abide in Christ, being the vine, we will be nourished as a branch by the Holy Spirit, just as a physical branch is nourished by the energy and water and strength that comes from the trunk of the tree.

We as human beings, by being totally grafted into the trunk of the tree, Jesus Christ; are nourished spiritually by Christ through the agency of the Holy Spirit.

Then we will grow, even as a physical branch grows because of the nutrients it receives from the trunk; we grow because of the spiritual nutrients we receive from our trunk or our vine, Jesus Christ. And if we abide faithfully in Christ we will be nourished by him through his Spirit. We will be given the Holy Spirit and the Bread of Life. We will be nourished by Christ and we will grow and we will bear fruit.

If we do not abide in Christ, which is a Christ-like zeal to live by every Word of God the Father, we are cut off from our source of spiritual nourishment we are cut off from our source of spiritual growth.

We have to always put God the Father and Jesus Christ, and that means the whole Word of God, FIRST.

All scripture was recorded and preserved for our instruction and we really need to stand on all the scriptures, not just pick and choose what we like or don't like.

Jesus said in **John 15:3 Now ye are clean through the word which I have spoken unto you** [IF you live by those words]. Eleven were spiritually clean but the twelfth, Judas; was not spiritually clean, not being faithful.

The Word of God is not limited to the words that Jesus physically spoke in the gospels. The whole Word of God from Genesis to Revelation was inspired by the Being who became Jesus Christ. He inspired Moses and all the other writers of scripture, Isaiah, the Prophets, David and others, were all inspired by Christ.

The entire Word of God makes us spiritually clean, if we learn it and actually live by it. It makes us clean from sin because it teaches us what we need to avoid, which is sin.

The Word of God teaches us what sin is and it teaches us to avoid sin, so that we can become clean and pure, and free from sin.

If in our lives, we learn and actually live by every Word of God, we are copying God the Father and Jesus Christ; We become like God by internalizing the very nature of God.

John 15:4 Abide in me, and I [will abide] **in you. As the branch cannot bear fruit of itself, except it abide in the vine; no more can ye** [bear fruit except you] **abide in me. 15:5 I am the vine, ye are the branches:**

The branches refer to people, and the vine or the trunk of the tree is Jesus Christ.

. . . 15:5 He that abideth in me, and I in him, the same bringeth forth much fruit: . . .

Here Christ is talking about physical fruit as an allegory of spiritual fruit. When we are abiding in Christ, he is going to nourish us with the Word of God by the Holy Spirit and we are going to bear fruit.

. . . for without me ye can do nothing.

If we stand on our own ways we are going nowhere. We may get rich and popular in this world like some rock star, but in terms of our relationship with God we are going nowhere.

15:6 Now if a man abide not in me, [Christ], he will be cast forth as [like] a branch, [that does not bear fruit and he will be] withered; [and then] men gather them, and cast them into the fire, and they are burned.

Anyone who rejects full unity with God the Father and a Christ-like zeal to live by every Word of God; is going to be cut off from the tree, thrown out and burned up. He is going to be destroyed.

We all have to abide in Christ, and those who are not fully abiding in God the Father and Jesus Christ, needs to repent of that and return to God the Father and Jesus Christ in sincere repentance.

15:8 Herein is my Father glorified, that ye bear much fruit; so shall ye be my disciples.

The branches of trees represent people abiding in Christ and living by every Word of God being filled with the loving law of God. The law of God actually defines love and it defines the nature of God the Father and the nature of Jesus Christ. We must abide in Christ to live by every Word of God if we are to produce the Christ-like spiritual fruits of true godly righteousness.

The lesson for the Feast of the Ingathering of Nations, sometimes called Tabernacles, is that all nations will ultimately be grafted into God the Father and Jesus Christ and be brought into the family of God.

The Feast of the Ingathering of Nations or Tabernacles; represents the bringing in of the main harvest of humanity, the grafting in of the branches of the main harvest of humanity, into the true vine and the trunk of that great tree of eternal life, Jesus Christ and God the Father.

That is the lesson of the Feast of Tabernacles; that all humanity are branches, needing to be grafted into the true vine Jesus Christ and into God the Father, and into their Word and their ways which lead to the spiritual Promised Land of life eternal, if we remain steadfast in them.

These Feast of Tabernacles branches represent the main harvest of all of humanity who were not converted as a part of the first fruits; representing our unconverted mothers and fathers, sons and daughters, sisters and brothers, husbands, wives, dear friends, associates, all kinds of people, even our enemies in this life: being grafted into God the Father and Jesus Christ and the New Covenant of godliness, with the potential to receive the gift of eternal life.

When we understand what this means; that our dearly beloved ones who have been separated from God for a wink of time in eternity; are going to have their chance to be grafted into God the Father and Jesus Christ, then we can really REJOICE at the Feast of Tabernacles.

As everyone reconciles with God and with each other, all of these past hurts are going to vanish away in a wondrous time of really super, rejoicing.

Seven days, at a day for a thousand years, represents seven thousand years; and people can be raised up in their courses, just like they were born over the past thousands of years.

Deuteronomy 16:14, And thou shalt rejoice in thy feast, thou, thy son, thy daughter, thy manservant, thy maidservant, and the Levite, the stranger [that is the unconverted person] **and the fatherless, and the widow, that are within thy gates.**

16:15 Seven days shalt thou keep a solemn feast unto the LORD thy God in the place which the LORD shall choose: because the LORD thy God shall bless thee and all thine increase, and all the works of thine hands, therefore thou shalt surely rejoice.

The place that God chose was the temple at Jerusalem, and the people went up to the Feast year by year after God chose Jerusalem. But Jesus knew that the temple would be destroyed and that Judea would be occupied and that terrible things would happen; and so He said in Matthew 18— wherever two or three are gathered together I will be there among you.

If we are gathered together in his name and by God's command, he promised that he will be among us through God's Spirit.

The presence of God is what makes a convocation holy. Just meeting together is not holy. Holy is when God is present.

In addition if we are there, kind of doing our own thing, and rejecting knowledge and rejecting truth, rejecting spiritual growth, rejecting some of the commandments, and not keeping the Feast on the day God commands and not keeping it in the way that God commands; the Feast is not holy because God is not going to be there.

The whole family is to go to the Feast whenever possible. Of course, God understands if there is a pregnancy or an illness, things like that, and there are some people of great age who have reached the point where they are frail in terms of traveling: But certainly every effort should be made whenever possible and God understands all these things, but he wants everyone possible to come before him.

The Feast is to be a gathering of God's people in the place that God chooses.

God chose Jerusalem, however knowing that the temple would be destroyed and his faithful scattered, Jesus said: **Matthew 18:20 For where two or three are gathered together in my name, there am I in the midst of them.**

If we are gathered together to serve God and we are gathered according to God's commandment, and we are seeking to live by every Word of God, God the Father and Jesus Christ will be there through the agency of the Holy Spirit.

Today, God dwells in his people; we have become the spiritual temple of the Holy Spirit, we are now the spiritual temple of God.

So in effect, all truly converted people have Christ dwelling in them through God's Spirit, if we are faithful to him. Therefore, we can keep the Feast together in an area outside Jerusalem because we are still the temple, and we are now a spiritual temple where God has placed his name [his presence]. The temple of Jerusalem is gone but God has placed his name in his faithful; God is dwelling in the godly faithful.

1 Corinthians 3:16 Know ye not that ye are the temple of God, and that the spirit of God dwelleth in you? 3:17 If any man defile the temple of God [by sinning], him shall God destroy; for the temple of God is holy, which temple ye are.

How do we defile the temple of God? By deliberately accepting false teachings and false doctrine; by clinging to false things when we know they are false, or by making excuses to justify false things, or by being spiritually lazy and not questioning what we are taught by the whole Word of God..

For example, Nehemiah said we must not buy food or drink on the Sabbath day. And I have heard it from more than one minister who said; "oh, that was just for those days, or that was just for the Jews, or they were having a revival in those days."

We most certainly are in need of a revival today!

In Conclusion

- During the seven days of the Feast of Ingathering [Tabernacles], we are to dwell in dwellings which are not our permanent dwellings; so that we might learn that like Abraham in Palestine and Israel in Sinai, the godly are strangers in this wicked physical world, looking to enter a much better and permanent world of godliness.

Hebrews 11:13 These all died in faith, not [yet] having received the promises, but having seen them afar off, and were persuaded of them, and embraced them, and confessed that they were strangers and pilgrims on the earth.

- We are to cut branches on the first day of the Fest of Tabernacles, and we are to rejoice with them for the whole seven days; acting out bringing in the main harvest of humanity into the family of God with great rejoicing.

- We may keep the Feast, wherever God's faithful can gather together, until Christ comes and builds the Ezekiel Temple and gives us further instructions.

Ecclesiastes

Introduction

The book of Deuteronomy is appointed to be read at the Feast of Tabernacles every seventh year (Deu 31:10). The Deuteronomy study can be found under the Deuteronomy Joshua title.

Ecclesiastes concerns the temporary transitory nature and pointlessness of physical things, teaching us that the only things that have lasting value are the eternal spiritual things of God.

The Book of Ecclesiastes was appointed to be read at the Feast of Tabernacles by Ezra and was probably written by Solomon, to be read during the Feast of Tabernacles.

Ecclesiastes is a lesson that all physical things ultimately end and that the only permanent things are spiritual, and that therefore we should be concerned with the spiritual as our priority. The lesson is that while we are to enjoy our physical lives, our focus should be on learning the spiritual lessons and principles that will bring the gift of eternal life and will last forever.

Those who have been called of God now, should be willing to give up everything physical for the spiritual gift of that pearl of great price, eternal life, seeking to internalize the nature of God through sincere repentance from all sin and a solid commitment to go forward to live by every Word of God.

If we dedicate ourselves to live by every Word of God in Christ-like zeal, using our physical lives to learn the spiritual things of God, then and only then will the sacrifice of the Lamb of God will be applied to us and the gift of God's Spirit will be given to enable us to become godly people.

The remainder of mankind who have not yet been called to God having their eyes opened to godliness, will after actual experience with life the first time around.

Then after dying and being resurrected back to physical life the main harvest of humanity will fully realize the temporary transitory nature of physical things, and will realize that only godliness has eternal and intrinsic lasting value.

Wiki: "Ecclesiastes takes its Hebrew name from the main speaker, Qoheleth, (also Koheleth), a word related to the root which means "to assemble". The idea behind the name was that probably the Teacher caused a group of students to assemble and hear his words; the Greek title is a modification of Ekklesia in an attempt to translate this, and the English is taken directly from the Greek. Qoheleth introduces himself as "son of David, king in Jerusalem," implying that he is Solomon.

The book is in the form of an autobiography, at times expressed in aphorisms and maxims, telling of his investigation into the meaning of life and the best way of life. The work emphatically proclaims all the actions of man to be inherently transitory, "vain", "futile", "empty", "meaningless", "temporary", "fleeting," or "mere breath," depending on translation, because the lives of both wise and foolish men end in death.

Qoheleth clearly endorses wisdom as a means for a well-lived earthly life, and the book is an instruction that the transitory nature of physical life, points us to the pressing need to seek the spiritual, while doing our best to enjoy the blessings God has provided in our present physical existence.

The teacher comes to this final conclusion: Let us hear the conclusion of the whole matter: Fear God, and keep his commandments: for this is the whole duty of man. (Ecc 12:13)."

The author Solomon was born to be king and grew up in his father's shadow, personally taught by a man after God's own heart, his own father king David, how to be a king.

When Solomon became king he asked God for wisdom as Solomon had been taught to seek wisdom above all else by his father David, and God respected that choice and also gave Solomon many other blessings.

Yet, Solomon had one big hole in his education, he had not grown up in adversity fleeing for his life like his father David had, or being imprisoned like Joseph, or working as a slave in Egypt; instead Solomon was born with the proverbial silver spoon.

Solomon had not learned to resist temptation or to persevere through trials; and as the years passed Solomon became infatuated with his own wisdom and slowly began to forget the commandments of God which are true wisdom. He began to make decisions based on what he thought looked right to him, and even the super-wise Solomon was NOT as wise as God and God's Word.

As Solomon began to rely on his own wisdom; he tried out and engaged in all manner of sin; and with the wisdom given him he began to understand the truth and ultimately came to repentance before God.

All of humanity is also being called [in their appointed times] to learn the same lesson, learning to deeply value, hunger and thirst after the spiritual things which are of far more value than gold or rubies because they will last forever.

The story of Solomon's journey to repentance is one of the most misunderstood Books of the Bible.

The Book of Ecclesiastes was written by a man of great wisdom, and in his experiences of his own ways, Solomon learns how little real meaning and lasting value physical things have in comparison to eternity, and the wisdom of God's Word; and he comes to a place of repentance.

Living by every Word of God is the ONLY way that brings eternal life.

We MUST learn the lesson that only by internalizing the very nature of God through faithfully living by every Word of God can we live forever as God lives forever.

When we repent of living contrary to the Word of God or compromising with even the very least commandment, and we then commit to live by every Word of God forever [which is what baptism is]; only then will the sacrifice of the Lamb of God Jesus Christ be applied to us, atoning for PAST sins, reconciling us to God the Father and bringing the birthright of eternal life.

Only when we learn the lesson that Solomon learned, that the purpose of physical existence is to provide an environment for learning spiritual lessons and principles, and then we dedicate ourselves to godliness, will we be fit to receive the gift of eternal life.

Ecclesiastes 12:13 Let us hear the conclusion of the whole matter: Fear God, and keep his commandments: for this is the whole duty of man. **12:14** For God shall bring every work into judgment, with every secret thing, whether it be good, or whether it be evil.

Solomon

- **WIKI "Solomon** (Hebrew: שְׁלֹמֹה, Modern *Shlomo* Tiberian *Šəlōmō* ISO 259-3 *Šlomo*; Arabic: سليمان *Sulaymān*, also colloquially: *Silimān*; Greek: Σολομών *Solomōn*), also called **Jedidiah** (Hebrew יְדִידְיָה), was, according to the Book of Kings and the Book of Chronicles, a king of Israel and the son of David. The conventional dates of Solomon's reign are circa 970 to 931 BC. He is described as the third king of the United Monarchy, and the final king before the northern Kingdom of Israel and the southern Kingdom of Judah split. Following the split, his patrilineal descendants ruled over Judah alone.

Solomon was loved by God from his birth:"

2 Samuel 12:24 And David comforted Bathsheba his wife, and went in unto her, and lay with her: and she bare a son, and he called his name Solomon: and the Lord loved him. **12:25** And he sent by the hand of Nathan the prophet; and he called his name Jedidiah [meaning "Beloved of YHVH"], because of the Lord.

Solomon had been made heir apparent in his youth; probably because he was the son of Bathsheba David's favorite, and probably because Solomon was diligent to learn of God and God's commandments from his father David. The Eternal did not call Solomon his beloved as a young child for nothing; the child must have been faithful and diligent learning of God from David his father, as David educated him to become king over Israel.

1 Kings 1:11 Wherefore Nathan [the prophet] spake unto Bathsheba the mother of Solomon, saying, Hast thou not heard that Adonijah the son of Haggith doth reign, and David our lord knoweth it not?

1:12 Now therefore come, let me, I pray thee, give thee counsel, that thou mayest save thine own life, and the life of thy son Solomon.

1:13 Go and get thee in unto king David, and say unto him, **Didst not thou, my lord, O king, swear unto thine handmaid, saying, Assuredly Solomon thy son shall reign after me, and he shall sit upon my throne?** why then doth Adonijah reign?

1:14 Behold, **while thou yet talkest there with the king, I also will come in after thee, and confirm thy words.**

When Solomon became king and had secured the realm he proposed to build a House for God as his father David had wanted [I have no doubt that they discussed this often together, and made plans together; for David laid up a vast sum for Solomon to build with.]. Solomon was full of love for God and his Word; having been zealous for these things from his birth.

At about that time, God who loved Solomon for his love of God's law from childhood, offered Solomon a blessing, and Solomon being humble before God, as taught by David; asked for wisdom to rule God's people.

Psalm 111:1 The fear of the Lord is the beginning of wisdom: a good understanding have all they that do his commandments: his praise endureth for ever.

Solomon had been taught the fear and love of God by his father David.

God granted this request and further blessed Solomon with many other things, for wisdom has her fruits.

Solomon started his rule, very wise in the things and commandments of God, however he began to slowly lose his humility and be ensnared by pride.

Solomon then set out to test God and God's Word, and to test also his own wisdom and ways, by considering everything that this world has to offer and judging physical things for their real value.

The Book of Ecclesiastes is about what Solomon learned from his testing and inquiries into all the greatness that this world has to offer.

Ecclesiastes is about pride or humility, worldliness or godliness; and about transitory physical things without lasting value or spiritual things which have true lasting eternal value.

This book is very, very, vital to those claiming to be God's people today. God deeply loved Solomon and therefore allowed Solomon to make his mistakes and learn from them.

The same is true today; God deeply loves all his called out, and he is allowing us to do what we think is right so we may make our mistakes and learn from them, in order to perfect us so that we might be zealous for all eternity!

Oh, how God has loved us, but very many of us are like rebellious children, preferring our own wisdom to the wisdom of God our Father; preferring our own ways and traditions to the truth and commandments of our loving Father.

God is warning his beloved children of the way that they should go, and we had better heed his warning, before we are destroyed by the wisdom of men and the traditions of men.

Ecclesiastes was written at the end of Solomon's inquiries, and was inspired by God to teach us the same lesson that Solomon learned; so that we might come to the same conclusion as Solomon; and dedicate ourselves to the ONLY things that really matter and have lasting value; God and his commandments.

The lessons of Ecclesiastes are an analogy of humanity who try out all their own ways to finally learn that only that the ways of God are all that is truly permanent and all that really matters. Some will learn this lesson now while the vast majority of mankind will understand these things when they are raised up to physical life and God opens their eyes to spiritual understanding in the main Feast of Tabernacles harvest of humanity.

Ecclesiastes 1

Ecclesiastes 1:1 The words of the Preacher, the son of David, king in Jerusalem.

After deep and lengthy study, the Teacher emphatically proclaims all the actions of man to be inherently *hevel*, a word meaning "vain", "futile", "empty", "meaningless", "temporary", "transitory", "fleeting," or "mere breath," depending on translation, as the lives of both wise and foolish men end in death.

Why do men seek physical fame, power or wealth in this life? Why do they seek their own ways which are vanity and will come to nothing, and reject the truth of God?

1:2 Vanity of vanities, saith the Preacher, vanity of vanities; all is vanity.
1:3 What profit hath a man of all his labour which he taketh under the sun?
1:4 One generation passeth away, and another generation cometh: but the earth abideth for ever.

Physical things never satisfy for long.

1:5 The sun also ariseth, and the sun goeth down, and hasteth to his place where he arose. **1:6** The wind goeth toward the south, and turneth about unto the north; it whirleth about continually, and the wind returneth again according to his circuits. **1:7** All the rivers run into the sea; yet the sea is not full; unto the place from whence the rivers come, thither they return again. **1:8** All things are full of labour; man cannot utter it: the eye is not satisfied with seeing, nor the ear filled with hearing.

Physical thing do not last and never satisfy for long.

1:9 The thing that hath been, it is that which shall be; and that which is done is that which shall be done: and there is no new thing under the sun. **1:10** Is there any thing whereof it may be said, See, this is new? it hath been already of old time, which was before us. **1:11** There is no remembrance of former things; neither shall there be any remembrance of things that are to come with those that shall come after.

The Preacher or Instructor in Wisdom, is identified as king Solomon.

1:12 I the Preacher **was king over Israel in Jerusalem**.

Solomon seeks out the meaning of life, and seeks out wisdom concerning all things physical. He seeks out all the wisdom and pleasures of man, as many others before and after him have done.

1:13 And I gave my heart to seek and search out by wisdom concerning all things that are done under heaven: this sore travail hath God given to the sons of man to be exercised therewith.

Solomon learns what all people will eventually learn; that there is nothing lasting or satisfying in this very temporary physical existence; ONLY the things of God are permanent and satisfying.

1:14 I have seen all the works that are done under the sun; and, behold, all is vanity and vexation of spirit. **1:15** That which is crooked cannot be made straight: and that which is wanting cannot be numbered.

Solomon sought out wisdom and realized that human wisdom is vexation and madness, for wisdom reveals the emptiness and futility of physical existence.

1:16 I communed with mine own heart, saying, Lo, I am come to great estate, and have gotten more wisdom than all they that have been before me in Jerusalem: yea, my heart had great experience of wisdom and knowledge. **1:17** And I gave my heart to know wisdom, and to know madness and folly: I perceived that this also is vexation of spirit.

When we understand that we shall all surely die and our existence will end, all other things become empty, meaningless and hopeless folly.

1:18 For in much wisdom is much grief: and he that increaseth knowledge increaseth sorrow.

Solomon then seeks out wealth and the pleasures of life to see if he will find meaning there.

Ecclesiastes 2

Solomon sought to find meaning in life through pleasure seeking because wisdom revealed that he would eventually die and cease to exist anyway.

Ecclesiastes 2:1 I said in mine heart, Go to now, I will prove thee with mirth, therefore enjoy pleasure: and, behold, this also is vanity.

Solomon then learned that pleasure seeking is pointless and ultimately proves to be empty and meaningless.

2:2 I said of laughter, It is mad: and of mirth, What doeth it? **2:3** I sought in mine heart to give myself unto wine, yet acquainting mine heart with wisdom; and to lay hold on folly, till I might see what was that good for the sons of men, which they should do under the heaven all the days of their life.

Then he sought riches and building projects, only to find them ultimate meaningless as all physical things will ultimately perish.

2:4 I made me great works; I builded me houses; I planted me vineyards: **2:5** I made me gardens and orchards, and I planted trees in them of all kind of fruits: **2:6** I made me pools of water, to water therewith the wood that bringeth forth trees:

2:7 I got me servants and maidens, and had servants born in my house; also I had great possessions of great and small cattle above all that were in Jerusalem before me:

2:8 I gathered me also silver and gold, and the peculiar treasure of kings and of the provinces: I gat me men singers and women singers, and the delights of the sons of men, as musical instruments, and that of all sorts.

2:9 So I was great, and increased more than all that were before me in Jerusalem: also my wisdom remained with me.

2:10 And whatsoever mine eyes desired I kept not from them, I withheld not my heart from any joy; for my heart rejoiced in all my labour: and this was my portion of all my labour.

2:11 Then I looked on all the works that my hands had wrought, and on the labour that I had laboured to do: and, behold, all was vanity and vexation of spirit, and there was no profit under the sun.

Solomon tests wisdom against foolishness.

2:12 And I turned myself to behold wisdom, and madness, and folly: for what can the man do that cometh after the king? even that which hath been already done.

Wisdom is far greater than foolishness, yet what is its advantage at the end of physical life?

2:13 Then I saw that wisdom excelleth folly, as far as light excelleth darkness.

2:14 The wise man's eyes [are open see and understand] are in his head; but the fool walketh in darkness: and I myself perceived also that one event happeneth to them all.

Then Solomon understood that both the humanly wise and the foolish die and cease to exist.

2:15 Then said I in my heart, As it happeneth to the fool, so it happeneth even to me; and why was I then more wise? Then I said in my heart, that this also is vanity.

2:16 For there is no remembrance of the wise more than of the fool for ever; seeing that which now is in the days to come shall all be forgotten. And how dieth the wise man? as the fool.

Solomon learns that at the end of life, the age old question remains: "Is that all there is?" If so then life itself is foolishness for it has no lasting value.

2:17 Therefore I hated life; because the work that is wrought under the sun is grievous unto me: for all is vanity and vexation of spirit.

Solomon despairs that his heirs will be successful to maintain his projects.

2:18 Yea, I hated all my labour which I had taken under the sun: because I should leave it unto the man that shall be after me. **2:19** And who knoweth whether he shall be a wise man or a fool? yet shall he have rule over all my labour wherein I have laboured, and wherein I have shewed myself wise under the sun. This is also vanity.

2:20 Therefore I went about to cause my heart to despair of all the labour which I took under the sun.

Solomon learns that all physical pursuits are empty and meaningless and loses all desire to pursue them further.

Solomon despairs as he realizes that the fruits of all his wisdom and labours will ultimate be left to another who probably does not deserve it and will make a big mess of them.

2:21 For there is a man whose labour is in wisdom, and in knowledge, and in equity; yet to a man that hath not laboured therein shall he leave it for his portion. This also is vanity and a great evil.

What has a man left for himself of all his labours when he dies?

2:22 For what hath man of all his labour, and of the vexation of his heart, wherein he hath laboured under the sun? **2:23** For all his days are sorrows, and his travail grief; yea, his heart taketh not rest in the night. This is also vanity.

Therefore in physical things, people should enjoy life to the full while they still live. Let men enjoy the fruits of their labours.

2:24 There is nothing better for a man, than that he should eat and drink, and that he should make his soul enjoy good in his labour. This also I saw, that it was from the hand of God. **2:25** For who can eat, or who else can hasten hereunto, more than I?

The wicked build up, so that God will take from them and give to the righteous. Therefore it is vexation [empty foolishness] of spirit to be wicked and break God's commandments. Those who compromise with God's commandments or teach tolerance for sin are foolish vain and spiritual empty men.

2:26 For God giveth to a man that is good in his [God's] sight wisdom, and knowledge, and joy: but to the sinner he giveth travail, to gather and to heap up, that he may give to him that is good before God. This also is vanity and vexation of spirit.

Ecclesiastes 3

There is a right time for everything and often patience is in order

Ecclesiastes 3:1 To every thing there is a season, and a time to every purpose under the heaven: **3:2** A time to be born, and a time to die; a time to plant, and a time to pluck up that which is planted;

3:3 A time to kill, and a time to heal; a time to break down, and a time to build up; **3:4** A time to weep, and a time to laugh; a time to mourn, and a time to dance;

3:5 A time to cast away stones, and a time to gather stones together; a time to embrace, and a time to refrain from embracing; **3:6** A time to get, and a time to lose; a time to keep, and a time to cast away;

3:7 A time to rend, and a time to sew; a time to keep silence, and a time to speak; **3:8** A time to love, and a time to hate; a time of war, and a time of peace.

The law may allow something, but it is not always expedient to do what the law allows. Wisdom must be exercised in what we do, even regarding lawful things. Carefully choose the right time and place for all your doings, so as to prosper in them.

What profit is there in our labours, except to take pleasure and be satisfied with our work? And to rejoice and enjoy its fruits.

3:9 What profit hath he that worketh in that wherein he laboureth? **3:10** I have seen the travail, which God hath given to the sons of men to be exercised in it.

No carnally minded person whose thoughts are on physical pursuits, can understand the works and Word of God.

3:11 He [God] hath made every thing beautiful in his time: also he hath set the world [worldliness and limited understanding to the carnal man] in their heart, so that no man can find out the work that God maketh from the beginning to the end.

3:12 I know that there is no good in them [worldliness and physical pursuits], but for a man to rejoice, and to do good [keep the commandments of God] in his life.

All good things including the fruits of our own labour and wisdom, are gifts of God, for he has made and sustains all things.

3:13 And also that every man should eat and drink, and enjoy the good of all his labour, it is the gift of God.

Only the godly things are eternal and have any real meaning, and no person can change what God has ordained. Men should fear God for only he is eternal and is of any importance in the larger scheme of things.

3:14 I know that, whatsoever God doeth, it shall be for ever: nothing can be put to it, nor any thing taken from it: and God doeth it, that men should fear before him. **3:15** That which hath been is now; and that which is to be hath already been; and God requireth that which is past.

Solomon saw that there was unequal justice and wickedness in the judgment and ruler-ship of men. And that in the physical priesthood and temple there was sin. Therefore man can only count on God for righteous judgment.

3:16 And moreover I saw under the sun the place of judgment, that wickedness was there; and the place of righteousness, that iniquity was there. **3:17** I said in mine heart, God shall judge the righteous and the wicked: for there is a time there for every purpose and for every work.

At God's judgments, God shall demonstrate that physical man is as the brute beasts who cannot understand. Therefore only the spiritual things and commandments of God have any value or really matter.

3:18 I said in mine heart concerning the estate of the sons of men, that God might manifest them, and that they might see that they themselves are beasts.

3:19 For that which befalleth the sons of men befalleth beasts; even one thing befalleth them: as the one dieth, so dieth the other; yea, they have all one breath; so that a man hath no preeminence above a beast: for all is vanity. **3:20** All go unto one place; all are of the dust, and all turn to dust again.

3:21 Who knoweth the spirit [Reuach, spirit, breath] of man that goeth upward, and the spirit [Reuach, spirit, breath] of the beast that goeth downward to the earth?

Serve God in the wisdom of God's Word and enjoy life to the full, for after death all our physical deeds and wealth will go to another.

3:22 Wherefore I perceive that there is nothing better, than that a man should rejoice in his own works; for that is his portion: for who shall bring him to see what shall be after him?

Solomon considers the state of man, between the oppressed and the oppressors.

Ecclesiastes 4

Ecclesiastes 4:1 So I returned, and considered all the oppressions that are done under the sun: and behold the tears of such as were oppressed, and they had no comforter; and on the side of their oppressors there was power; but they had no comforter.

It is better to be dead than to be oppressed and without relief.

4:2 Wherefore I praised the dead which are already dead more than the living which are yet alive.

The person who has not seen oppression or been an oppressor, is blessed to have been saved from exposure to such evil.

4:3 Yea, better is he [who has never seen evil and oppression] than both they [the oppressed and the oppressor], [better is the one who has not yet been born or seen such evil] which hath not yet been, who hath not seen the evil work that is done under the sun.

Solomon now considers the labours of men. Great and good accomplishments that make men famous, are pointless without God, because in the end they will come to nothing.

4:4 Again, I considered all travail [work, labour, trials], and every right work, that for this a man is envied of his neighbour. This is also vanity and vexation of spirit.

Yet, it is foolishness to be lazy and do nothing.

4:5 The fool foldeth his hands together, and eateth his own flesh.

It is better to have little, accompanied by peace and peace of mind; than to have much and be in interminable strife and stress.

4:6 Better is an handful with quietness, than both the hands full with travail and vexation of spirit.

4:7 Then I returned, and I saw vanity under the sun.

Greed for physical wealth is a sore and heavy burden, working men to death; and has no reward for all perish in the end.

4:8 There is one alone, and there is not a second; yea, he hath neither child nor brother: yet is there no end of all his labour; neither is his eye satisfied with riches; neither saith he, For whom do I labour, and bereave my soul of good? This is also vanity, yea, it is a sore travail.

It is better to work together with others.

4:9 Two are better than one; because they have a good reward for their labour. **4:10** For if they fall, the one will lift up his fellow: but woe to him that is alone when he falleth; for he hath not another to help him up.

4:11 Again, if two lie together, then they have heat: but how can one be warm alone? **4:12** And if one prevail against him, two shall withstand him; and a threefold cord is not quickly broken.

The following is especially true spiritually, for the Ekklesia is now full of old and foolish rulers who will not be admonished, while the kingdom of God shall be filled with the wisdom of faithful obedient children.

> **Matthew 18:2** And Jesus called a little child unto him, and set him in the midst of them,
>
> **18:3** And said, Verily I say unto you, Except ye be converted, and become as little children [humble and trusting in God], ye shall not enter into the kingdom of heaven.
>
> **18:4** Whosoever therefore shall humble himself as this little child, the same is greatest in the kingdom of heaven.

Ecclesiastes 4:13 Better is a poor and a wise child than an old and foolish king, who will no more be admonished.

The commandment breaking ruler, leader or elder; is foolish and imprisoned by wickedness, all his subjects will suffer for his wickedness.

4:14 For out of prison he cometh to reign; whereas also he that is born in his kingdom becometh poor.

The righteous obedient child shall grow up to take the ruler-ship from the foolish leader.

4:15 I considered all the living which walk under the sun, with the second child that shall stand up in his stead.

It is foolishness, not to rejoice in God and his commandments; for the physical works of men shall not be long remembered. The accomplishments of the mighty shall not long be remembered after their death.

4:16 There is no end of all the people, even of all that have been before them: they also that come after shall not rejoice in him. Surely this also is vanity and vexation of spirit.

Seek out the wisdom of God in his Word; rather than teaching what we do not really know and understand. The student should study and not teach until he is fully and properly prepared in his studies by inspiration of God.

Be very careful in your prayers and petitions to God. It is vanity and foolishness to pray for an hour each day, just to waste God's time with much speaking.

Make your prayers sincere and from the heart, and do not engage in empty ramblings to put in time. Better is a prayer of three minutes from the heart, than hours of empty words.

Ecclesiastes 5

It is far better to listen, learn and keep the whole Word of God, than to foolishly commit sin and be required to offer sacrifices for sin.

Ecclesiastes 5:1 Keep thy foot when thou goest to the house of God, and be more ready to hear, than to give the sacrifice of fools: for they consider not that they do evil.

Think before you speak and do not be over quick to answer a matter without thinking.

5:2 Be not rash with thy mouth, and let not thine heart be hasty to utter any thing before God: for God is in heaven, and thou upon earth: therefore let thy words be few. **5:3** For a dream cometh through the multitude of business [an active mind]; and a fool's voice is known by multitude of [empty] words.

5:4 When thou vowest a vow unto God, defer not to pay it; for he hath no pleasure in fools: pay that which thou hast vowed. **5.5** Better is it that thou shouldest not vow, than that thou shouldest vow and not pay.

Do not make promises to God, lest you fail to keep them, for if you make a promise to God, Satan will immediately work to make keeping your word a heavy burden to you. Instead fear God and do HIS will, making no promises to God, except for your baptismal marriage commitment.

5:6 Suffer not thy mouth to cause thy flesh to sin; neither say thou before the angel, that it was an error: wherefore should God be angry at thy voice, and destroy the work of thine hands? **5:7** For in the multitude of dreams and many words there are also divers vanities: but fear thou God.

You oppressors of the flock; you shall be judged of God.

5:8 If thou seest the oppression of the poor, and violent perverting of judgment and justice in a province, marvel not at the matter: for he that is higher than the highest regardeth; and there be higher than they [A higher one than the evil doer, who shall judge him.].

All things come out of the earth that God has made for humanity. Therefore all that humanity has, is a gift of God without which we could not even exist.

5:9 Moreover the profit of the earth is for all: the king himself is served by the field.

No matter what physical thing man desires, when he has achieved it; he will not be satisfied with it. for physical things are not of any real value; only the spiritual is satisfying and everlasting.

5:10 He that loveth silver shall not be satisfied with silver; nor he that loveth abundance with increase: this is also vanity.

What is the point of acquiring more than we can use; except to help others. Let the rich be generous to the poor and they will see treasures laid up for them in heaven.

5:11 When goods increase, they are increased that eat them: and what good is there to the owners thereof, saving the beholding of them with their eyes?

5:12 The sleep of a labouring man is sweet, whether he eat little or much: but the abundance of the rich will not suffer him to sleep.

5:13 There is a sore evil which I have seen under the sun, namely, riches kept for the owners thereof to their hurt.

5:14 But those riches perish by evil travail: and he begetteth a son, and there is nothing in his hand [there is nothing laid up for him in heaven when he dies].

Physical wealth is of no real lasting value, only the spiritual has lasting value. Those who seek the pleasures and wealth of this world shall die and have nothing laid up in heaven for themselves. it is better to do good and keep God's commandments always, then to lust after worldliness.

5:15 As he came forth of his mother's womb, naked shall he return to go as he came, and shall take nothing of his labour, which he may carry away in his hand.

5:16 And this also is a sore evil, that in all points as he came, so shall he go: and what profit hath he that hath laboured for the wind?

5:17 All his days also he eateth in darkness, and he hath much sorrow and wrath with his sickness.

Enjoy life and help others as God blesses you; but do not set your heart on ungodly lusts and pleasures.

5:18 Behold that which I have seen: it is good and comely for one to eat and to drink, and to enjoy the good of all his labour that he taketh under the sun all the days of his life, which God giveth him: for it is his portion.

Let us use what God has given us for godly purposes and keep his commandments always.

5:19 Every man also to whom God hath given riches and wealth, and hath given him power to eat thereof, and to take his portion, and to rejoice in his labour; this is the gift of God.

5:20 For he shall not much remember the days of his life; because God answereth him in the joy of his heart.

It is a sore burden to work hard and then have one's reward taken by another; in usury and taxes, or by fraud or theft, or by cunning words.

Ecclesiastes 6

Ecclesiastes 6:1 There is an evil which I have seen under the sun, and it is common among men:

6:2 A man to whom God hath given riches, wealth, and honour, so that he wanteth nothing for his soul of all that he desireth, yet God giveth him not power to eat thereof, but a stranger eateth it: this is vanity, and it is an evil disease.

If a man work hard all his life and enjoy none of it, and if he has not laid up a reward in heaven; it is a great evil.

6:3 If a man beget an hundred children, and live many years, so that the days of his years be many, and his soul be not filled with good, and also that he have no burial; I say, that an untimely [miscarried] birth is better than he.

6:4 For he cometh in with vanity, and departeth in darkness, and his name shall be covered with darkness.

6:5 Moreover he [that has not been born being miscarried and] hath not seen the sun, nor known any thing: this hath more rest than the other.

If a man is rich in physical things, and not knowing God or keeping his commandments, lives for a thousand years; he will still die; the physically rich, or carnally wise; shall still die, like the fool.

The ONLY things that has any real lasting value, are the commandments and teachings of God and our relationship with the Father and the Son!

6:6 Yea, though he live a thousand years twice told, yet hath he seen no [true good thing] good: do not all go to one place?

6:7 All the labour of man is for his mouth, and yet the appetite is not filled.

6:8 For what hath the wise more than the fool? what hath the poor, that knoweth to walk before the living?

It is better to have, than to desire and not have.

6:9 Better is the sight of the eyes than the wandering of the desire: this is also vanity and vexation of spirit.

Man cannot contend with God; it is better to keep God's Words and ways than to perish in foolishness.

6:10 That which hath been is named already, and it is known that it is man: neither may he contend with him that is mightier than he.

The day of death of the righteous, is in conscious thought, the day of his birth into the Family of God, therefore it is better than the beginning of his life and physical sorrows at his physical birth. The same is true of the unconverted, for they shall have a new life in the main harvest into the Family of God.

6:11 Seeing there be many things that increase vanity, what is man the better?

6:12 For who knoweth what is good for man in this life, all the days of his vain life which he spendeth as a shadow? for who can tell a man what shall be after him under the sun? [Only God!]

Ecclesiastes 7

A Few Proverbs

A good reputation is priceless, however there are many in this evil world who will lie, or use innuendo to destroy good names. Their deceitful work is in vain, for God will bring the truth out in his good time.

Ecclesiastes 7:1 A good name is better than precious ointment; and the day of death than the day of one's birth.

Mourning a loss helps put life in its proper perspective and bring us to God. Reveling in carnal events only encourages our carnal nature towards more worldliness and personal pride.

Sadness turns us to understand that the only things of real consequence are the things of God; therefore mourning brings us back to a good understanding of the transitory nature of the physical and the need for God.

7:2 It is better to go to the house of mourning, than to go to the house of feasting: for that is the end of all men; and the living will lay it to his heart.

7:3 Sorrow is better than laughter: for by the sadness of the countenance the heart is made better.

7:4 The heart of the wise is in the house of mourning [repentance]; but the heart of fools is in the house of mirth.

The correction of God's Word is better than precious jewels to the one who responds positively and corrects himself.

7:5 It is better to hear the rebuke of the wise, than for a man to hear the song of fools.

The joy of those who break God's law and compromise with God's commandments is the sound of fools running to their own destruction.

7:6 For as the crackling of thorns under a pot, so is the laughter of the fool: this also is vanity.

The godly man hates oppression, and a bribe destroys the righteousness of the godly.

The heart is representative of our nature and a bribe is a desire for physical wealth above well doing in keeping all of God's commandments.

7:7 Surely oppression maketh a wise man mad; and a gift destroyeth the heart.

It is better to have successfully completed a project, then to be only beginning and possible fail.

7:8 Better is the end of a thing than the beginning thereof: and the patient in spirit is better than the proud in spirit.

Control your temper and suppress and control anger; for an uncontrolled temper leads to much shame and evil.

7:9 Be not hasty in thy spirit to be angry: for anger resteth in the bosom of fools.

7:10 Say not thou, What is the cause that the former days were better than these? for thou dost not enquire wisely concerning this.

The greatest inheritance that a parent can give is wise instruction of his children, and the wise person who also inherits wealth with wisdom, will do much good with it.

7:11 Wisdom is good with an inheritance: and by it there is profit to them that see the sun.

7:12 For wisdom is a defence, and money is a defence: but the excellency of knowledge is, that wisdom giveth life to them that have it.

Do not oppose God in his will, for he gives blessings and takes them away, to teach us the vanity of all physical things.

7:13 Consider the work of God: for who can make that straight, which he hath made crooked?

7:14 In the day of prosperity be joyful, but in the day of adversity consider: God also hath set the one over against the other, to the end that man should find nothing after him.

Solomon now gets into self-righteousness and the pointlessness of man following the righteousness of men; by doing what he thinks is right, instead of doing what God commands.

7:15 All things have I seen in the days of my vanity: there is a just man that perisheth in his righteousness, and there is a wicked man that prolongeth his life in his wickedness.

Justice or wickedness according to the thoughts of what is right to a man, means nothing in the end; for both what appears just or evil to humanity will fail [men think that abortion and much wickedness is right]. It is those who fear God and are just, by the keeping of all of God's commandments, who have something of real value for eternity.

Therefore be not self-righteous, nor worldly wise; instead be godly righteous and godly wise, through the diligent keeping of all of his teachings and commandments.

This verse has been badly twisted by the wicked, who declare the zealous for God over righteous, when the verse is actually about the SELF-

RIGHTEOUSNESS of the wicked, who are zealous for their OWN ways and NOT zealous for the ways of God.

7:16 Be not righteous over much; neither make thyself over wise: why shouldest thou destroy thyself?

Do not depart from zeal for God and his Word like the wicked.

7:17 Be not over much wicked, neither be thou foolish: why shouldest thou die before thy time?

7:18 It is good that thou shouldest take hold of this; yea, also from this withdraw not thine hand: **for he that feareth God shall come forth of them all.**

A wise man is better than ten strong men who dissipate their strength in foolishness.

7:19 Wisdom strengtheneth the wise more than ten mighty men which are in the city.

> **Romans 3:23** For all have sinned, and come short of the glory of God;

Therefore let us look to God and not to men for righteousness.

Ecclesiastes 7:20 For there is not a just man upon earth, that doeth good, and sinneth not.

Do not eves drop or be so thin skinned and over sensitive that you take exception to every critical word. Learn to let little things slide or your life will be miserable and full of vexations.

7:21 Also take no heed unto all words that are spoken; lest thou hear thy servant curse thee:

7:22 For oftentimes also thine own heart knoweth that thou thyself likewise hast cursed others.

Solomon proved out these things by wise thought, but found little understanding of the things of God by human wisdom.

7:23 All this have I proved by wisdom: I said, I will be wise; but it was far from me.

Solomon found that the greatest evil to befall him was the enticements of wicked women who made his life a misery and were his downfall. In this he was speaking of his own desire for strange [unconverted] women.

The righteous man should seek out a righteous woman. This is true of Christ for he will not marry an unclean by sin bride.

7:24 That which is far off, and exceeding deep, who can find it out?

7:25 I applied mine heart to know, and to search, and to seek out wisdom, and the reason of things, and to know the wickedness of folly, even of foolishness and madness:

7:26 And I find more bitter than death the woman, whose heart is snares and nets, and her hands as bands: **whoso pleaseth God shall escape from her; but the sinner shall be taken by her.**

7:27 Behold, this have I found, saith the preacher [teacher], counting one by one, to find out the account:

7:28 Which yet my soul seeketh, but I find not [any righteous]: one [righteous] man among a thousand have I found; but a [good] woman among all those have I not found.

7:29 Lo, this only have I found, that God hath made man [to be] upright [godly]; but they have sought out many [wicked] inventions.

Ecclesiastes 8

A wise man respects authority and submits to the ruler, beginning with God; and then the rulers of the nations.

Ecclesiastes 8:1 Who is as the wise man? and who knoweth the interpretation of a thing? a man's wisdom maketh his face to shine, and the boldness of his face shall be changed.

We should keep the commandment of the physical king because he exercises physical power over us! How much more should we keep the commandments of the King of kings who has power of eternal life and death?

8:2 I counsel thee to keep the king's commandment, and that in regard of the oath of God.

8:3 Be not hasty to go out of his [to try and hide from the king's sight, by extension to leave the presence of God; in order to do evil] sight: stand not in an evil thing; for he doeth whatsoever pleaseth him.

8:4 Where the word of a king [God the Father is King of the universe and Christ is King over the earth] is, there is power: and who may say unto him, What doest thou?

8:5 Whoso keepeth the commandment [of God who is the ultimate King] shall feel no evil thing: and a wise man's heart discerneth both time and judgment.

Man has no power to achieve eternal life; which is the gift of God the King of those who obey him.

8:6 Because to every purpose there is time and judgment, therefore the misery of man is great upon him. **8:7** For he knoweth not that which shall be: for who can tell him when it shall be?

8:8 There is no man that hath power over the spirit to retain the spirit; neither hath he power in the day of death: and there is no discharge in that war; neither shall wickedness deliver those that are given to it.

Men rule over others, dominating and abusing; not believing that God rules over them and will call them to account.

8:9 All this have I seen, and applied my heart unto every work that is done under the sun: there is a time wherein one man ruleth over another to his own hurt.

All men die and there is no profit in the gain of the wicked. Let us obey our God and he shall give the gift of eternal life.

8:10 And so I saw the wicked buried, who had come and gone from the place of the holy, and they were forgotten in the city where they had so done: this is also vanity.

Because there seems to be no immediate bad result of much evil, short sighted men do not see the consequences of their evil deeds.

8:11 Because sentence against an evil work is not executed speedily, therefore the heart of the sons of men is fully set in them to do evil.

God's gift of eternal life in peace is reserved for those who love him and keep his commandments, while the end of the commandment breaker is his destruction.

8:12 Though a sinner do evil an hundred times, and his days be prolonged, yet surely I know that it shall be well with them that fear God, which fear before him:

8:13 But it shall not be well with the wicked, neither shall he prolong his days, which are as a shadow; because he feareth not before God.

The wicked who persecute the zealous for God: shall be destroyed.

> **Matthew 18:6** But whoso shall offend [persecute] one of these little ones **which believe in me**, it were better for him that a millstone were hanged about his neck, and that he were drowned in the depth of the sea.

When the just before God are attacked by the wicked, it is a great evil, and God will not hold the wicked guiltless.

Ecclesiastes 8:14 There is a vanity which is done upon the earth; that there be just men, unto whom it happeneth according to the work of the wicked; again, there be wicked men, to whom it happeneth according to the work of the righteous: I said that this also is vanity.

Solomon advises us to enjoy our lives with propriety and true godliness.

8:15 Then I commended mirth, because a man hath no better thing under the sun, than to eat, and to drink, and to be merry: for that shall abide with him of his labour the days of his life, which God giveth him under the sun.

Solomon considers the works of man and God.

8:16 When I applied mine heart to know wisdom, and to see the business that is done upon the earth: (for also there is [are those] that neither day nor night seeth sleep with his eyes: [but work always] .

The ways of God are far beyond carnal man's understanding:

1 Corinthians 2:11 For what man knoweth the things of a man, save the spirit of man which is in him? even so the things of God knoweth no man, but the Spirit of God.

Ecclesiastes 8:17 Then I beheld all the work of God, that a man cannot find out the work that is done under the sun: because though a man labour to seek it out, yet he shall not find it; yea farther; though a wise man think to know it, yet shall he not be able to find it.

Ecclesiastes 9

No man knows the things of God; except those to whom God has given his Holy Spirit of understanding.

Ecclesiastes 9:1 For all this I considered in my heart even to declare all this, that the righteous, and the wise, and their works, are in the hand of God: no man knoweth either love or hatred by all that is before them.

Death is a great evil in the earth.

9:2 All things come alike to all: there is one event to the righteous, and to the wicked; to the good and to the clean, and to the unclean; to him that sacrificeth, and to him that sacrificeth not: as is the good, so is the sinner; and he that sweareth, as he that feareth an oath.

9:3 This is an evil among all things that are done under the sun, that there is one event unto all: yea, also the heart of the sons of men is full of evil, and madness is in their heart while they live, and after that they go to the dead.

9:4 For to him that is joined to all the living there is hope: for a living dog is better than a dead lion.

9:5 For **the living know that they shall die: but the dead know not any thing**, neither have they any more a reward; for the memory of them is forgotten.

9:6 Also their love, and their hatred, and their envy, is now [will perish without repentance] perished; neither have they any more a portion for ever in any thing that is done under the sun.

The faithful to God will be accepted and given the gift of eternal life; therefore be diligent to be faithful to God and to keep ourselves free from the contamination of sin.

Let the called out be diligent to cleave to their espoused Husband and:

9:7 Go thy way, eat thy bread with joy, and drink thy wine with a merry heart; for God now accepteth thy works.

9:8 Let thy garments be always white [let our lives pure free from breaking God's commandments]; and let thy head lack no ointment [a type of God's Spirit].

Instructions for a happy and successful life

9:9 Live joyfully with the wife whom thou lovest all the days of the life of thy vanity, which he hath given thee under the sun, all the days of thy vanity: **for that is thy portion in this life**, and in thy labour which thou takest under the sun.

9:10 Whatsoever thy hand findeth to do, do it with thy might; for there is no work, nor device, nor knowledge, nor wisdom, in the grave, whither thou goest.

9:11 I returned, and saw under the sun, that the race is not to the swift, nor the battle to the strong, neither yet bread to the wise, nor yet riches to men of understanding, nor yet favour to men of skill; but time and chance happeneth to them all.

9:12 For man also knoweth not his time: as the fishes that are taken in an evil net, and as the birds that are caught in the snare; so are the sons of men snared in an evil time, when it falleth suddenly upon them.

The wise words of a poor man are despised, for men look to the great. Men look after the seeing of their eyes, and not according to the wisdom of the spirit of righteousness.

9:13 This wisdom have I seen also under the sun, and it seemed great unto me:

9:14 There was a little city, and few men within it; and there came a great king against it, and besieged it, and built great bulwarks against it:

9:15 Now there was found in it a poor wise man, and he by his wisdom delivered the city; yet no man remembered that same poor man.

9:16 Then said I, Wisdom is better than strength: nevertheless the poor man's wisdom is despised, and his words are not heard.

Wisdom is found in the quiet of prayer and the careful consideration of the words of God; NOT in partying, or in seeking our own ways.

9:17 The words of wise men are heard in quiet more than the cry of him that ruleth among fools.

There is great strength and much good in wisdom; but one sinner can cause much damage; therefore do not allow the openly unconverted in your assemblies.

> **Titus 3:10** A man that is an heretick after the first and second admonition reject; **3:11** Knowing that he that is such is subverted, and sinneth, being condemned of himself.

Ecclesiastes 9:18 Wisdom is better than weapons of war: but one sinner destroyeth much good.

Ecclesiastes 10

Here we begin to come to the conclusion of Solomon; which is that the pursuit of our own ways and of physical things is an empty meaningless struggle which has no lasting value.

It is the things of God which are eternal; and the only value of the present physical life is to learn that following and living by every Word of God is the only thing that has meaning and lasting value.

The next three chapters contain what Solomon has learned in his pursuit of all physical things; which is what the Ekklesia needs to learn today.

In truth our own ways are empty, meaningless, transitory; while eternity, keeping the whole Word of God, is all that really matters. The only value that this physical life has, is as a practical lesson in that truth.

Only a little sin, a little compromise with God's law, teachings and will; causes the otherwise good man to stink in God's nostrils.

Those who teach tolerance of sin for the sake of organizational unity, instead of teaching unity with God through the enthusiastic keeping of God's commandments; are an unclean nauseating odor to God and will be rejected by Christ (Rev 3:16).

Ecclesiastes 10:1 Dead flies cause the ointment of the apothecary to send forth a stinking savour: so doth a little folly him that is in reputation for wisdom and honour.

A wise man will always focus on and look to keep God's commandments with his strong right hand; while the compromising foolish will turn aside out of the ways of God for his heart is not with God.

10:2 A wise man's heart is at his right hand; but a fool's heart at his left.

10:3 Yea also, when he that is a fool walketh by [out of] the way, his [he has no godly wisdom] wisdom faileth him, and he saith to every one that he is a fool.

Do not resist the ruler of all things which is God, by resisting his commandments; for there is no escape from his judgment. When God warns and corrects you repent quickly before him.

10:4 If the spirit of the ruler rise up against thee, leave not thy place; for yielding pacifieth great offences.

It is a great folly for a ruler to teach men to tolerate sin and compromise with God's commandments for organizational unity or for any other purpose. In that organization the spiritually rich in wisdom are brought low and wickedness is exalted above the people.

10:5 There is an evil which I have seen under the sun, as an error [false doctrine] which proceedeth from the ruler:

10:6 Folly [sin] is set in great dignity [by wicked men], and the rich [spiritually rich who are zealous for God and his commandments] sit in low place.

When wickedness rules; the evil are lifted up, while the faithful to God are brought low.

10:7 I have seen servants upon horses, and princes walking as servants upon the earth.

The man who lays snares for the faithful zealous followers of God shall ultimately fall into his own traps and be destroyed in his own pit [the grave].

10:8 He that diggeth a pit shall fall into it; and whoso breaketh an hedge, a serpent shall bite him.

Various Proverbs

10:9 Whoso removeth stones [Physical work can be dangerous but is necessary to prosper] shall be hurt therewith; and he that cleaveth wood shall be endangered thereby.

Think before acting and you will save yourself much labour.

10:10 If the iron [the ax] be blunt, and he do not whet the edge [sharpen the tools], then must he put to more strength: but wisdom is profitable to direct [saving much work].

A person, who spouts out everything they hear and has no discretion, is no better than a serpent lying in wait to bite, for their words of indiscretion will surely bite many.

10:11 Surely the serpent will bite without enchantment; and a babbler is no better.

A wise man will speak wise things, teaching the wisdom of God's commandments; but a foolish man will teach foolish rebellion against zeal for God's commandments, that may appear wise to worldly men, but is foolishness just the same.

10:12 The words of a wise man's mouth are gracious; but the lips of a fool will swallow up himself.

10:13 The beginning of the words of [the compromiser with God's law] his mouth is foolishness: and the end of his talk is mischievous madness.

The wicked often bury their false doctrine in a multitude of words.

10:14 A fool also is full of words: a man cannot tell what shall be; and what shall be after him, who can tell him?

10:15 The labour of the foolish wearieth every one of them, because he knoweth not how to go to the city [of God, the temple of God and God's gift of life eternal].

10:16 Woe to thee, O land, when thy king is a [ignorant and lacking knowledge like a] child, and thy princes [leaders feed themselves first] eat in the morning!

10:17 Blessed art thou, O land, when thy king is the son of nobles [When the king is the son of righteous and Godly wise advisors], and thy princes eat [feed the people and take only what is appropriate for themselves and not to make themselves intoxicated with wealth or worldly pleasures: and in the spiritual sense feed on God's Word] in due season, for strength, and not for drunkenness!

We have been lax, lukewarm and slothful about our spiritual house and we have had a misguided zeal for the physical.

10:18 By much slothfulness the building decayeth; and through idleness of the hands the house droppeth [collapses] through.

One cannot feast or drink wine without wealth. Therefore let us lay up spiritual wealth that we may rejoice in our God.

10:19 A feast is made for laughter, and wine maketh merry: but money answereth all things.

God knows all our heart and he knows the thoughts of our minds. Therefore discipline your very nature to zealously keep all of God's commandments and internalize them as a part of our very natures.

10:20 Curse not the king, no not in thy thought; and curse not the rich in thy bedchamber: for a bird of the air shall carry the voice, and that which hath wings shall tell the matter.

Ecclesiastes 11

If we are generous to others we shall make friends and have our reward from God

Ecclesiastes 11:1 Cast thy bread upon the waters: for thou shalt find it after many days.

11:2 Give a portion to seven, and also to eight; for thou knowest not what evil shall be upon the earth.

Be generous to others as God is generous to us, but give out of our blessings, and do not give what we do not have. Also give unto those who have claims on us; providing what is needed to our families and creditors.

When we give to the needy [BOTH physically and the spiritual gifts of teaching God's truth], and obey God; then in due time God will give to us spiritual riches and eternal life; therefore the gift really remains with us as the fallen tree remains in its place.

11:3 If the clouds be full of rain, they empty themselves upon the earth: and if the tree fall toward the south, or toward the north, in the place where the tree falleth, there it shall be.

The lazy man [physically or spiritually] who will not put effort into his work; shall not reap physical or spiritual gain

> **Matthew 25:24** Then he which had received the one talent came and said, Lord, I knew thee that thou art an hard man, reaping where thou hast not sown, and gathering where thou hast not strawed: **25:25** And I was afraid, and went and hid thy talent in the earth: lo, there thou hast that is thine.
>
> **25:26** His lord answered and said unto him, Thou wicked and slothful servant, thou knewest that I reap where I sowed not, and gather where I have not strawed: **25:27** Thou oughtest therefore to

have put my money to the exchangers, and then at my coming I should have received mine own with usury.

25:28 Take therefore the talent from him, and give it unto him which hath ten talents.

25:29 For unto every one that hath shall be given, and he shall have abundance: but from him that hath not shall be taken away even that which he hath. **25:30** And cast ye the unprofitable servant into outer darkness: there shall be weeping and gnashing of teeth.

Brethren, we have been deceived and distracted into doing a business

Brethren, I tell you the truth. Unless we become zealous to live by every Word of God and to study to learn and grow in repentance and knowledge; we shall NOT be in the resurrection of first fruits.

Ecclesiastes 11:4 He that observeth the wind shall not sow; and he that regardeth the clouds shall not reap.

Man with the spirit of a man, knows nothing of God. It is only by the Spirit of God, given to those who commit to obeying God; that godly things are understood.

11:5 As thou knowest not what is the way of the spirit, nor how the bones do grow in the womb of her that is with child: even so thou knowest not the works of God who maketh all.

Work night and day as David did [Psalm 119] to seek out God and learn of God's ways to zealously keep them.

11:6 In the morning sow thy seed, and in the evening withhold not thine hand: for thou knowest not whether shall prosper, either this or that, or whether they both shall be alike good.

The light [scriptures and law] of God is sweet to convert the soul; just remember the days of darkness from which God's Word has liberated us, so that we do not return to spiritual Egypt.

11:7 Truly the light is sweet, and a pleasant thing it is for the eyes to behold the sun:

11:8 But if a man live many years, and rejoice in them all; yet let him remember the days of darkness; for they shall be many. All that cometh is vanity.

Live life to the full according to the commandments of God; for we shall all be judged by the same God, out of the same books; according to our works.

> **Revelation 20:12** And I saw the dead, small and great, stand before God; and the books were opened: and another book was opened, which is the book of life: and the dead were judged out of those things which were written in the books, according to their works.

Ecclesiastes 11:9 Rejoice, O young man, in thy youth; and let thy heart cheer thee in the days of thy youth, and walk in the ways of thine heart, and in the sight of thine eyes: but know thou, that for all these things God will bring thee into judgment.

Put away the evil and excess of youth and learn of God to zealously keep all of his commandments.

11:10 Therefore remove sorrow from thy heart, and put away evil from thy flesh: for childhood and youth are vanity.

Ecclesiastes 12

Remember God and his law in your youth; before you are old and your eyes be dimmed and there is no more pleasure in life

Ecclesiastes 12:1 Remember now thy Creator in the days of thy youth, while the evil days come not, nor the years draw nigh, when thou shalt say, I have no pleasure in them;

12:2 While the sun, or the light, or the moon, or the stars, be not darkened, nor the clouds return after the rain:

12:3 In the day when [death approaches] the keepers of the house shall tremble, and the strong men shall bow themselves, and the grinders cease because they are few and those that look out of the windows be darkened, [eyesight is] be darkened,

12:4 And the doors shall be shut in the streets, when the sound of the grinding is low, and he shall rise up at the voice of the bird, and all the daughters of musick shall be brought low;

12:5 Also when they shall be afraid of that which is high, and fears shall be in the way, and the almond tree shall flourish, and the grasshopper shall be a burden, and desire shall fail: because man goeth to his long home [of the grave], and the mourners go about the streets:

12:6 Or ever the silver cord be loosed, or the golden bowl be broken, or the pitcher be broken at the fountain, or the wheel broken at the cistern.

The spirits of the dead return to God to be kept in his care for the resurrections; when they shall be placed in new bodies.

12:7 Then shall the [people] dust return to the earth as it was: and the spirit shall return unto God who gave it.

12:8 Vanity of vanities, saith the preacher; all is vanity.

Even though Solomon was vexed with the vanity of physical life, he still taught the people in many Proverbs. This seems to indicate that the proverbs may have been written after Ecclesiastes.

12:9 And moreover, because the preacher was wise, he still taught the people knowledge; yea, he gave good heed, and sought out, and set in order many proverbs.

12:10 The preacher sought to find out acceptable words: and that which was written was upright, even words of truth.

12:11 The words of the wise are as goads [to do the righteousness of God's commandments], and as nails fastened by the masters of assemblies, which are given from one shepherd.

The study of physical things is endless; the things of real value are the things of God.

12:12 And further, by these, my son, be admonished: of making many books there is no end; and much study is a weariness of the flesh.

12:13 Let us hear the conclusion of the whole matter: Fear God, and keep his commandments: for this is the whole duty of man.

12:14 For God shall bring every work into judgment, with every secret thing, whether it be good, or whether it be evil.

Ezekiel 37 and the Resurrection to Flesh

Ezekiel 37 pictures the main harvest represented by the Feast of Tabernacles being resurrected to physical life and judgment.

Remember that the early harvest is resurrected to spirit at the end of the sixth day of the Feast of Unleavened Bread, or at the end of the first six thousand years; but this harvest of Ezekiel 37 is resurrected to flesh, and we know that no resurrection to flesh takes place before the early resurrection to spirit and the millennial 1,000 year Sabbath are completed.

Revelation 20:5 But the rest of the dead lived not again until the thousand years were finished. This is the first resurrection.

Ezekiel 37 is a prophecy of the main fall harvest of Israel and by extension of all humanity as they are grafted into spiritual Israel

While this prophecy is specific to Israel, we know that Israel is the forerunner to what will ultimately be offered to all humanity. Therefore this prophecy also pertains to all humanity; for which during the Feast of Tabernacles of the fall main harvest, a bullock is sacrificed for each one of the seventy families [primary racial groups of the Genesis 10 Table of Nations] of mankind.

God commands three harvest feasts for his people based on the harvests in Judea.

The first is the Feast of Unleavened Bread which pictures the early harvest being called out of the Egypt of bondage to Satan and sin.

The calling out of physical Israel from Egypt and their journey for six days capped by a seventh day High Holy Day is a type of a kind of spiritual Israel being called out of sin beginning with Abel for 6,000 years and then the resurrection from the Red Sea of death to eternal life and a millennial Sabbath in the presence of our Creator.

After physical Israel entered the land and began to till the soil, the harvest could not be reaped until the Wave Offering was lifted up to God the Father, picturing the beginning of the spiritual harvest with the resurrection and ascension of Jesus Christ during the Feast of Unleavened Bread.

Late on the sixth day of Unleavened Bread Israel come up out of the sea, and then celebrated God's Victory High Day Sabbath of the seventh day of that Feast. This day pictures the harvest of the spiritually called out of the past six thousand years who have overcome and been chosen; being changed to eternal life and raised up from the Red Sea of death [the grave] to the Victory of God and eternal life.

Then at Pentecost at Sinai all of physical Israel entered into a Covenant with God; this being an instructional type that all Israel and all of humanity would later enter into a NEW Covenant (Jer 31:31) at the beginning of the millennial Sabbath of rest on a future Day of Pentecost; and God's Spirit will be poured out on all flesh (Joel 2:28), as happened in a fore-type on that first century Pentecost.

The Feast of Pentecost pictures the establishment of the theocracy of physical Israel, and represents the establishment of the reign of Jesus Christ as King of kings of the Kingdom of God over all the earth.

The seventh day is still a part of the week! Therefore those who live during the millennial seventh day are a part of the early harvest and will be changed or die in their sins at the age of 100.

Isaiah 65:20 There shall be no more thence an infant of days, nor an old man that hath not filled his days: for the child shall die an hundred years old; but the sinner being an hundred years old shall be accursed.

The scriptures tell us that the resurrection of the chosen overcomers will take place at the end of the sixth day and before the High Holy seventh day which pictures the millennium [thousand years], and that there will be no more resurrections from that point until AFTER the millennium!

Revelation 20:5 But the rest of the dead lived not again until the thousand years were finished

Please visit the Festivals categories for detailed explanations.

Then AFTER the millennium; the main harvest of the Feast of Tabernacles will begin in a seven thousand year great judgment and bringing in of the whole of remaining humanity which had died in sin.

Revelation 20:13 And the sea gave up the dead which were in it; and death and hell delivered up the dead which were in them: and they were judged every man according to their works

The main physical harvest celebrated by Tabernacles, represents the main fall harvest of lives for God.

No! The seven days of the Feast of Tabernacles does NOT picture a 1,000 year millennium which is absolutely contrary to scripture (2 Peter 3:8)! We have been taught falsely on these things in direct contradiction to the Word of God! The early harvest is not resurrected in the fall! That is inherently contradictory [oxymoronic]!

Ezekiel 37 pictures that main harvest of humanity who have all died in their sins, being resurrected to physical life and judgment represented by the seven day Feast of Tabernacles. Remember that the early harvest is resurrected to SPIRIT to begin the millennium, but this harvest of Ezekiel 37 is resurrected to FLESH.

Ezekiel 37:1 The hand of the LORD was upon me, and carried me out in the spirit of the LORD, and set me down in the midst of the valley which was full of bones, **37:2** And caused me to pass by them round about: and, behold, there were very many in the open valley; and, lo, they were very dry [very ancient].

37:3 And he said unto me, Son of man, can these bones live? And I answered, O Lord GOD, thou knowest.

37:4 Again he said unto me, Prophesy upon these bones, and say unto them, O ye dry bones, hear the word of the LORD.

After the end of the millennium Jesus Christ will resurrect the long dead who had died in their sins; back to physical life

37:5 Thus saith the Lord GOD unto these bones; Behold, I will cause breath to enter into you, and ye shall live: **37:6** And I will lay sinews upon you, and will bring up flesh upon you, and cover you with skin, and put breath in you, and ye shall live; and ye shall know that I am the LORD.

The dead who have never known godliness will be restored back to physical life and will then receive an opportunity to reconciled to God and receive his gift of eternal life.

37:7 So I prophesied as I was commanded: and as I prophesied, there was a noise, and behold a shaking, and the bones came together, bone to his bone. **37:8** And when I beheld, lo, the sinews and the flesh came up upon them, and the skin covered them above: but there was no breath in them.

This is a process where physical bodies are created first, after which the spirits of the dead are placed back into the new bodies made for them, their own spirits are taken out of storage as it were; and the breath of air given to them so that they might breath and live.

37:9 Then said he unto me, Prophesy unto the wind, prophesy, son of man, and say to the wind, Thus saith the Lord GOD; Come from the four winds, O breath, and breathe upon these slain, that they may live.

37:10 So I prophesied as he commanded me, and the breath came into them, and they lived, and stood up upon their feet, an exceeding great army.

Here we are told that these are the dead of all Israel, and since all humanity will be grafted into Israel this refers to all who have ever died not knowing or understanding godliness.

37:11 Then he said unto me, Son of man, these bones are the whole house of Israel: behold, they say, Our bones are dried, and our hope is lost: we are cut off for our parts.

God will resurrect all Israel [and all humanity] who has ever lived and has not yet been changed to spirit; to physical life and they shall dwell in their own land.

37:12 Therefore prophesy and say unto them, Thus saith the Lord GOD; Behold, O my people, I will open your graves, and cause you to come up out of your graves, and bring you into the land of Israel.

When people who in their last conscious instant knew they were dying, often horribly, are brought back to life from death: They will KNOW the power and greatness of the Eternal God!!!

They will KNOW that he is the Life-Giver and that he can be their salvation if only they will follow him!!!

They will know and they will turn to him in sincere repentance to live by every Word of God and they will be brought into the spiritual Temple [Family] of God, and their teachers [the laborers of the already spiritually changed] will rejoice greatly as they bring the sheaves of the harvest of humanity into the family of God; as pictured by the Feast of the Ingathering of Nations [Tabernacles]!!!

Please do visit our Festival category articles.

37:13 And ye shall know that I am the LORD, when I have opened your graves, O my people, and brought you up out of your graves, **37:14** And shall put my spirit in you, and ye shall live, and I shall place you in your own land: then shall ye know that I the LORD have spoken it, and performed it, saith the LORD.

While this prophecy is specific to Israel, and we know that Israel is the forerunner to what will ultimately be offered to all humanity. Therefore this prophecy also pertains to all humanity for during the Feast of Tabernacles of the fall main harvest, a bullock is sacrificed for each one of the seventy families [primary racial groups of the Genesis 10 Table of Nations] of mankind.

God the Light of the World

Throughout the scriptures darkness is used as an allegory of ignorance and spiritual blindness; while light is a reference to the light of spiritual understanding. We see that at the creation of this present world, the earth was in darkness and God brought light to the earth.

Genesis 1:1 In the beginning God created the heaven and the earth. **1:2** And the earth was without form, and void; and darkness was upon the face of the deep. And the Spirit of God moved upon the face of the waters.

1:3 And **God said, Let there be light: and there was light. 1:4** And God saw the light, that it was good: and God divided the light from the darkness.

As light casts out darkness, the spiritual light of God the Father and Jesus Christ and an understanding of the Word of God given by Christ through his reconciling sacrifice and the gift of the Holy Spirit, casts out the darkness of spiritual ignorance.

This analogy of light is found in the Menorah or lampstand in the Temple, which pictures the pure olive oil as an allegory of the Holy Spirit burning in the lamps to provide light.

The Spiritual Ekklesia are to be a light of godly example to humanity, through their godly zeal to live by every Word of God, powered by the Holy Spirit.

In reference to the ceremony of light in the Temple as inspired by God's Spirit to Ezra, on the beginning of the first day of the Feast of Tabernacles, Jesus said that the Ekklesia were to be like the light on a hill which cannot be concealed; like the physical temple on the holy hill.

Matthew 5:14 Ye are the light of the world. A city that is set on an hill cannot be hid **5:15** Neither do men light a candle, [lamp] and put it under a bushel [basket], but on a candlestick; and it giveth light unto all that are in the house. **5:16 Let your light so shine before men, that they may see your good works, and glorify your Father which is in heaven.**

The Feast of Tabernacles Light Ceremony

In the second temple era Ezra and Nehemiah established the temple service; and from that time, at sunset on the beginning of the first day of the Feast of Tabernacles the worshipers descended to the Court of the Temple where great preparations had been made before the Feast.

Before the Feast four golden Menorah lamp-stands of seven branches each, were set up and against them rested four ladders, four youths of the priesthood, each with a pitcher of oil capable of holding one hundred twenty log. (one log is about 1/3 liter; about 12 liters to a gallon; so that is 120 divided by 12 is about four pitchers of about 10 gallons each).

At sunset as the Feast of Tabernacles began, the Menorahs were lighted and there was a great light shining all through the temple courtyard, the temple area; and shining so brightly on the temple hill, that you could see it from far outside the city!

That blazing light from the temple was what Christ referred to in his instructions to his disciples; that they should be a brilliant light on a hill [the temple mount], in their example of zeal for the whole Word of God!

This was all prepared before the holy day and as the flaming torches were lighting these olive oil burning lamps, the Levites sang songs of praise, playing harps and lutes and cymbals and trumpets and instruments of music of all types and they stood upon the fifteen steps [15 psalms of degrees (Psalms 120-134) were written by David for the Feast of Tabernacles to be sung on these steps.] which led down from the Court of Israel to the Court of Women.

As the sun set the Levitical singers sang the fifteen Songs of Degrees [Ascents] in the Book of Psalms; the Levitical singers standing on the fifteen steps of the temple, standing with their instruments of music and singing these hymns.

As the sun set, two priests sounded their silver trumpets in a threefold blast and then ascending the fifteen steps they sounded their trumpets as they mounted each of the fifteen steps; on the tenth step they sounded another three-fold blast.

Then as they came to the eastern gate they turned around towards the west to face the Most Holy Place, so they would no longer face the east. They turned to face the west which is the Most Holy Place, turning away from the east and the sun.

The Illumination of the Temple was regarded as a part of, and having a symbolic meaning in the Feast of Tabernacles, as was the pouring out of water ceremony.

The light shining ceremony at the temple was so bright that it lit up the whole city from on top of that hill, so that it was seen from a great distance.

Isaiah 9:2 The people that walked in darkness have seen a great light: they that dwell in the land of the shadow of death, upon them hath the light shined.

That prophecy was about Christ and we read in the Book of John, beginning at chapter one, that Christ came and he was the light of the world, but most people rejected him.

This fulfillment of Isaiah through this ceremony in the temple symbolized that great light which was to shine upon Israel, the light of Messiah and godliness. The priests and scribes, Ezra, these people knew Isaiah, and they knew that this great light was going to shine out of darkness. So they set up this ceremony, looking forward to that light.

Isaiah 60:1 Arise and shine; for thy light is come, and the glory of the Lord is risen upon thee. 60:2 For, behold, the darkness shall cover the earth, and gross darkness the people:

People who are in spiritual darkness due to a blindness and ignorance of spiritual things, ignorance of God, and enslavement and bondage to Satan; will have their eyes opened to the light of God in due time.

. . . but **the Lord shall arise upon thee and His glory shall be seen upon thee, and the Gentiles shall come to thy light and the kings to the brightness of thy rising.**

This prophecy concerns the soon coming of Messiah to be the light of the world, and God's light is to be shed on the whole world including the Gentiles. Israel will turn back to God and the Gentiles will be drawn to that great light and they shall seek God.

John 8:12. Jesus said, I am the light of the world. He that followeth Me shall not walk in darkness, but shall have the light of life.

Jesus Christ is the whole Word of God which was inspired by Him in the scriptures, Jesus Christ is the light of the world, and the whole Word of God is God's light in print; while spiritual blindness and darkness.is rebellion against, or anything contrary to the whole Word of God.

This physical light and physical darkness, is an analogy of spiritual light and spiritual darkness. And the spiritual light is Jesus Christ and every Word of God which is Christ in print.

This light came when Jesus began his ministry on the earth, and it is coming again in a much greater way and in a greater fullness when He comes again and establishes the kingdom of God over all the earth.

This ceremony was to represent the light of God being made available to ALL nations and all people during the millennium and in the latter harvest of humanity!

Then after the millennium, at the time of the main harvest of humanity; all those who have lived and died not knowing God, and not living by every Word of God, will be resurrected in their order, during their courses for the full seven days or seven thousand years of the Feast of Tabernacles and brought into the family of God.

During the millennium and after in the main harvest, men will see the light of Christ and the ways of God and the commandments of God shining forth from Jerusalem. As it is written, the law shall go forth from Jerusalem and the Word of God from the temple—paraphrasing here.

And after that, when the New Jerusalem comes down from heaven; the LIGHT of God shall fill the whole earth FOREVER!!!

Healing the Blind

John 9:1 [On the seventh day of the Feast of Tabernacles] And as Jesus passed by, he saw a man which was blind from birth **9:2** And his disciples asked him, saying, Master, who did sin, this man, or his parents, that he was born blind? **9:3** Jesus answered, Neither hath this man sinned, nor his parents: but that the works of God should be made manifest in him.

Through the healing of this man, the works of God were made known to everyone.

9:4 I must work the works of him that sent me, [that is, the works of God the Father] while it is day: the night cometh, when no man can work. **9:5 As long as I am in the world,** [said Jesus] **I am the light of the world.**

The Father and the Son are the Light of the World, casting out the darkness of ignorance, wickedness and evil. Those who reject the truth are also rejecting the light of godliness.

9:6 When he had thus spoken, he spat on the ground, and made clay of the spittle, and anointed the eyes of the blind man with the clay, **9:7** And said to him, Go, wash in the pool of Siloam, (which is by interpretation, Sent.) He went his way therefore, and washed, and came seeing.

Siloam is the pool which was the source of the water for the water pouring ceremony.

This is about the light of TRUTH saving humanity from the darkness of ignorance, slavery to sin and death!

The Ceremony of Light is about the Light of the whole Word of God; which is opened to men by repentance and the application of the reconciling sacrifice of Christ; it is about those who repent and go on to sin no more, being zealous for the Word of God and shining in an example of passionate godliness for all to see!

The Light Ceremony is about those who persevere and overcome, who will be changed to spirit; becoming teachers and leaders, helping to provide the Light of God and the Light of the Word of God to all humanity during the millennium and then in the main harvest of humanity, bringing humanity into a relationship with God the Father, and reconciling all people to the Father through the teaching of the truth, sincere repentance and the reconciling sacrifice of Christ.

The holy days of the seventh month represent the reaping of the main harvest of humanity and the bringing in of the main harvest into the temple and family of God.

Isaiah speaks of Messiah in this way:

Isaiah 42:6, I the Lord have called thee in righteousness, and will hold thine hand, and will keep thee, and will give thee for a covenant of the people for a light of the Gentiles;

Now who did the Father give to establish the covenant with the people? His Son, Jesus Christ, who died for our sins so that we could be reconciled with God the Father. This is a prophecy of Christ.

And what else is Christ to do?

42:7 To open the blind eyes, which was illustrated at the Feast by Christ healing the blind; eyes, that healing was a symbolic act. This man was blind from birth, not because of any sin, but so that Christ could heal him and demonstrate to the world that He would at the appropriate time when He returns, open the blind eyes of humanity to the light of God. To call people to God, to open the eyes of the spiritually blind, to bring them to repentance, to teach them the ways of God, to apply himself as a sacrifice for the sins of humanity and to reconcile a repentant humanity to God the Father.

The Lamb of God came to open the blind eyes as an allegory that he would open the eyes of those blinded by spiritual darkness and ignorance; spiritually blinded and enslaved by Satan and

. . . To bring out the prisoners from the prison [deliver people from bondage to sin] **, and them that sit in darkness** [spiritual ignorance] **out of the prison house** [of death and the grave],

That is, the light liberates humanity from the darkness of spiritual ignorance and from the bondage of spiritual Egypt, from the bondage of Satan.

Christ was to deliver all people who were imprisoned and in bondage to Satan in this world. He is going to bring them out, put away Satan and deliver all people from the spiritual darkness of blindness and ignorance and bondage to sin; into the light of God's righteousness.

The light of Christ is also the whole Word of God, because the whole Word of God is Jesus Christ in print. It was all, every word of it, inspired by Jesus Christ. I am talking about as originally written. Obviously there are a few details in translation that we have to figure out, but if we put all scriptures on the same subject together, with the Holy Spirit we can understand, given enough time and God's Spirit.

Jesus Christ is the light of the world! and if we do not accept that light and instead choose our own false traditions, we have rejected the Light of the knowledge of God and the Light of Truth; for spiritual darkness, spiritual ignorance and spiritual blindness!

Let us all be zealous for the whole Word of God and be quick to repent of any departure from the Truth and Light of the Word of God; that we may be a shining light of example to others, that they might do the same thing and exalt the Eternal above all else!

The early harvest of first fruits have been called into the marvelous light of godliness, and in due time all nations will also be called into that light!

1 Peter 2:9 But ye are a chosen generation, a royal priesthood, an holy nation, a peculiar people; **that ye should shew forth the praises of him who hath called you out of darkness into his marvellous light;**

In Conclusion

Brethren, we have been called to shine the light of faithful godliness through enthusiastically zealously living by every Word of God, so that we are living examples of true godliness! In doing so we are learning and qualifying to be resurrected into the first fruits as priests of the High Priesthood of Melchizedek [Jesus Christ]. Then we will fulfill all of the duties of the priesthood; leading people to reconcile with God the Father, and teaching mankind the way to peace and life eternal; in the millennium, the main harvest of humanity and for all eternity!

When Messiah the Christ comes, he will build the Ezekiel Temple and the LIGHT of godliness will shine forth to the whole earth during the millennium and after that throughout the seven thousand years of the main harvest of humanity pictured by the Feast of the Ingathering of Nations called Tabernacles!

Isaiah 2:2 And it shall come to pass in the last days, that the mountain of the Lord's house shall be established in the top of the mountains, and shall be exalted above the hills; and all nations shall flow unto it. **2:3** And many people shall go and say, Come ye, and let us go up to the mountain of the Lord, to the house of the God of Jacob; and **he will teach us of his ways, and we will walk in his paths: for out of Zion shall go forth the law, and the word of the Lord from Jerusalem.**

The 70 Feast of Tabernacles Sacrifices

The 70 Feast of Tabernacles Sacrifices Represent Bringing all Nations into the Family of God

On the Feast of Tabernacles, that was a sin offering every day for each of the seven days of one kid of the goats: And a burnt offering each day consisting of bullocks, rams and lambs with their appropriate unleavened bread and drink offerings.

The number of bullocks offered decreased every day. The first day thirteen bullocks were offered, on the second day twelve, and so on.

If you add up all of the bullocks offered over the seven days, they total seventy: And if we go to the table of nations in Genesis, after the dispersion of the Tower of Babel, we find that humanity was divided into seventy basic families or nations.

In modern times there may be more subdivisions like different tribes of the same people, but there are seventy fundamental nations, and during the Feast of Tabernacles one bullock was offered as a burnt offering for each nation.

A burnt offering is wholly burned on the altar and represents wholehearted service to God. Seventy burnt offerings represent every one of the seventy nations of mankind wholeheartedly serving God

This is a very interesting thing, and it points very strongly to the work of Christ, as the sacrificial animals represented Christ in His work and His service and atonement for sin, and in the burnt offering; rep[resents Christ bringing all people to God the Father and reconciling them.

These seventy bullocks, one for each of the nations of humanity, picture Christ working hard and reconciling them with God the Father and bringing each of them into wholehearted service to God.

An interesting point is that the number of the burnt sacrifices, whether we are taking the bulls or the lambs or rams or any of the animals that were sacrificed during the Feast of Tabernacles is always divisible by the number seven. And a total of all those sacrificed together is divisible by the number seven.

Seventy bullocks, fourteen rams, ninety-eight lambs were sacrificed at the Feast of Tabernacles, all together 182 sacrifices during the Feast of Tabernacles, which is twenty-six times seven, to which must be added the 336 tenths of ephahs of flour for the unleavened bread offering. And that is forty-eight times seven.

The offerings are divided by the seven days of the feast, offering thirteen bullocks the first day, twelve bullocks the second, eleven the third, right through to a total of seventy.

Sacrifices on the First Day of Tabernacles

Numbers 29:12 And on the fifteenth day of the seventh month ye shall have an holy convocation; ye shall do no servile work, [which is work of any kind] and you shall keep a feast unto the Lord seven days: **29:13** You shall offer a burnt offering, a sacrifice made by fire, of a sweet savor unto the Lord; thirteen young bullocks, two rams and fourteen lambs of the first year; they shall be without blemish.

The above are the sacrifices for the first day of the Feast of Tabernacles. They are not the sacrifices offered on every day, or the total, they are only what is offered on the first day.

In the burnt offering made by fire, the smoke ascends up to heaven, picturing the prayers, efforts and the faithful service of Christ and of Christ-like people rising up to God the Father, and being accepted by God the Father as something very sweet and acceptable to Him.

Numbers 29:17 And **on the second day ye shall offer twelve young bullocks**, two rams, fourteen lambs of the first year without spot. And in **Numbers 29:20** And **on the third day eleven bullocks**.

Thirteen bulls killed on the first day, twelve on the second, eleven on the third, and so forth through the seven days, totaling seventy bullocks.

At Babel God divided humanity into seventy families with seventy different basic languages and races; therefore one bullock is burned as a burnt offering for each family of man, and the bullock in the burnt offering pictures patiently wholeheartedly serving God with strength and commitment.

These Burnt Offerings of Bullocks represent all the families of man being brought into reconciliation with God the Father and then serving Him over the course of the Feast of Tabernacles. These sacrifices are offered in their courses with so many being resurrected to flesh and converted on the first day, so many on the second day, so many on the third day etc throughout the seven days [representing a seven thousand year period] of resurrections to flesh in batches or courses pictured by the Feast of the Ingathering of Nations [Tabernacles].

We know that this is a FALL seven day festival, therefore it has to refer to the fall, or main harvest of humanity, which comes AFTER the millennium; and the number of bullocks picture the seventy families of man being brought into the family of God in the main harvest of lives.

The Feast of Tabernacles is definitely a picture of the fall main harvest of humanity.

The branches represent the nations being brought into the family [temple] of God, and the seventy bullocks represent the patient service of Christ in bringing the seventy nations of humanity into the family of God; and the marching around the altar pictures the evil of this world crashing down, somewhat like the people marched around Jericho; and the Light of the World ceremony, and the water pouring ceremony of pouring out the Holy Spirit on all people during the main fall harvest; all of these things point inescapably to a meaning of the Feast of Tabernacles which is greater than simply "we are going to get ours in the Millennium."

This is about the saving of humanity. It is about those who have been spiritually changed and chosen as first fruits becoming teachers and leaders, providing the Light of God and the light of the Word of God to all humanity, and reconciling humanity into a proper relationship with God the Father, and reconciling all people to the Father through the teaching of the truth, sincere repentance and the sacrifice of Christ.

Jesus Christ is the light of the world. He spoke to the woman in Samaria at the well, talking to her about living water and about how He would give her living water and she would nevermore thirst. He was talking about God's Spirit which gives the understanding of the whole Word of God and leads us into all truth. And that is what the water, the living water is. It is the Word and Holy Spirit of God. This is a really wonderful thing when you understand it.

For years, people went to the Feast and they heard sermon after selfish sermon about how great it is going to be for us and how we are going to dominate and get all the good things and be above everybody.

No, that is totally false! We were not called to rule as the Gentiles rule. As Jesus said to the disciples; the Gentile rulers rule with authority and you shall not do so. You shall not bully the people and seek your own advantage. When God's people rule, they are going to be teaching, guiding, leading, helping.

And when people stumble the teachers are going to reach down and help them up and say; this is the way, walk ye in it. And they are going to lead people to the light of God and through the sacrifice of Christ, the repentant people will begin to realize how much better this way is than the way they had lived in the past. And they will be eager, starving for the bread of life.

They will be thirsting for the water of life, and they will be willing to seek it out. If someone who died of a terrible cancer or was hacked up in a battle, in their next instant when they are raised up, with their injuries healed, the blind eyes are opened and they are shown a better way. You don't have to hurt one another and kill one another and there is a way of peace.

Today look around you. The whole world longs for peace. And the Pope is making a big case for himself by presenting himself as a champion of peace. And there are millions, billions of people who really want peace. They want an end to the suffering.

The end of suffering is coming, but first there is going to be a final chapter, so that everybody gets their belly so full of their own ways that no one will ever want any part of this wicked way again.

Then after the Millennium the main harvest will be brought in, during the Feast of the Ingathering of Nations [Tabernacles]; all those people who died not having had an opportunity for salvation will be raised up to flesh. The long dead of physical Israel will be raised up and with them the long dead of the Gentiles will be raised up and grafted into a new, inclusive of all humanity, spiritual Israel.

The Feast of Tabernacles is about that better way of the New Covenant (Jeremiah 31:31); being offered to all humanity in the main harvest after Satan and his wicked angels are removed forever on the Day of Atonement.

The Living Waters of the Holy Spirit

Hoshanna Rabbah: The Last Great Day of: The Feast of Tabernacles!

In a semi-arid or desert region, water is a very scarce and valuable commodity essential to life.

Psalm 114:8 Which turned the rock into a standing [pool of] water, the flint into a fountain of waters

Psalm 114 speaks about that physical rock where Moses spoke and God brought water gushing out of it, and that is a picture - an allegory - of Jesus Christ, the rock of our salvation, and out of Him comes forth the Living Waters of Salvation.

Just like the waters in the desert came out of the rock and saved the people from dying of physical thirst; so the water, the spiritual water of salvation, comes forth out of Jesus Christ to bring us spiritual salvation, to save us from a lack of the water of God's Word and Spirit.

We should be hungering and thirsting after the Word of God; Jesus Christ came and gave himself for us and poured out the water of the Word, out of himself for us. The whole earth will tremble at His presence when He returns to the earth, the mountains and highlands are going to shake and tremble at the presence of His power and His glory when He comes with His saints.

1 Corinthians 10:4 And did all drink the same spiritual drink: [the people who left Egypt all drank the same water in the desert - a type of the spiritual water of the Word and Spirit of God], **for they drank that spiritual rock that followed them: and that Rock was Christ.**

In the wilderness desert, they came to a fountain of living waters

The living waters that came out of the rock in the wilderness, were a type of the living waters of the Spirit of Salvation, that come out of Jesus Christ in the spiritual sense.

In the wilderness we find two occasions where water came out of the rock.

On the first occasion Moses was commanded to strike the rock and the water came forth. And that is a picture of the death of Christ, of Jesus Christ the Lamb of God being struck down and giving his life for the sins of humanity.

Christ was crucified so that salvation could be opened up to the world and so that the living water of salvation, the salvation of Christ, could be poured out on humanity; just as the striking of that rock in the wilderness brought physical water gushing out to save the people.

The second time, Moses was commanded to speak to the rock and water will come out; which speaks of the water of salvation being given freely to the sincerely repentant who being baptized and committing to go and sin no more; need only speak asking in prayer and the Water of Salvation [the Holy Spirit] would be poured out on us.

Moses was commanded to speak to the rock, and he did make an error there in striking it the second time. He was only to speak to the rock a second time because Jesus Christ the Lamb of God was only to die once.

The second time Moses was only to speak to the rock, for Christ only died once; and after that at the appointed time: all who call on the name of the Lord shall be saved.

When we sincerely repent of past law breaking and commit to go and sin no more can ask that the water of salvation [the Holy Spirit] be poured out on us. Christ died as an effectual sacrifice atoning for our sins, so that we can be washed clean when we sincerely repent.

Ephesians 5:25 Husbands, love your wives, even as Christ also loved the church [the faithful godly brethren, the collective spiritual bride], and gave himself for it;

5:26 That he might sanctify and cleanse it [cleanse God's faithful from all sin] with the washing of water by the word [washing away all sin by his sacrifice and giving his Spirit to empower the sincerely repentant to live by every Word of God, replacing sin with godliness],

5:27 That he might present it to himself a glorious church [spiritual body of faithful] , not having spot, or wrinkle [of the uncleanness of sin], or any such thing; but that it should be holy and without blemish.

Right now the water of the Holy Spirit and Word of Salvation - which is living by every Word of God - is only being offered to a few called out, but when Christ comes with His resurrected saints and the Kingdom is established over all the earth; all who call on the name of the Lord shall be saved.

During the days of Moses the water pouring ceremony of Tabernacles was not commanded, but later during the restoration under Ezra, this water pouring ceremony was instituted, based on Moses bringing water from the Rock; and it was later revealed by Paul that the true Rock was the one who became Jesus Christ who led Israel in the desert (1 Cor 10:4).

The water pouring ceremony and rejoicing with branches

These ceremonies began at the temple during the days of Ezra and that great revival, and these things were used as instructional tools by Jesus Christ in His earthly ministry.

In the second temple celebration, on every day of the Feast of Tabernacles, the people in the temple courtyard would hold their clusters of branches, waving them before the Lord and making a circular procession around the altar.

The altar is a symbol; it is the table of the Lord. It is where the sacrifices are made - representing the sacrifice of the Lamb of God, Jesus Christ - and it is the table of the Lord.

Ezekiel 41:22 The altar of wood was three cubits high, and the length thereof two cubits; and the corners thereof, and the length thereof, and the walls thereof, were of wood: and he said unto me, **This is the table that is before the Lord.**

Malachi speaks about people today calling the table of the Lord contemptible. Spiritually this is about people not being zealous to live by every Word of God and departing from a zeal to keep the whole Word of God;.

To reject a zealous living by every Word of God to do as we think right, is in fact exalting our own ways above the Word of God and amounts to calling the altar and the sacrifice of Christ; unworthy and contemptible.

The false idea that Jesus paid for our law breaking and we do not have to be zealous, or we do not have to care that much; and we can just kind of float along justifying our sins instead of changing our lives. What that attitude really is, is holding the table of the Lord, the altar of God and the atoning sacrifice of the Lamb of God contemptable.

To say that we do not have to really stop sinning and we can continue living our own way, is expressing contempt for the sacrifice of Jesus Christ.

People say they love God, but they continue in sin: Which is holding the table of the Lord and the sacrifice of Christ, in contempt.

God brought water out of the rock for Israel in the wilderness, first by commanding Moses to strike the rock to bring forth water.

Exodus 17:6 Behold, I will stand before thee there upon the rock in Horeb; and thou shalt smite the rock, and there shall come water out of it, that the people may drink. And Moses did so in the sight of the elders of Israel.

Striking the rock signified the sacrificial death of the Rock of Salvation - Messiah the Christ - for the sins of the world, opening the way for the gift of the Holy Spirit, symbolized by the Living Waters of Salvation.

1 Corinthians 10:4 And did all drink the same spiritual drink: for they drank of that spiritual Rock that followed them: and that Rock was Christ.

Later God brought water out of the rock by commanding Moses to speak to the Rock:

Numbers 20:8 Take the rod, and gather thou the assembly together, thou, and Aaron thy brother, and speak ye unto the rock before their eyes; and it shall give forth his water, and thou shalt bring forth to them water out of the rock: so thou shalt give the congregation and their beasts drink.

Thus signifying that ultimately all who call upon the LORD in sincere repentance, will receive the waters of the Holy Spirit freely; giving them understanding and enabling them to internalize the Word of God; and they will be saved.

Joel 2:28 And it shall come to pass afterward, that I will pour out my spirit upon all flesh;

Through the scriptures the pouring out of water before the LORD was considered to seal a Covenant of dedication to God in a most solemn manner

The water essential for life itself, representing an acknowledgment that life itself came by the blessing of God; and the pouring out of water represented a complete Covenant and commitment to live by every Word of God, the giver of the life giving water.

When Israel repented and turned to God in the days of Samuel, they poured out water as a sign of their repentance and commitment to live by every Word of God.

1 Samuel 7:6 And they gathered together to Mizpeh, **and drew water, and poured it out before the Lord, and fasted on that day, and said there, We have sinned against the Lord.** And Samuel judged the children of Israel in Mizpeh.

David also poured out water as representative of the lives of his three friends. Water is essential for life and is life.

2 Samuel 23:16 And the three mighty men brake through the host of the Philistines, and drew water out of the well of Bethlehem, that was by the gate, and took it, and brought it to David: nevertheless he would not drink thereof, but **poured it out unto the Lord. 23:17** And he said, Be it far from me, O Lord, that I should do this: is not this the blood of the men that went in jeopardy of their lives? therefore he would not drink it.

From these examples we can see clearly that God uses physical water as representative of the Holy Spirit of eternal life and the cleansing nature of the Word of God, which casts out all sin and replaces that sin with the nature of God, if we live by that Word. The pouring out of water is therefore a prophecy of that pouring out of God's Spirit on the people in God's due time.

From the days of at least Ezra and Nehemiah; water and willows were brought to the temple before the first High Day of the Feast of Tabernacles began [bringing it before the Holy Day began] and the water was poured out on every Feast day.

Far from criticizing these things; Jesus used these things to instruct us further in the truth of God.

The willows with their long-hanging supple branches, give a whooshing sound when whipped about; and this waving of willow branches was used on Holy Days and during the Festivals to produce the whooshing sound like that of a rushing wind of the Holy Spirit.

Acts 2:1 And when the day of Pentecost was fully come, they were all with one accord in one place. **2:2** And suddenly there came **a sound from heaven as of a rushing mighty wind,** and it filled all the house where they were sitting.

This whooshing sound was to represent the sound of the wind or the Holy Spirit, the Ruach.

When the Spirit came down; there was a sound of a mighty rushing wind, as well as the appearance of fire. This whoosh-whoosh sound was to represent the pouring out of the Spirit of God in the temple ceremony; inspired by Christ to be done in the temple from at least the time of Ezra and Nehemiah.

While the priests gathered the willows, the other priest would proceed to come back from the Pool of Siloam from which the high priest had taken a flask-full of living water as they termed it.

The water was then poured out on every day of the Feast of Tabernacles.

During the intermediate festival days they would go to get the water and fresh willows on the morning of that day and pour it out the same day. On the Sabbath and the High Day they would go out the day before and gather the water and willows, so as not to do even that much work on the Sabbath or High Day, and the water was then kept in the temple and poured out when the High Day or Sabbath came.

When both groups returned to the temple, the one with their willows would circle the altar, waving their willows to make a whoosh-whoosh sound; the sound of the rushing of wind or the rushing of the Holy Spirit.

Then the high priest with his flask of water and his assistant with a flask of wine; wine in the sacrificial system, pictures the pouring out of the blood of Christ the Lamb of God in sacrifice which atones for sin and opens the way for the washing of water of the Holy Spirit and the Word of God. Hence the wine and water were poured out together.

The physical high priest was a type of our spiritual High Priest, Jesus Christ. And the physical high priest physically poured out this water during the ceremony, as a type that Jesus Christ our spiritual High Priest, would pour out his blood in atoning sacrifice for the people and also pour out the Water of Salvation [the Holy Spirit] upon humanity.

The two priests would both go to the altar as the whooshing was taking place, and pour out their pitchers on the southeast corner of the altar, the whooshing picturing the coming of the Holy Spirit, and the pouring out of water pictured the living water of salvation coming from Christ, and the wine pictured the sacrificial blood of the Lamb of God, the blood of reconciliation and atonement.

Wine, is a type of blood and the physical life of Jesus Christ the Lamb of God being shed for us, while water which was made directly by God is a type of the Holy Spirit of God being poured out on the sincerely repentant to bring eternal life in the spirit.

These things indicate that a very deep spiritual inspiration by God was given to Ezra and those people who came from Babylon and began to rebuild the temple and set up these ceremonies.

The seventh day of the Feast of Tabernacles is the: Hoshanna Rabbah, The Great Day of Salvation, because Tabernacles or Sukkot was a festival celebrating the final harvest of the year. As such, it pictures the main harvest of humanity.

This daily ceremony was a thanking of God for the main physical harvest and an allegorical instruction about the pouring out of the Holy Spirit and the Word of God, and the final harvest of humanity, which is represented by the Feast of Tabernacles.

Before the Feast of Tabernacles there were weeks of Sabbath lessons going through every passage of the scripture dealing with water. During the water drawing ceremony at the pool of Siloan (Hebrew shiloach, literally "sending forth," from shalach "to send."), the high priest would recite

Isaiah 12:1-3 And in that day you shall say, O LORD, I will praise you: though you were angry with me, your anger is turned away, and you have comforted me. **12:2** Behold, God is my salvation [the word meaning salvation being shortened from Yehoshua to Yeshua (Strong's H3444) also see Nehemiah 8:17]; I will trust, and not be afraid: for the LORD is my strength and my psalm; he also is become my salvation. **12:3** Therefore with joy shall you draw water out of the wells of salvation.

Those who are sharp right now can recognize in part of this quote from Isaiah, the song of Moses, which Moses sang, when Israel came up out of the Red Sea and Moses sang this song about the glory of God and His deliverance.

The word salvation in the Hebrew was Yehoshua which originated in Joshua *"But Ho-shea, son of Nun, Moses called Yeho-shua" (Num 13:1-16)*. This name was later shortened to "Yeshua" (Is 12:1-3, Neh 8:17). And the name of Messiah the Christ, His personal name that His parents called Him by; was Yeshua which was the short form of Yehoshua.

Yeshua means salvation. The direct English variation of that is Joshua, and the English variation which came from the Hebrew Yeshua through the Greek Iesous, is the English word Jesus. Jesus is the same as Yeshua. It means salvation.

Isaiah says **"with joy shall you draw water out of the wells of salvation** [Draw salvation from Yeshua]."

Salvation comes from Jesus Christ coupled with our own sincere repentance. We draw the water of salvation [The Holy Spirit] from Jesus Christ. It is through Jesus Christ that we receive the Water of Salvation, which is the Word of God and the Holy Spirit.

This is the Water of Salvation which gives life eternal by washing us clean from sin, making us purer and purer as we overcome, and bringing us closer and closer to full spiritual unity with God the Father, to ultimately become like God the Father.

The ceremony itself was quite a sight to see. If you can imagine what this was like: There was this tremendously beautiful temple and many thousands of priests dressed in their priestly robes looking so impressive, and all the people there with their bunches of branches dressed in their best, as we do today; and they are gathered in the courtyard of the temple, with tens of thousands of people there, and with all the priesthood.

The whole ceremony, with the parade and the musicians and the singing of the Psalms of Ascent and people dancing joyfully to the Lord, was a tremendously joyful occasion.

The gates of the temple were thrown open soon after midnight each day of Tabernacles and the ceremony began in the early morning.

The time till the beginning of the early morning daily sacrifice was spent in examining the sacrifices and offerings that were to be brought for this special day.

When the morning sacrifice had been prepared, a priest accompanied by a joyous procession with music went down to the Pool of Siloam to draw the water and bring it back, close to three logs, which is about three liters or quarts. On the Sabbath and High Holy Day they fetched this in a golden vessel to the temple itself on the previous day.

The priesthood served in stages by courses through the year. But at the Holy Festivals they were all present, and of course they were the whole body of the descendants of Aaron, which was many thousands of priests at various times in history.

In one court of the temple stood the altar with all the thousands of priests, and fifteen steps below that, in the court[yard] of Israel; many hundreds of thousands of people were gathered.

The Ceremony

The group of worshipers were led by flutists [wind instruments] also representing the "Rushing Wind" of the Holy Spirit.

Acts 2:1 And when the day of Pentecost was fully come, they were all with one accord in one place. **2:2** And **suddenly there came a sound from heaven as of a rushing mighty wind,** and it filled all the house where they were sitting.

The Levites were playing music on **wind instruments** and they along with many people followed the high priest as he went down to the pool to get the water. following as he goes and returns with a pitcher of water and his associate brings the wine, each in golden pitchers.

As the priestly procession left the temple for Siloam, another procession left the temple for a place in the Kidron Valley close by, where they cut willow branches.

There were two groups, one going to Kidron to get the willows and the other going to Siloam to get the water.

The one group brought back a pitcher of wine which represents the blood representing the atoning sacrifice of Christ; and a pitcher filled with water from the pool of Siloam, which represents the Living Waters of Salvation, the Holy Spirit and the whole Word of God; flowing out from the effectual sacrifice of Jesus Christ!

The other group brought back willow branches, which were whipped about, making a whooshing sound of the wind of the Holy Spirit; **the willow also being specifically commanded to be cut and rejoiced with at this Feast** (Lev 23:40).

As the two groups were returning, there were continual blasts of the priests' trumpets, the singing of Psalm 136; and the whoosh-swooshing of the willows, to represent the sound of the rushing wind of the Holy Spirit.

Amid the blasts of the trumpets, when the **morning daily was about to be offered**; [burned at dawn] the priests arrived with the water and the wine, and as the water and wine arrived those who had the willows stuck them in the ground and bent them over to form a canopy over the altar.

The ordinary daily sacrifice proceeded; while the priest who had gone to Siloam to get the water, timing his arrival so that he returned just as his brethren carried up the pieces of the daily sacrifice to lay them on the altar.

The morning and evening burnt offerings represented the work and sacrifice of Jesus Christ on behalf of all Israel into which ultimately all humanity will be spiritually grafted! Although the whole process of the daily offerings took many hours each morning and again each evening, the morning sacrifice was offered [burned] at dawn, and the evening sacrifice was offered [burned] at sunset.

As the regular daily was being burned on the altar, the two groups of priests arrived to the accompaniment of the flutes and the whooshing of the willows symbolizing the presence of the Holy Spirit, and a choir of thousands of Levites sang the Great Hallel (Psalm 136) as the whole procession entered into the Temple through the Water Gate [named after this event].

As they reached the temple the shofars and silver trumpets blasted loudly, and the high priest approaches the altar where there are two silver basins waiting.

As the high priest entered by the Water Gate, [that is why that particular gate was called the Water Gate]; the priests with the water and the wine were received with a threefold blast from the silver trumpets.

Then the priests went up the steps to the level to where the altar was, and turned to the left where there were two silver basins which had narrow holes in them.

They then poured the water in one, and poured the wine in the other, and filled the basins so that the liquids would dribble in a small stream through the holes in the bottom of the basins. The eastern had a hole a little wider for the wine and the western basin a somewhat narrower hole for the water, so that when the same amount was poured in, because of the different densities, they would all flow out completely at the same time.

The physical high priest, representative of the spiritual High Priest Jesus Christ, then poured out the drink offering or wine offering, and at the same time the water from Siloam was poured into the other basin; as the daily morning sacrifice began to burn!

The wine representing the shed blood of Christ, and the water from the Pool of Siloam representing the salvation of the whole Word of God through the Holy Spirit from Jesus Christ were poured out as the morning daily picturing Christ's faithful wholehearted service began to burn!

Now, as soon as the wine and the water were poured out, the temple musicians began again and the "Hallel", [the second Hallel is Psalm 113 to Psalm 118] was sung to the accompaniment of wind instruments and flutes. This again was to represent the whooshing of the wind of the Holy Spirit. These instrumental sounds represented the Holy Spirit while they sang Psalm 113 to 118.

It should be noted that these same Psalms celebrating the main fall harvest were also a feature of the Spring Festivals.

On the Sabbath and on the first day of the Feast of the Ingathering of Nations [Tabernacles] they did not play the flute instruments, because they considered that too much physical work, offending the sanctity of the Sabbath and the Holy Day.

When the choir and the singers came to the words of Psalm 118:1, "O give thanks to the Lord", and again when they sang Psalm 118:25, "O work then now salvation, Yeshua" and once again at the close [this is three times in Psalm 118:29,] "O give thanks unto the Lord". Then all the worshipers shook their branches toward the altar, the emphasis here in the three verses was: To give thanks, to give thanks before God and to rejoice; and they shook their branches toward the altar.

Leviticus 23:49 And ye shall take you on the first day the boughs of goodly trees, branches of palm trees, and the boughs of thick trees, and willows of the brook; and ye shall rejoice before the Lord your God seven days.

This is alluded to when Jesus entered Jerusalem six days before his crucifixion. He entered Jerusalem and the people cut down branches from the trees and strewed them in the way and cried, saying "O then work now salvation to the Son of David". (Matthew 21:8-9 and John 12:12-13).

When Christ entered Jerusalem for that last week, they threw down the palms which were representative of the palms they used in the temple during the Feast of Tabernacles to rejoice before God and to give thanks to God. And they strewed those down in the way as Christ entered the city. And they said "work now salvation", the same as what they said during the Feast of Tabernacles, "give salvation."

The name for the seventh day of the Feast of Tabernacles is; The Last Great Day, or Hoshana Rabbah.

The priests asked: Why is it called, The drawing out of water? And they answered, because of the pouring out of the Holy Spirit, according to what is said: **"With joy shall you draw water out of the wells of salvation."** And that is what we just read in Isaiah.

The Feast of Tabernacles and the peculiar joyousness of it are designated as 'the drawing out of the water of Salvation'; the pouring out of the water of salvation on all the people, as represented by the pouring out of water at the altar, being done on behalf of all the people and for all the people.

And these ceremonies and celebrations and the singing and blasting of trumpets continued throughout the entire seven days of the Feast of Tabernacles!

This was a time of great rejoicing, of singing Psalms and the pouring out of the water, of marching around the altar and rejoicing, celebrating salvation and victory over sin and the salvation of and the gathering of the main harvest of humanity into the family of God!

The Feast of Tabernacles really was an incredible seven day ceremony, if you can imagine all these vast numbers of people doing this during the days of Christ.

The fall of Jericho as a type of victory over sin; through Messiah our Salvation

Israel marched around Jericho one time each day for six days and on the the seventh day; instead of circling Jericho once, they circled it seven times and turned and shouted, and the city of Jericho fell.

This is why Ezra began the ceremony of circling the altar once each day of the Feast of Ingathering [Tabernacles] and on the seventh day the priests circled the altar seven times, turning and rejoicing: Acting out the final fall of sin on that Great Day of Tabernacles, which the fall of Jericho represented.

The Astounding Allegorical Prophecy of JERICHO

The people were to march around the city of Jericho which represent sin, for six days, remaining silent except for the blasting of the trumpets of God; and on the seventh day the trumpets were to sound and the people were to shout in rejoicing at the fall of Jericho.

The march around Jericho was reenacted at the Feast of Tabernacles from the Ezra restoration and revival, as an instructional allegory of the final victory over all sin being completed on the seventh and Last Great Day of the Feast of the Ingathering of Nations called Tabernacles!

Joshua 6:3 And ye shall compass the city, all ye men of war, and go round about the city once. Thus shalt thou do six days.

The priests were to sound their seven trumpets daily during the once daily march and they were to march around Jericho the city representing Sin, once each day; and then they were to march around the city seven times on the seventh day; and the city representing sin would come crashing down!

The sounding of trumpets and the shouting of rejoicing on the seventh day, the Last Great of the Feast of Tabernacles; pictures the end of God's plan for man as flesh and total victory over sin!

6:4 And seven priests shall bear before the ark seven trumpets of rams' horns: and **the seventh day ye shall compass the city seven times, and the priests shall blow with the trumpets.**

6:5 And it shall come to pass, **that when they make a long blast with the ram's horn, and when ye hear the sound of the trumpet, all the people shall shout with a great shout; and the wall of the city shall fall down flat, and the people shall ascend up every man straight before him.**

6:6 And Joshua the son of Nun called the priests, and said unto them, Take up the ark of the covenant, and let seven priests bear seven trumpets of rams' horns before the ark of the LORD. **6:7** And he said unto the people, Pass on, and compass the city, and let him that is armed pass on before the ark of the LORD.

6:8 And it came to pass, when Joshua had spoken unto the people, that the seven priests bearing the seven trumpets of rams' horns passed on before the LORD, and **blew with the trumpets: and the ark of the covenant of the LORD followed them. 6:9** And the armed men went before the priests that blew with the trumpets, and the rereward came after the ark, the priests going on, and blowing with the trumpets.

6:10 And Joshua had commanded the people, saying, **Ye shall not shout, nor make any noise with your voice, neither shall any word proceed out of your mouth, until the day I bid you shout; then shall ye shout.**

6:11 So the ark of the LORD compassed the city, going about it once: and they came into the camp, and lodged in the camp. **6:12** And Joshua rose early in the morning, and the priests took up the ark of the LORD. **6:13** And seven priests bearing seven trumpets of rams' horns before the ark of the LORD went on continually, and blew with the trumpets: and the armed men went before them; but the rereward [a rear guard followed the Ark of the Covenant] came after the ark of the LORD, the priests going on, and blowing with the trumpets. **6:14** And **the second day they compassed the city once, and returned into the camp: so they did six days.**

Right here please notice that the people OBEYED God, even though it would not have made any sense to them!

It is to the zealous faithful followers of Jesus Christ who live by every Word of God the Father in heaven; that the V I C T O R Y over DEATH; and the gift of the Promised Land of eternal life comes!

6:15 And it came to pass on the seventh day, that they rose early about the dawning of the day, and compassed the city after the same manner seven times: only on that day they compassed the city seven times. **6:16** And it came to pass at the seventh time, when the priests blew with the trumpets, Joshua said unto the people, Shout; for the LORD hath given you the city.

At the end of the main harvest of humanity all flesh now changed to spirit will Shout for Joy, for God has given us total victory over bondage to sin!

Which person having been changed to spirit and received the gift of eternal life in peace and prosperity, being brought into the family of God; will not be overflowing with joy and humility before the great power of our Mighty God on that day?

The word "accursed" means receiving total destruction. Nothing of Jericho representing sin was to be taken or saved; except the repentant Rahab and her family.

The city of Jericho was to be accounted accursed because it represented unrepentant sin and the wickedness of rebellion against God!

This symbolic city was accursed and destroyed, so shall all those who refuse to repent from acting contrary to the Word of God during their opportunity also be destroyed.

6:17 And the city shall be accursed, even it, and all that are therein, to the LORD: only Rahab the harlot shall live, she and all that are with her in the house, because she hid the messengers that we sent.

Joshua warns that to take of the accursed thing [a type of partaking in any sin] which was condemned to destruction; will make the partaker of the accursed thing accursed (condemned to destruction) himself. This why Paul reminded Timothy not to be a partaker of other men's sins.

1 Timothy 5:22 . . . neither be **partaker of** [participate in] **other men's sins: keep thyself pure.**

Joshua 6:18 And ye, in any wise keep yourselves from the accursed thing, lest ye make yourselves accursed, when ye take of the accursed thing, and make the camp of Israel a curse, and trouble it.

When we partake of other men's sins like patronizing restaurants on Sabbaths and High Days, we make ourselves anathema to God Almighty!

On the Last Great Day of the Feast of Tabernacles when the priests circled the altar seven times on the seventh day, they sang with loud voices a song of repentance, redemption and salvation — **Save now, I pray, O Lord; O Lord, I pray, send now prosperity; Blessed is He who comes in the name of the Lord. . .**(Psalm 118:25-26).

Of course this temple ceremony is nowhere commanded in the scripture - except in the command to Israel at Jericho - yet its principles are fully scriptural and Jesus Christ had no problem with it.

Jesus from His childhood, would have been very familiar with these things as He went up to Jerusalem with His parents for the Feast, and would have seen this year by year, and growing up would have learned all about this. Then in His ministry He used this water pouring ceremony, magnifying its meaning, from Moses getting water from the rock as a lesson in the pouring out of the Holy Spirit.

Jesus used the figures of blindness and the light of the world, the water of salvation and the Bread of Life, to teach about the plan of salvation and Christ's central role in the salvation of humanity.

The Waters of Salvation and the Woman at the Well

John 4:7 There cometh a woman of Samaria to draw water [from a well in Samaria]:, and Jesus said to her, Give me a drink. **4:8** (For His disciples had gone away [Jesus was sitting there alone]. **4:9** Then said the woman of Samaria to Him, How is it that thou, being a Jew, asks water of me which am a woman of Samaria? for the Jews have no dealings with the Samaritans. **4:10** Jesus answered her and said, If you knew the gift of God, and who is it that says to you, Give me to drink; you would have asked of Him [to give drink to you], **that He would give to you living water. 4:11 The woman said unto Him, Sir, thou has nothing to draw up water with, and the well is very deep: from whence, then, hast thou this living water? 4:12 Art thou greater than our father Jacob, who gave us the well, and drank thereof himself, and his children, and his cattle?**

4:13 Jesus answered and said unto her, Whosoever drinks of this water shall thirst again: 14 But whosoever drinks of the water that I give him shall never thirst [again],

Whoever drinks physical water is going to get thirsty again. When we drink of physical water after a while we get thirsty again; and we drink again, and we get thirsty again and so on.

4:14 But whosoever drinks of the water that I shall give him shall never thirst; for the water that I shall give him shall be in him a well of water, springing up into everlasting life.

The water that Jesus Christ gives is the Word of God and the Holy Spirit, which leads us into eternal life. The water of the Holy Spirit will be in us and growing in us because we were called by God the Father and have sincerely repented, committing to go and sin no more; to live by every Word of God following God's Spirit.

We took the gift of God's Holy Spirit represented by the living water into ourselves when we sincerely repented and committed to follow and be cleanses by the Water of the Word of God.

The person who is zealous for the Word of God and thirsts after the living water of Salvation; has eternal life dwelling in him, unless he later rejects God's Spirit and quenches it, but as long as he is faithful, he has eternal life living in him.

Jesus' Last Feast of Tabernacles

The awesome reality of John 7:37 is much better understood when we understand the context.

The occasion of the seventh or last day of the Feast of Tabernacles - on the last Feast of Tabernacles that Jesus observed before He was crucified the next spring - was used by Christ to teach that He was the Messiah, the source of salvation, the source of the Living Water of Salvation for all Israel and for all mankind.

We can understand this from the event in John 7:37.

The sixth day of the Feast of Tabernacles was drawing to a close and toward the seventh day of the Feast of Tabernacles which was the Last Great Day of the Feast of Tabernacles, not because it was a holy convocation, but because it was the "Day of the Great Hosanna".

It was on this day, as the priests had come from Siloam with the golden pitcher, pouring it through the basin and causing it to run down onto the base of the altar, and the Psalms had been sung to the sound of the wind instruments,; the people responding and worshiping and rejoicing as the priests three times sounded three full blasts upon the two silver trumpets: that Jesus cried out loudly in the temple to all the people.

With hundreds of thousands of people present and many thousands of priests dressed in their priestly vestments, all of them singing, rejoicing and praising God; as the water and wine were poured out [the wine typifying the pouring out of the life of Christ the Lamb of God, for the salvation of the people as a sacrifice for their sins and the water being poured out representing the gift of the Word of God, salvation and the

Holy Spirit]; and with the willows whooshing, making the sound of the rushing of the Holy Spirit.

Suddenly as all of this was happening, just as Psalm 118 had been completed: out from the midst of the congregation came a loud, strong, clear voice declaring loudly: **John 7:37 In the last day, that Great Day of the Feast [of Tabernacles], Jesus stood and cried out, saying, If any man thirst, let him come unto Me and drink. 7:38 He that believeth on Me, as the scriptures hath said, out of his belly shall flow rivers of living water.**

David now begins to quote the song of Moses (Ex 15, Rev 15) which is to be sung by the resurrected bride at the Marriage of the Lamb before the throne of God the Father in heaven!

Our God is mighty, He is valiant, He is gloriously victorious over all his enemies [Satan and sin]: He is great and greatly to be honored and praised!

Psalm 118:14 The LORD is my strength and song, and is become my salvation. **118:15** The voice of rejoicing and salvation is in the tabernacles of the righteous: the right hand of the LORD doeth valiantly. **118:16** The right hand of the LORD is exalted: the right hand of the LORD doeth valiantly.

David did die physically, Here he refers to the resurrection to eternal life after which he will eternally declare the mighty works of YHVH, the Eternal.

118:17 I shall not die, but live, and declare the works of the LORD.

God will correct his people who go astray, in order to bring them back to him, but God will not give up on those he has called, or willingly give us over to the flames. Only we can choose the eternal death of fire by our adamant refusal to repent from our departure from living by every Word of God.

118:18 The LORD hath chastened me sore: but he hath not given me over unto death.

God is righteousness; and the Word of God defines the righteousness of God!

When we are called and we sincerely repent of sin, we enter into the gates of righteousness [godly righteousness is living by every Word of God], and we enter into the gates of righteousness which is the salvation of God.

118:19 Open to me the gates of righteousness: I will go into them, and I will praise the LORD: **118:20** This gate of the LORD, into which the righteous shall enter.

God hears our sincere repentance and he gives us his merciful salvation, by applying the sacrifice of the Lamb of God to us.

118:21 I will praise thee: for thou hast heard me, and art become my salvation.

David prophesies of Jesus Christ the Lamb of God and how he would be rejected for a time. David prophesies of the day of salvation, speaking of the Passover when the Lamb of God was sacrificed for the salvation of all sincerely repentant people.

118:22 The stone which the builders refused is become the head stone of the corner. **118:23** This is the LORD's doing; it is marvellous in our eyes. **118:24** This is the day which the LORD hath made [the Passover which God has ordained]; we will rejoice and be glad in it. **118:25** Save now, I beseech thee, O LORD: O LORD, I beseech thee, send now prosperity.

Blessed are all those who are faithful in their complete submission to live by every Word of God.

118:26 Blessed be he that cometh in the name of the LORD: we have blessed you out of the house of the LORD.

The Lamb of God, Jesus Christ in the flesh, brought the light of spiritual understanding; and he was bound by his promise to die for the sins of humanity like the sacrifices were bound on the altar.

118:27 God is the LORD, which hath shewed us light: bind the sacrifice with cords, even unto the horns of the altar.

Here we have a most fitting end to the Passover service; a praise of God for his eternal mercies for his creation!

118:28 Thou art my God, and I will praise thee: thou art my God, I will exalt thee. **118:29** O give thanks unto the LORD; for he is good: for his mercy endureth for ever.

This Psalm speaking of Christ leading physical Israel through the Red Sea, defeating Pharaoh in Egypt and delivering physical Israel from bondage to sin; in type represents a future spiritual salvation for all of humanity from bondage to sin.

Just as the final pouring of water on the seventh day of Tabernacles began to run down the altar, picturing the gift of the Word of Salvation and the pouring out of the Holy Spirit, and the wine flowed down, picturing the sacrifice of Christ, to give us salvation and atone for sin: A powerful voice cried out from among the hundreds of thousands, a strong voice resounded through the temple:

Yeshua [Jesus Christ] cried out **John 7:37…'If any man thirst, let him come unto me and drink.'** With those words, He was clearly telling all the people: I am your salvation, I am Messiah, I am the Christ. It is through Me that you receive salvation! and that impressed the people and it shocked the leaders.

Now when Jesus said this, He said if ANY man thirst. He did not say if any Jew thirst or any Israelite, He said ANY man, thereby revealing that salvation was being opened up to ALL humanity, and that the Feast of Tabernacles refers to the main harvest of humanity.

And He cried out in the midst of the seventh day of the Feast of Tabernacles, not on the Feast of the Eighth Day as some wrongly suppose, because they misunderstand the term "the Great Day of the Feast."

John 7:37 In the last day, that Great Day of the Feast [of Tabernacles], Jesus stood and cried out, saying, If any man thirst, let him come unto Me and drink. 7:38 He that believeth on Me, as the scriptures hath said, out of his belly shall flow rivers of living water.

God pours His Spirit on the sincerely repentant who zealously work to live by every Word of God; they will be filled with the Holy Spirit, the spiritual Water of eternal life (Joel 2:28).

Then as the Spirit of God fills the people, they will be enabled to follow God and to live by every Word of God.

. . . (But of this spake he of the Spirit [This is a direct quote; revealing that this Living Water represents the Holy Spirit]**, 7:39 But this spake He of the Spirit, which they that believe on Him should receive: for the Holy Spirit was not yet poured out or not yet given; because that Jesus was not yet glorified.)**

He had not yet been sacrificed and raised up. **7:40** Many of the people [many of them]**,** when they heard this saying, [they] said, **Of a truth this is that Prophet.**

The term 'that prophet' is a reference to the prophecy of Moses, who said 'behold the day will come when a prophet will arise like unto myself, him you shall follow, him you shall obey.'

They remembered the words of Moses and they said, 'of a truth, this is that prophet that Moses spake of.' And that prophet was Jesus Christ. "That Prophet" refers to Jesus the Christ ONLY! **'This spake He of the spirit which they that believe on Him should receive.'** This is clearly explaining the water as representing the Holy Spirit; and revealing Jesus the Christ as "That Prophet."

Again, **'In the last day, that Great Day of the Feast** [The seventh day of Tabernacles]**, Jesus stood and cried and said if any man thirst, let him come unto Me and drink, and he that believes on Me as the scripture hath said, out of his belly shall flow rivers of living water.'**

He cried out in the middle of all those hundreds of thousands of people, in the middle of this incredibly impressive ceremony: The effect was probably electric in that huge assembly.

Jesus Christ was saying that He was the fulfillment of the various types and prophecies of scripture. And many people, were impressed and they wanted to follow Him. But the high priests and the Pharisees and the top people immediately were struck with jealousy and envy, and they said, no way are we going to give up our high offices to this man. So they became very angry.

Even the temple guard, whose duty it was to maintain order and arrest someone who interrupted the services like that, dared not lay hands on Him. When the chief priests and the Pharisees ordered the security people to go and arrest Him, they just said, 'Never did a man speak like this man;' how can we do this when all the people are influenced by him and think Him to be a prophet? That is all that they could answer to their masters. They did not want to believe, but they asked how can we arrest this guy when all the people are counting Him a prophet? If we arrest Him, it will make a greater disturbance than if we leave Him alone.

Nicodemus was a member of the Sanhedrin and also a follower of Christ, and when the Sanhedrin immediately met to condemn Christ for creating a disturbance during the ceremonies and for calling himself the Messiah and "That Prophet", Nicodemus stood up and defended Christ with a declaration, **'Doth our law, judge a man before it hears him,' and knows what he does?**

Nicodemus said, how can you sit here as a court and condemn this man unless he is brought before you and testifies before you and you hear the whole case? It is not lawful for you to condemn him without hearing the whole case.

And so the Sanhedrin made some comments, and condemned Christ, but they did not do anything of a legal nature since they could not arrest Him because they were not about to cause a riot.

Yet from this time they began to earnestly seek ways to stop and kill him.

****

Right now those who are called to God the father through the Son, called to zealously live by every Word of God and do His will and please Him; all those called to God through history, right from righteous Abel until now; have had God's Spirit poured out on them in direct proportion to how we use that Spirit, how we follow it and live by every Word of God.

The more zealously we study and learn and live by every Word of God, the more of God's Spirit and the more understanding we will be given.

The less we study and the less we zealously keep the Word of God, and the more we compromise; the more God's Spirit will be held back from us, and we will be quenching that Spirit, and over time will have less and less.

On the seventh day of the Feast of Tabernacles, when the wine was poured out representing the shed blood of Christ, and the water was poured out representing the Holy Spirit of Salvation; the whooshing of the branches and wind instruments representing the sound of a wind of the Holy Spirit coming—all these things, represent the main harvest of humanity; the Ingathering of the Nations into the family of God.

All of this ceremony was condoned by Jesus Christ, and all of it was used by Jesus Christ to present himself as the fulfillment of all of these things on that seventh day of the Feast of Tabernacles.

All of this symbolism is clear and it is correct and it is godly and it is right, and although it may not be directly commanded in scripture, it is certainly based on and backed up by scripture and it is not in any way contrary to scripture.

Just as Psalm 118 was concluded, Jesus stood up and cried out with a loud voice so that the many thousands of people in the temple heard Him.

The Feast of Tabernacles pictures the fall harvest and rejoices over the fall harvest, and it pictures the fall harvest, as the main harvest of souls, salvation being extended, the sacrifice of Christ being extended; to all of humanity.

Eternal Salvation, not just for the few called out for the early harvest; but now eternal Salvation extended to all of humanity.

As Christ said, 'whosoever who believeth in me', **anyone, everyone that believes in Christ, not just believes but acts on that belief having the works of faith, because faith without works is dead.** Anyone who believes on Christ and starts to live by every Word of God will have the living waters of salvation poured out upon them.

That is what the seven days of Tabernacles is about, with the thirteen bullocks the first day and the twelve on the second day, and so on, making seventy sacrificial bulls, picturing all of mankind, all the families of mankind serving God. And the Holy Spirit being given to repentant humanity, with the water of salvation poured out on every sincerely repentant person.

If you can just imagine that temple and these thousands of priests and tens of thousands of worshipers all singing Psalm 118, singing I will praise you, I will give thanks to God for he is good. His mercy endures forever. The Eternal is God and his mercy endures forever. It must have been awesome and people would have gone home on a very positive note, thinking very positively about God and the greatness of God and how poor we are spiritually and how much we need God.

We need to realize how much we need God, because we cannot save ourselves. It is impossible. And no other man can save us either.

Salvation is a direct personal responsibility. We as individuals have to respond to the call and go to God the Father and to the Word of God through Christ. Focus on that. Do not focus on anyone just because he says he is somebody; but take those words and test them by the Word of God and always the Word of God MUST come first.

Jesus Christ is the Fountain of the Holy Spirit and the Living Waters of Salvation:

Jeremiah 17:13 O Lord, the hope of Israel, all that forsake thee shall be ashamed, and they that depart from me shall be written [judged as carnal] in the earth, because they have forsaken **the Lord, the fountain of living waters** [the Living Waters being God's Holy Spirit].

The Eighth Day

The Feast of The Eighth Day

In any seven day cycle the eighth day is always the beginning of a new cycle of seven. The Eighth Day ALWAYS represents "A NEW BEGINNING"!

The seven days of the Feast of the Ingathering of Nations are completed when the last person is changed to spirit or destroyed for unrepentant wickedness at the end of the seventh day of the Feast of Tabernacles.

After the seven thousand years of the Feast of Tabernacles [the Ingathering of Nations], the earth itself will be cleansed by fire, destroying the full surface of the planet and purifying it, and the surface of the earth and atmosphere will be re-created for the coming of God the Father and the New Jerusalem; coming down from heaven to dwell with mankind, now in peaceful unity of spirit with God the Father and the Son.

Isaiah 65:17 For, behold, I create new heavens and a new earth: and the former shall not be remembered, nor come into mind.

During the seven thousand years of the main harvest of humanity, the Ingathering of Nations, all those resurrected to flesh and given their opportunity will live to the age of one hundred years old and will then be judged. Those who have learned to live by every Word of God will be rewarded with a a change to spirit and the gift of eternal life, and the incorrigibly unrepentant wicked will be cast into the lake of fire.

Isaiah 65:20 There shall be no more thence an infant of days, nor an old man that hath not filled his days: for the child shall die an hundred years old; but the sinner being an hundred years old shall be accursed.

The plan of God for physical humanity will be completed at the end of the Feast of Tabernacles main harvest and the earth itself will then be cleansed from all impurity and evil by fire, as the lake of fire is allowed to grow and cover the whole earth.

The Feast of the Eighth Day then begins at the close of the Feast of Tabernacles, picturing a New Beginning with mankind and God going forward into eternity in peace and harmony, free from all sin and spiritual impurity.

A New Beginning in peace and harmony; KNOWING the way to peace and LIVING the way of peace: All pain, suffering and disease vanquished by a LOVING FATHER: Even death itself destroyed!!!

Read very carefully through Revelation 21 and 22 and see the glory of and the meaning of: The Feast of the Eighth Day.

After the millennial Sabbath of rest, and then after the seven thousand year Feast of Tabernacles main harvest of humanity; the earth will be cleansed by fire.

2 Peter 3:7 But the heavens and the earth, which are now, by the same word are kept in store, reserved unto fire against the day of judgment and perdition [destruction] of ungodly men.

People who scoff at the prophets are scoffing at over one third of the Christ breathed Word of God!

3:8 But, beloved, **be not ignorant of this one thing, that one day is with the Lord as a thousand years, and a thousand years as one day.**

Here we have a profound key to unlock much prophecy including the Feast days. A key that is rejected by most today; who try to teach that seven days is as one thousand years, when they give their false take on the Feast of Tabernacles.

One day is as ONE thousand years; and seven days are NOT equal to one thousand years; therefore seven days MUST refer to either just seven days, or to SEVEN thousand years. There is NO WAY that the Feast of Tabernacles could refer to a one thousand year millennium!

This FALSE teaching has been driven into the minds of people for generations and has prevented an understanding of the true meaning of the Festivals and much prophecy.

Many don't realize that what is a very long period of time to man, is a very short period of time with God. And God will fulfill his Word. He will keep his promises. These things are coming and are now at the door!

All Scripture must fit together. There are many who say the Seven Day Feast of Tabernacles represents a thousand year millennium. And yet what does Peter say here? One day is with the Lord as a thousand years, and a thousand years is as one day.

How could the Seven Day Feast of Tabernacles picture one thousand years? According to Scripture, it must picture 7,000 years or it must have nothing whatsoever to do with years.

According to God's Word, the Seven Day Feast of Tabernacles pictures 7,000 years. It does not picture any one thousand year millennium. The same thing is true of the Feast of Unleavened Bread and the seven day week! We know because God inspired Peter to say so.

3:9 The Lord is not slack concerning his promise, as some men count slackness; but is longsuffering to us-ward, not willing that any should perish, but that all should come to repentance.

Then Peter writes about the end of the plan for physical humanity and the cleansing of the earth by fire before God the Father and the New Jerusalem come down to the earth; represented by The Feast of the Eighth Day; which will be a new beginning for all humanity, going forward into all eternity as the spirit children of God.

Using the concept of duality with the coming of Christ as a precursor to the coming of God the Father, Peter uses the term "Day of the Lord" to refer to information about the final total cleansing of the earth; before eternity with God the Father for all humanity, then changed to eternal spirit.

. . . .in the which the heavens [atmosphere] shall pass away with a great noise, and the elements shall melt with fervent heat, the earth also and the works that are therein shall be burned up.

3:11 Seeing then that all these things shall be dissolved, what manner of persons ought ye to be in all holy conversation [words and deeds] and godliness, **3:12** Looking for and hasting unto the coming of the day of God, wherein the heavens being on fire shall be dissolved, and the elements shall melt with fervent heat? **3:13 Nevertheless we, according to his promise, look for new heavens and a new earth, wherein dwelleth righteousness.**

This refers to that time after the plan for PHYSICAL humanity has been completed when the whole earth will be cleansed by fire to purify it from all uncleanness so that the New Jerusalem and God the Father may come to dwell with his spirit children on this earth!

Peter is revealing the great power of Almighty God and encouraging all people to remain true to God the Father and to enthusiastically live by every Word of God; and by internalizing the very nature of God through pleasing him, we can look forward to spending eternity in perfect peace and harmony with God and with our spiritual brethren!

That is the true meaning of The Feast of the Eighth Day: A New Beginning, going forth into eternity in peace with God; through total unity with Jesus Christ and God the Father!

3:14 Wherefore, beloved, seeing that ye look for such things, be diligent that ye may be found of him [God] in peace [with God], without spot, and blameless [without even a hint of sin].

3:15 And account that the longsuffering [God's patience with us] of our Lord is salvation; even as our beloved brother Paul also according to the wisdom given unto him hath written unto you;

Peter here warns the brethren to be on the lookout for those who would twist the words of Paul to lead men away from their zeal to live by every Word of God.

3:16 As also in all his epistles, speaking in them of these things; in which are some things hard to be understood, **which they that are unlearned and unstable wrest, as they do also the other scriptures, unto their own destruction.**

The whole earth is cleansed by fire, then comes The Feast of the Eighth Day

A New Beginning with all wickedness including Satan himself with his spirits and every person who does not live by EVERY WORD of God DESTROYED; and the earth itself cleansed by fire!

Then finally God the Father himself coming down to live with his redeemed children on a newly re-created planet now cleansed by fire and re-created pure from all evil; and God and humanity going forward into eternity in the peace and prosperity that living by Every Word of God brings!

Revelation 21:1 And I saw **a new heaven and a new earth: for the first heaven and the first earth were passed away;** and there was no more sea.

21:2 And I John saw **the holy city, new Jerusalem, coming down from God out of heaven**, prepared as a bride adorned for her husband.

21:3 And I heard a great voice out of heaven saying, **Behold, the tabernacle of God is with men, and he will dwell with them, and they shall be his people, and God himself shall be with them, and be their God.**

The Wondrous Meaning of the Feast of the Eighth Day!

No more suffering or tears of pain. All people at peace united with God and therefore at peace with and united with all others who are united with God!

The way to peace, is for the ultimate deceiver to be removed and the truth and the true way to peace followed by all.

The longing of humanity is for a peace that we cannot achieve without the wisdom of God. Real peace is not imaginary; IT IS COMING!

21:4 And **God shall wipe away all tears from their eyes; and there shall be no more death, neither sorrow, nor crying, neither shall there be any more pain: for the former things are passed away.**

21:5 And he that sat upon the throne said, **Behold, I make all things new**. And he said unto me, Write: for these words are true and faithful.

21:6 And he said unto me, It is done. I am Alpha and Omega, the beginning and the end. **I will give unto him that is athirst of the fountain of the water of life [the Holy Spirit of God] freely.**

21:7 He that overcometh [to learn to live by Every Word of God] shall inherit all things [the entire universe is included in the term "All Things"]; and I **will be his God, and he shall be my son.**

Those who think they can sin with impunity will be destroyed for the good of the whole; so that they do not damage the peace of others. It is an ignorant and foolish person who claims to be godly and justifies his sins by claiming that God is love and will overlook his willful sins.

It is because God is love, that he will NOT overlook our sins! Because our sins hurt ourselves and they hurt others and God loves ALL people! Almighty God will not permit any self justifying willful sinner to enter his spiritual family!

21:8 But the fearful [those too afraid of men to follow and obey God], and unbelieving [those who will not believe that we must stop sinning], and the abominable [the self justifying willful perpetrators of any sin are an abomination to God], and murderers, and whoremongers, and sorcerers, and idolaters [as in making idols of men and corporate organizations to exalt their words above the Word of God], and all liars [including those who tell partial truths to deceive], shall have their part in the lake which burneth with fire and brimstone: which is the second death.

Those who say that we should not expose and condemn sin: Hear the Word of the Lord:

Proverbs 17:15 He that justifieth the wicked, and he that condemneth the just, even they both are abomination to the Lord.

Isaiah 58:1 Cry aloud, spare not, lift up thy voice like a trumpet, and shew my people their transgression, and the house of Jacob their sins.

The New Jerusalem is presented as the bride of the Lamb of God, because the resurrected bride will dwell in the New Jerusalem with her Husband and with His Father!

Revelation 21:9 And there came unto me one of the seven angels which had the seven vials full of the seven last plagues, and talked with me, saying, Come hither, I will shew thee the bride, the Lamb's wife.

21:10 And he carried me away in the spirit to a great and high mountain, and shewed me that great city, the holy Jerusalem, descending out of heaven from God,

21:11 Having the glory of God: and her light was like unto a stone most precious, even like a jasper stone, clear as crystal;

21:12 And had a wall great and high, and had **twelve gates**, and at the gates twelve angels, and names written thereon, which are **the names of the twelve tribes of the children of Israel:**

21:13 On the east three gates; on the north three gates; on the south three gates; and on the west three gates.

21:14 And the wall of the city had **twelve foundations, and in them the names of the twelve apostles of the Lamb.**

21:15 And he that talked with me had a golden reed to measure the city, and the gates thereof, and the wall thereof.

A furlong being 1/8 of a mile makes the city a 1,500 mile cube.

21:16 And the city lieth foursquare, and the length is as large as the breadth: and he measured the city with the reed, twelve thousand furlongs. The length and the breadth and the height of it are equal.

21:17 And he measured the wall thereof, an hundred and forty and four cubits, according to the measure of a man, that is, of the angel.

21:18 And the building of **the wall of it was of jasper**: and **the city was pure gold, like unto clear glass.**

The walls had on them the gems representing each tribe of Israel.

21:19 And the foundations of **the wall** of the city were garnished with all manner of precious stones. The first foundation was jasper; the second, sapphire; the third, a chalcedony; the fourth, an emerald;

21:20 The fifth, sardonyx; the sixth, sardius; the seventh, chrysolyte; the eighth, beryl; the ninth, a topaz; the tenth, a chrysoprasus; the eleventh, a jacinth; the twelfth, an amethyst.

21:21 And the twelve gates were twelve pearls: every several gate was of one pearl: and **the street of the city was pure gold, as it were transparent glass.**

This may be a clue as to the meaning of the "sea of glass" of the courtyard before the throne of God. The sea [expanse] of glass [crystal or gold] - the Heavenly Temple Courtyard - is quite likely paved with translucent gold or crystal which reflects and refracts the light emanating from God into all the shimmering colors of the rainbow.

21:22 And I saw no temple therein: for the Lord God Almighty and the Lamb are the temple of it.

21:23 And the city had **no need** of the sun, neither of the moon, to shine in it: for the glory of God did lighten it, and the Lamb is the light thereof.

"No need" does not mean that the sun and moon will no longer exist, and no night does not mean that the earth will not be turning; it means that God will be a continual light over all the earth.

After ALL MANKIND has been brought into the Family of God during the Feast of Tabernacles harvest of humanity. The earth will be cleansed and the New Jerusalem will descend from Heaven.

The Father Himself shall dwell on the earth with His children. His children will be spiritually healed and given the gift of eternal life.

The river of water of life coming out from the throne of God is a picture of the Holy Spirit of life eternal flowing out from God.

Revelation 22:1 And he shewed me a pure river of **water of life**, clear as crystal, proceeding out of the throne of God and of the Lamb.

The tree of life nourished by the water; as a type of eternal life coming from the Holy Spirit and the keeping of the whole Word of God, bears the fruits of the Spirit of God. The leaves which give life to a tree are represented as giving spiritual healing [eternal salvation] to the nations.

22:2 In the **midst of the street** [growing up out of the river and overspreading to both sides is the tree of eternal life] of it, and on either side of the river, was there the tree of life, which bare twelve manner of fruits, and yielded her fruit every month [these tree[s] bore a new kind of fruit each month]: and the leaves of the tree were for the [spiritual] healing of the nations.

22:3 And there shall be no more curse [sin or the decay and death that sin brings]: but the throne of God and of the Lamb shall be in it; and his servants shall serve him:

22:4 And they [the people now changed to spirit] shall see his face; and his name shall be in their foreheads.

The nature of God [the Holy Spirit] will dwell in the minds of all people who were changed to spirit; absolutely no sin allowed.

22:5 And there shall be no night there; and they need no candle, neither light of the sun; for the Lord God giveth them light: and **they** [the chosen and changed] **shall reign for ever and ever.**

22:6 And he said unto me, These sayings are faithful and true: and the Lord God of the holy prophets sent his angel to shew unto his servants the things which must shortly be done.

The saying "I come quickly" is addressed to those in the later day when knowledge and understanding shall be increased, and the wise shall receive an understanding of these things (Dan 12). The blessing on those who "keep the sayings of the book" is a blessing on those who keep the instructions to "Live by EVERY WORD of God."

22:7 Behold, I come quickly: **blessed is he that keepeth the sayings of the prophecy of this book.**

The Promise of our Father in heaven: CANNOT BE BROKEN. Therefore let us strive diligently to serve our Magnificent Father on high!!!

Thy Will Be Done!!!

The Eighth Day Represents a New Beginning for Humanity, Going Forward into Eternity

Revelation 22:1 **And he showed me a pure river of water of life, clear as crystal, proceeding out of the throne of God and of the Lamb.**

This pure water is a symbol of the Holy Spirit of God, which will be given freely to all who ask; for all who keep the Commandments of God will have a right, to this gift, which will be freely available throughout eternity (Rev 22:14). Only the faithfully obedient will have a right to enter the gates of the City.

Only those who keep all of the commandments and every Word of God will be received into eternal life as spirit and have the right to enter the true eternal city.

Revelation 22:14 Blessed are they that do his commandments, that they may have right to the tree of life, and may enter in through the gates into the city.

The Eighth Day is the first day after a cycle of seven. An eighth day ALWAYS pictures a New Beginning.

When God is finished with His plan for Physical Humanity, He will totally destroy the surface of the earth and cleanse it completely, from all uncleanness and sin.

After this He will create a New Heavens and a New Earth, [probably meaning the atmosphere and surface of the planet, rather than the starry heavens] as Peter tells us.

This New Heavens and New Earth are described in Revelation 21 and 22. All unrepentant sinners (commandment breakers 1 Joh 3:4) will be destroyed along with this old earth.

Only the righteous will be allowed entry into the gates of the City. Only the obedient will have the right to partake of the water of life (the Holy Spirit of God) freely.

That is, no wicked person will be on the new earth or will enter the New Jerusalem, because they will all have been destroyed in the fire which cleansed the earth.

No one who sins, or compromises with the commandments of God will be changed to spirit or allowed into eternity with God the Father; they ALL of the unrepentant will be destroyed in the lake of fire!

The Eighth Day of the Feast: being the first day after a complete seven days; pictures a New Beginning for humanity.

All evil and wickedness shall be destroyed, BEFORE the Eighth Day begins! All those who break God's commandments and the teachings of Christ will be destroyed; if they do not repent and change their behavior.

All those who replace the love of God [which is defined by every Word of God] with mere emotional feelings: Shall be destroyed!

God is love and his law is love. The commandments of God define his nature, and if we compromise with those commandments and teachings, we rebel against the very nature of God and we SHALL BE DESTROYED if we replace the nature of God with the nature of sin.

If we do what WE THINK IS RIGHT, if we live as we decide; instead of DEFINING LOVE AS GOD DEFINES LOVE; THROUGH HIS COMMANDMENTS: We are NOT living by every word of God and we shall be destroyed for separating ourselves from God.

Those who ARE WILLING TO LISTEN TO THEIR FATHER AND THEIR HUSBAND, who are willing to submit to and obey the far greater wisdom of God, who are willing to live a life of passionate love for God and his law with love and concern for others; will be changed fully to Spirit and given Eternal Life.

They will have a right to drink of the Water of Life, to take of the Holy Spirit of God freely. They will be changed to spirit and given eternal life, entering the gates of the New Jerusalem freely.

They will dwell on a New Earth; going forward into Eternity; in perfect Peace and Harmony with Almighty God, and with each other. The Eighth Day: pictures an eternity of Peace, Happiness, Harmony, and Satisfying Productivity; as part of a truly Loving, Supportive and Caring Family: THE FAMILY OF GOD!

To the congregations making up the People of God

The Eighth Day, which is the first day AFTER the Feast of Tabernacles: Is a High Holy Day, Leviticus 23:36. It is a Holy Convocation. You shall do no servile work (work of any kind) therein.

For generations now, many People of God has made it a practice to hold services early, on the Eighth Day to facilitate the travel plans of their members. People claiming to be converted Godly people: have paid bills, packed belongings, cleaned their temporary dwellings and travelled on this High Holy Day. And their ministers have encouraged this in word and deed.

The servants of God: Serve God!

Anyone who says I can do anything I want and Jesus Christ has to back me up is either a fool or a liar. Jesus Christ is not going to back up anybody in sin. And He is not going to back up anybody who is not serving him but who is serving Satan and their own lusts and passions.

If we are the servants of Christ we will not be doing what we want. We will be doing what Jesus Christ wants. Even Moses was taught the lesson that he was not above the commandments of God, and was refused entrance into the land of promise.

Paul taught us: **Romans 6:16** Know ye not, that to whom ye yield yourselves servants to obey, his servants ye are to whom ye obey; whether of sin unto death, or of obedience unto righteousness?

Jesus said: **John 8:34** Jesus answered them, Verily, verily, I say unto you, Whosoever committeth sin is the servant of sin.

After all mankind has been brought into the family of God during the main harvest of the Feast of Tabernacles, the earth will be cleansed by fire, then:

1. The New Jerusalem will descend with God the Father from heaven
2. God the Father Himself will come to dwell on the earth with His children, now changed to spirit.
3. God's children now changed to spirit will have been healed of all sin, of all wickedness, of all evildoing, of all the suffering which they have endured in this physical life; and they will have been changed to spirit and given eternal life.

Consider that ONLY those who are zealous to internalize the whole Word of God will be changed into spirit at the early harvest, and that they are called out ahead of time **to become laborers to help in bringing in the main harvest of all humanity.**

The first fruits are training in this life on the earth today; not so that they can get their own way and bully and abuse and get all the best things during the millennium or during the main harvest.

This life and our calling to God in this Life; is to train us and teach us and prepare us to be laborers to help bring in the main harvest. We are not called to some self-aggrandizement. We are called to hard work, and the reason we often suffer much, is so that we will be able to empathize and understand the sufferings that people will have gone through in their previous physical life, after they are raised up back to flesh and given their opportunity.

We are learning through our experiences now, so that we will be able to understand their sufferings. We will be able to empathize with them. We will be able to say; yes, you suffered this and that, now here is a better way.

God's plan is a way that will banish all suffering, and if we are reconciled with God the Father, in future we will aid Christ in reconciling the rest of humanity to God the Father and bringing the rest of humanity into the temple and family of God.

When the main harvest of Tabernacles is all over, then all taint of defilement, of uncleanness and wickedness will be wiped off this earth through an intense fire.

And then will come eternity, a new heavens, a new atmosphere, a new resurfaced earth with no more sea, and God the Father coming down with His magnificent New Jerusalem; and the New Jerusalem and the earth being the capital of the universe forever.

Forever more: No more death. No more cancer. No more emphysema. No more malaria or polio. No more war and horrible injuries and mutilations of war. No more suffering and pain; and we will be reconciled and fully at one with God the Father and Christ: And because everyone existing will then be fully at one with God the Father and Christ. We will also be reconciled with each other!

Those who persecuted us, thinking they were doing God a service, those who rejected us and hated us for this way, will realize they made a mistake and they will come to us and reach out to us and say teach us of God's ways, because we know and we remember your example and we know that you were right and we know that you know God and God knows you, so teach us of the ways of God.

Then we will be reconciled to God, and also reconciled with parents, beloved children, brothers or sisters, and dear friends, who are also reconciling to God Almighty! Everything will come together during the main harvest of Tabernacles and then the family of God reconciled and united: will go forward into eternity in peace!

There will be no more tears of sorrow or agony of pain. Any tears there will be, will be tears of joy and happiness, as we are totally one with God the Father and totally one with each other. That is unity. Unity is not glossing over our divisions, so that we can appear united because we do not have any public arguments. That is not unity, that is just glossing over and hiding and deceiving people that we have unity when we are really deeply divided from God!

True unity is for each person to be at one with God the Father and Jesus Christ, by diligently studying and enthusiastically internalizing and keeping the whole word of God; so that we become like God, internalizing the nature of God. When we do that we become one in total unity with God. And we become one in unity with all others who are in the same unity with God the Father and Jesus Christ.

The Feast of the Eighth Day pictures a new beginning. It pictures eternity coming after the physical plan of God has been completed. It pictures no more sorrow, no more pain, no more suffering. It pictures eternal life with security of person and security of our efforts.

That is to say, when we work to do something, we do not have to worry about people stealing it. We will be totally secure with God in everything that we do, secure in our person, secure in the things that we do, secure in every way and we can then be at peace with a full peace of mind, a full peace of spirit, a full confidence in God the Father, knowing that everything is perfect and is going forward in perfection for all of eternity.

The Eighth Day, what an incredible reality!

The Tree of Life

In Genesis 3 two trees are described. The first tree was the Tree of the Knowledge of Good and Evil and it was forbidden to the man and woman.

This tree was symbolic of deciding right and wrong for ourselves and the command forbidding eating from this tree was a test command to see if the man and woman would obey God or decide right and wrong for themselves.

Disobeying God in eating from this tree [or in anything else] represents and consists of deciding for ourselves what us right and wrong instead of living by every Word of God; and the ultimate fruits of this tree is death.

To decide for ourselves to act and live contrary to what God has commanded, is to exalt ourselves above the Word of God and the end of this decision is death. Therefore this tree could also be called the Tree of Death.

A second tree, the Tree of Life, was the exact opposite of this symbolic tree of death. The Tree of Life brought LIFE; just as rejecting obedience to God and taking of the forbidden fruit brought death.

Romans 6:23 For the wages of sin is death; but the gift of God is eternal life through Jesus Christ our Lord.

What is this sin that brings death?

1 John 3:3 Whosoever committeth sin transgresseth also the law: for sin is the transgression of the law.

What is this law which brings long life then? Is it not the whole Word of God?

Exodus 20:12 Honour thy father and thy mother: that thy days may be long upon the land which the Lord thy God giveth thee.

Who then is our father? Ultimately our Father is our Creator; first God the Father as the Executive Authority of the creation and then Jesus Christ as the Implementing Authority of the creation. The one who became Jesus Christ called God in heaven his Father and commanded us to live by every Word of that God the Father.

Matthew 4:4 But he answered and said, It is written, **Man shall not live by bread alone, but by every word that proceedeth out of the mouth of God.**

Matthew 4:10 Then saith Jesus unto him, Get thee hence, Satan: for it is written, **Thou shalt worship the Lord thy God, and him only shalt thou serve.**

Deciding right and wrong for ourselves as Eve and Adam did when they failed the test in the garden, is sin and brings death. While diligently LIVING by EVERY WORD of God is life eternal!

Therefore as the fruit or end result of partaking of the Tree of the Knowledge of Good and Evil by rejecting God's Word for our own ways is death. Living by EVERY WORD of GOD brings life eternal.

Satan said that man could become God, simply by deciding right and wrong for himself. And while man could be the decider for himself as God decides things; man living by his own ways could not have eternal life! Only faithful passionate obedience to the way of life that God had and that man outside of God cannot have, can bring eternal life.

Because the man would now decide what was wrong and right for himself, instead of listening to the words of eternal life; the man was rejected from eternal life and the paradise of God. The Creator denied man eternal life as long as man decided for himself what was right and wrong.

As Adam rejected the Word of God to decide for himself; today the Ekklesia reject any zeal to live by every Word of God in order to live by their own ways and false traditions. As Adam was rejected from eternal life and eternity with God; so the unrepentant who have rejected zeal to passionately live by every Word of God, shall also be kept from entering the Promised Land of eternal life.

3:22 And the LORD God said, Behold, the man is become as one of us, to know [to decide for himself] good and evil: and now, lest he put forth his hand, and take also of the tree of life, and eat, and live for ever: **3:23** Therefore the LORD God sent him forth from the garden of Eden, to till the ground from whence he was taken.

The way into eternal life and the eternal paradise of God has been shut up and closed and man has been cut off from God by the command of God; except for those specifically called out by God the Father as a kind of early first fruits to God.

Man was cut off from repentance and from turning back to obey God, so that man could learn a lesson through experience, that the way of God is the way of life and that any other way brings death.

This cutting off of mankind from God was essential to prevent the man from repenting and after being changed to spirit with eternal life, sinning again in future. The whole purpose of cutting man off from God was to allow man to live by his own ways until he had thoroughly learned that there is no other way to eternal life in peace other than the way of God.

God cut man off from himself, or rather it was the sins of man that cut man off from God

Isaiah 59:1 Behold, the Lord's hand is not shortened, that it cannot save; neither his ear heavy, that it cannot hear:**59:2** But your iniquities have separated between you and your God, and your sins have hid his face from you, that he will not hear.

When mankind was cut off from the Tree of Life and rejected from the presence of God God's plan for salvation started up. That plan was for the Implementing Creator Jesus Christ to give up his God-hood and be made flesh and to live a perfect sinless life at the end of which he would give his life as the sacrificial Lamb of God for humanity, so that he could be a DOOR through which man could be reconciled to God the Father.

We are to live by EVERY WORD of GOD the Father, which is eternal life; but the door to reconciliation to God the Father is our sincere repentance after thoroughly learning that God is the ONLY way to life; a commitment to go and sin no more and to live by every Word of God from henceforth and forever more; and then the Door of Reconciliation which is the sacrifice of the Lamb of God will be applied to us and we shall be reconciled to God our Father in Heaven receiving the gift of the Holy Spirit, and if we continue and overcome we shall inherit the gift of eternal life.

From Adam to the ascension of Christ on Wave Offering Sunday in 31 A.D., mankind was cut off from God except for a very few called out in faith that Christ would fulfill his mission; and from 31 A.D. to today mankind has been cut off from God except that more have also been called out to have faith in the efficacy of that sacrifice and to live by every Word of God; this is the early Spring Harvest to eternal life. The Fall Festivals picture another harvest, the main of all humanity who has lived through the past being cut off from God and from the tree of Life.

John 10:9 I am the door: by me if any man enter in, he shall be saved, and shall go in and out, and find pasture.

John 5:11 And this is the record, that God hath given to us [those faithful to live by every Word of God] **eternal life, and this life is in his Son. 5:12 He that hath the Son hath life; and he that hath not the Son of God hath not life.**

The bread of manna was another allegory of the true Bread of Life, Jesus Christ; who came down from heaven to give himself as our Bread of Life, for our salvation.

Salvation is not just saying "I repent" and consenting to being dunked in a pool of water, or attending some organizational meetings, while continuing in sin.

Salvation requires the internalization of the nature of God; through diligent study, and the practical application of the whole Word of God in our own minds and in all our deeds! It i s essential for us to OVERCOME and to "Go and sin no more," and for us to live as Christ lived!

John 6:47 Verily, verily, I say unto you, He that believeth on me [and lives as Christ lives] hath everlasting life.

Jesus Christ being ONE in full unity with God the Father, was sent by the Father as the Bread of Life, for all God the Father would call.

Carefully consider these words given just before Passover and Unleavened Bread.

6:48 I am that bread of life. 6:49 Your fathers did eat manna in the wilderness, and are dead. 6:50 This is the bread which cometh down from heaven, that a man may eat thereof, and not die. 6:51 I am the living bread which came down from heaven: if any man eat of this bread, he shall live for ever: and the bread that I will give is my flesh, which I will give for the life of the world.

Jesus explains what the wine and unleavened bread of Passover and the Feast of Unleavened Bread mean.

6:52 The Jews therefore strove among themselves, saying, How can this man give us his flesh to eat? **6:53** Then Jesus said unto them, Verily, verily, I say unto you, Except ye eat the flesh of the Son of man, and drink his blood, ye have no life in you.

6:54 Whoso eateth my flesh, and drinketh my blood, hath eternal life; and I will raise him up at the last day. **6:55** For my flesh is meat indeed, and my blood is drink indeed. **6:56** He that eateth my flesh, and drinketh my blood, dwelleth in me, and I in him.

We are to take the nature of Christ into ourselves and we are to live as Christ lived; We are to live by God the Father's Word in enthusiastic passionate zeal, just like Jesus did!

6:57 As the living Father hath sent me, and **I live by the Father**: so he that eateth me, even he shall live by me. **6:58** This is that bread which came down from heaven: not as your fathers did eat manna, and are dead: he that eateth of this bread shall live for ever.

6:59 These things said he in the synagogue, as he taught in Capernaum.

John 14:6 Jesus saith unto him, I am the way, the truth, and the life: no man cometh unto the Father, but by me.

John 17:3 And this is life eternal, that they might know [be one with] thee the only true God, and Jesus Christ, whom thou hast sent.

Jesus used the example of a tree, like the example of the Tree of Life [which is to live by EVERY WORD of God] to teach that HE is the way to God the Father and to eternal life.

John 15 The Vine and Branches

This is a powerful; explanation of the meaning of the command to cut branches and bring them into the temple at the Feast of Tabernacles. Bringing in the branches with great rejoicing represents bringing in of the harvest of humanity into the Family of God.

Jesus teaches that he is the vine [or trunk] of the tree of life; and that the called out to him are the branches. As a branch receives its nourishment from the vine and trunk of the tree; so we receive our spiritual nourishment from the Bread of Life, the true VINE; Jesus Christ!

To have eternal life; we MUST be in FULL UNITY with Christ; and if we turn away from any of the teachings of Christ, which teaching is that we must live by every Word of God the Father in the letter and in the spirit and intent of the law; we will be rejected by Christ and by God the Father, because we have already rejected their Word.

If we remain faithfully loyal to Jesus Christ and God the Father by diligently studying and zealously KEEPING and living by every Word of God; we will still be tried, tested and given experiences bad and good, to increase our spiritual growth and development into FULL UNITY with Christ.

John 15:1 I am the true vine [trunk of the tree, the Logos the whole Word of God], and my Father is the husbandman. **15:2 Every branch in me that beareth not fruit** [is NOT faithful and zealous to live by every Word of God as Christ does] **he** taketh **away: and every branch that** beareth **fruit** [living by EVERY WORD of GOD], **he** purgeth [trims and trains] **it, that it may bring forth more fruit.**

If we abide in the Word of God, doing those things that please Christ and God the Father; they will abide in us through the Spirit of God. If we are NOT zealous to KEEP the Word of God; WE ARE NONE OF HIS!

Remember that, when you are asked by your elder to pollute the Sabbath; take Passover and observe High Days on the wrong dates, or in the wrong ways; or are told that you need not eat Unleavened Bread every day of the Feast as God has commanded.

Remember that after washing the disciple's feet; they were all clean except one. That one being the person who did not spiritually abide in Christ the true VINE

15:3 Now ye are clean through the word which I have spoken unto you. **15:4 Abide in me, and I in you. As the branch cannot bear fruit of itself, except it abide in the vine; no more can ye, except ye abide in me.**

Beware of false Christ's who tolerate sin and are not filled with Christ-like zeal to live by every Word of God; Because without a firm close FULL UNITY with the true Christ who lives by every Word of God; our religion is vain and meaningless, and falls to the status of a human social club.

15:5 I am the vine, ye are the branches: He that abideth in me, and I in him, the same bringeth **forth much fruit: for without me ye can do nothing.**

To be grafted into the true vine of Christ; we MUST be called by God the Father; we must believe, repent and be baptized for the remission of sins to be granted; And IF we remain abiding in God; with him dwelling us; IF we follow the Holy Spirit's lead into all truth diligently living by every Word of God, then we shall bear much fruit!

15:6 If a man abide not in me [living in Christ-like zeal to live by EVERY WORD of GOD], **he is cast forth as a branch, and is withered; and men gather them, and cast them into the fire, and they are burned.**

Those who compromise with any part of the whole Word of God, which Christ loves because he IS the Logos then Word; and who tolerate sin, which Christ hates; will be rejected and cast into the furnace of affliction; and if they still do not repent, cast into the fire of ultimate destruction.

15:7 If ye abide in me, and my words abide in you, ye shall ask what ye will, and it shall be done unto you. 15:8 Herein is my Father glorified, that ye bear much fruit; so shall ye be my disciples.

15:9 As the Father hath loved me, so have I loved you: continue ye in my love.

"Continue in my love" means that Christ wants our loving relationship with HIM to continue, through our learning and keeping the Word that he preached; which is to do God the Father's will and to live by every Word of God.

Watch Out! Many will teach to keep the commandments, but by commandments they mean their own false traditions and not every Word of God.

15:10 If ye keep my commandments, ye shall abide in my love; even as I have kept my Father's commandments, and abide in his love.

What did Christ command us? He kept the whole Word of God fully and we are to do likewise, living as he lived and as he will live in us.

Jesus Christ lived a life of perfect obedience to his beloved Father, and he will live a life of perfect obedience to God the Father dwelling in us!

Matthew 19:17 . . . . but if thou wilt enter into life, keep the commandments

John 15:11 These things have I spoken unto you, that my joy might remain in you, and that your joy might be full.

15:12 This is my commandment, That ye love one another, as I have loved you. **15:13** Greater love hath no man than this, that a man lay down his life for his friends.

We are to be willing to lay down our lives for God the Father and Jesus Christ; as Christ laid down his life for us! Our HEAD is Jesus Christ and His Head is God the Father! How long will we squabble over who gets to lead; and over who gets what?

1 Corinthians 11:3 But I would have you know, that the head of every man is Christ; and the head of the woman is the man; and the head of Christ is God.

And our spiritual mother is not some corporate entity, but is the Holy Jerusalem of God the Father from which the Word of God goes forth to the entire universe!

Galatians 4:26 But Jerusalem which is above is free [from bondage to sin], **which is the mother of us all.**

As the Word of God on this earth will go forth from Jerusalem, so the Word of God the Father goes forth to the entire universe from the heavenly Jerusalem above.

Isaiah 2:3 And many people shall go and say, Come ye, and let us go up to the mountain of the Lord, to the house of the God of Jacob; and he will teach us of his ways, and we will walk in his paths: for **out of Zion shall go forth the law, and the word of the Lord from Jerusalem**.

As God is our Father; the spiritual Jerusalem above is our mother, because the wisdom and Word of God the Father flows from her.

How can a city be our mother? The heavenly Jerusalem is the city of God, from which the Word of God and the Holy Spirit comes forth; and TEACHES and NOURISHES the brethren in godliness like a mother nourishes her child.

This idea that some corporate church is the mother of the faithful and must be obeyed in place of the Word of God is a lie; the mother of the faithful is the heavenly Jerusalem from which flows the Spirit and Word of God the Father!

Is the woman [corporate church] who teaches her child to commit fornication [follow false teachings], when the father has taught us not to commit fornication, a fit mother?

Absolutely NOT! and a corporate "church" which teaches us to live contrary to any part God's Word is NOT a fit spiritual mother!

A mother nourishes and brings up her children according to the word of their father, and spiritually speaking, the mother of the faithful consists of those who nourish the brethren in EVERY WORD of GOD the Father!

Proverbs 1:8 My son, hear the instruction of thy father, and forsake not the law of thy mother:

How has the love of God disappeared from us? where has our zeal to live by every Word of God gone? Where is our unity with the Word of God and with God our Father?

John 15:14 Ye are my friends, if ye do whatsoever I command you.

Amos 3:3 Can two walk together, except they be agreed?

Our prayers are answered in direct proportion to our diligent keeping of the whole Word of God!

John 15:15 Henceforth I call you not servants; for the servant knoweth not what his lord doeth: but I have called you friends; for all things that I have heard of my Father I have made known unto you. **15:16** Ye have not chosen me, but I have chosen you, and ordained you, that ye should go and bring forth fruit, and that your fruit should remain: **that whatsoever ye shall ask of the Father in my name, he may give it you.**

All God's people, all the called of God the Father are to be filled with the love of God.

Love for God our Father is to live by every Word of God, which Word is Jesus Christ. What is love? God is love; and the KEEPING of the Word of God is love.

HOW do we love? By internalizing Jesus Christ and God the Father, through following the example of Jesus Christ, and sincere repentance from acting contrary to the Word of God; and a diligent, passionate, enthusiastic Christ-like zeal to live by every Word of God.

It is then that we shall be united with God the Father and Jesus Christ through a zeal to live by their Word, as they are of ONE mind with each other! It is then that we shall be called "the friends of God:" like our spiritual father, Abraham!

15:17 These things I command you, that ye love one another.

The law in its full purpose, spirit and intent; defines the love of God!

If we keep the whole Word of God in all its spirit, purpose and intent, we become like God; we become fully united with Jesus Christ and God the Father.

IF we loved God, we would DO what God's Word says, we would do those things which are pleasing in his sight. Like little children we would want to become LIKE our Father!

Falling into the lukewarmness of Laodicea, is to become offensive and disgusting to Christ; who will spew us out of his body, like a dead branch cut off from a vine.

Godly Love

The Greek word agape is often translated "love" in the New Testament. The essence of agape love is giving one's self fully to God first and then acting in the best interests of others even the undeserving. Unlike our English word love, agape is not used in the New Testament to refer to romantic or sexual love. Nor does it refer to close friendship or brotherly love, for which the Greek word philia is used. Agape love involves faithfulness, commitment, and an act of personal will to strive to be like and please God at any personal cost. It is distinguished from the other types of love by its lofty moral nature and strong character. Agape love is beautifully described in 1 Corinthians 13.

Agape is used to describe the love that is of and from God, whose very nature is love itself: "God is love" (1 John 4:8). God does not merely love; He is love itself. Everything God does flows from His love. Agape is used to describe our love for God (Luke 10:27) and a faithful servant's love for his master (Matthew 6:24) as a type of our love for God.

The type of love that characterizes God is not an evangelical sappy, sentimental feeling of belonging to some group. God loves not because we deserve to be loved or because of any excellence we possess, but because it is His nature to love and He must be true to His nature.

Agape love is always shown by what it does, not by how we feel. God's demonstration of agape love led to the sacrifice of the Son of God for those He loves, and we demonstrate agape love by living by every Word of God.

We are to love others with agape love, whether they are fellow believers (John 13:34) or bitter enemies (Matthew 5:44). Agape love as modeled by Jesus Christ is not based on feelings; rather, it is a determined act of the will to live by every Word of God above our own will.

There remains one more Biblical Festival, the Feast of Purim; which is found in the book of Esther. This Feast is about the deliverance of Judah and is an allegory of the called out of spiritual Judah. No series on the Festivals would be complete without a study of Purim which is well worthy of being kept by the faithful of spiritual Judah in the twelfth month of God's Biblical Calendar

Psalms for The Feast of the Eighth Day

Psalms 145 to 150 are songs of praise and rejoicing in the LORD by all people then living in the millennium; after Christ comes to deliver mankind from Satan, sin and death.

These Psalms are mainly about **the Feast of the Eighth Day**, when all peoples and nations will sing the praises of the LORD forevermore after the main harvest of humanity is brought into the Family of God.

God will give every person an opportunity to be delivered from bondage to Satan, sin and death; those who embrace that opportunity will receive the gift of life everlasting while the incorrigible unrepentant wicked will perish and the earth will be cleansed by fire. God the father will then come down to the earth and His children will inherit the universe under the Father's leadership.

Mankind which has been redeemed and saved from eternal death, to be given the gift of eternal life in peace, with no more war, suffering or death, and the gift of a universe to complete and perfect; will praise their Maker and Deliverer and their Father for all His goodness, all His mercy and all His love forevermore!

Revelation 21:4 And God shall wipe away all tears from their eyes; and there shall be no more death, neither sorrow, nor crying, neither shall there be any more pain: for the former things are passed away.

The time has come to prepare the bride, for the time is close at hand and the bridegroom is ready to come for his wife!

Let the bride awake, arise and prepare herself, for the table of the LORD is being set with the solid meat of sound doctrine so that she might make herself ready by removing every spot and blemish of sin through internalizing every Word of her Beloved Husband and His Father in heaven!

If she is not ready her Husband will not wait for her, but will leave her standing alone and ashamed while he takes those who are ready to the Marriage of the Lamb. May the brethren be made ready by zealously, enthusiastically; LEARNING, INTERNALIZING and LIVING by EVERY WORD of God!

Psalm 145

Psalm 145:1 I will extol thee, my God, O king; and I will bless thy name for ever and ever. **145:2** Every day will I bless thee; and I will praise thy name for ever and ever. **145:3** Great is the LORD, and greatly to be praised; and his greatness is unsearchable.

145:4 One generation shall praise thy works to another [every generation will praise God to all others], and shall declare thy mighty acts. **145:5** I will speak of the glorious honour of thy majesty, and of thy wondrous works. **145:6** And men shall speak of the might of thy terrible acts: and I will declare thy greatness. **145:7** They shall abundantly utter the memory of thy great goodness, and shall sing of thy righteousness.

The LORD will yet save humanity!

145:8 The LORD is gracious, and full of compassion; slow to anger, and of great mercy. **145:9** The LORD is good to all: and his tender mercies are over all his works. **145:10** All thy works shall praise thee, O LORD; and thy saints [all sincerely repentant people] shall bless thee.

145:11 They shall speak of the glory of thy kingdom, and talk of thy power; **145:12** To make known to the sons of men his mighty acts, and the glorious majesty of his kingdom. **145:13** Thy kingdom is an everlasting kingdom, and thy dominion endureth throughout all generations.

145:14 The LORD upholdeth all that fall, and raiseth up all those that be bowed down. **145:15** The eyes of all wait upon thee; and thou givest them their meat in due season. **145:16** Thou openest thine hand, and satisfiest the desire of every living thing.

145:17 The LORD is righteous in all his ways, and holy in all his works. **145:18** The LORD is nigh unto all them that call upon him, to all that call upon him in truth. **145:19** He will fulfil the desire of them that fear him: he also will hear their cry, and will save them.

145:20 The LORD preserveth all them that love him [enough to live by every Word of God]: but all the wicked will he destroy.

145:21 My mouth shall speak the praise of the LORD: and let all flesh bless his holy name for ever and ever.

Psalm 146

Psalm 146:1 Praise ye the LORD. Praise the LORD, O my soul. **146:2** While I live [the godly will live forever] will I praise the LORD: I will sing praises unto my God while I have any being.

Do not trust in the words of men but test every word of men by the Word of God, and hold fast only to what is consistent with every Word of God (1 Thess 5:22): No matter what temporal or ecclesiastical title men may claim.

146:3 Put not your trust in princes, nor in the son of man, in whom there is no help. **146:4** His breath goeth forth, he returneth to his earth; in that very day his thoughts perish.

No man can save us and no words of men can save us: Only God the Father, King of the Universe and the Creator, can deliver men from Satan, sin, death and the grave.

146:5 Happy is he that hath the God of Jacob for his help, whose hope is in the LORD his God: **146:6** Which made heaven, and earth, the sea, and all that therein is: which keepeth truth for ever: **146:7** Which executeth judgment for the oppressed: which giveth food to the hungry. The LORD looseth the prisoners:

The Eternal will open the eyes of the spiritually blind and will deliver those stooped down in bondage to sin. The righteousness of God is to live by every Word of God.

146:8 The LORD openeth the eyes of the blind: the LORD raiseth them that are bowed down: the LORD loveth the righteous:

The Eternal will save those cast out of the Assemblies for their zeal to live by every Word of God, and God will save those cut off from their physical families for their zeal for godliness.

146:9 The LORD preserveth the strangers; he relieveth the fatherless and widow: but the way of the wicked he turneth upside down.

The Feast of the Eighth Day pictures a humanity changed to spirit, going forward into eternity with God, in the righteousness of living by every Word of God. Eternity as represented by the Feast of the Eighth Day will begin when the New Jerusalem comes down to the earth from heaven.

146:10 The LORD shall reign for ever, even thy God, O Zion, unto all generations. Praise ye the LORD.

Psalm 147

Praises to God for the coming and deliverance of Christ the Messiah, and for the opportunity of eternal salvation!

Psalm 147:1 Praise ye the LORD: for it is good to sing praises unto our God; for it is pleasant; and praise is comely.

When Christ comes, Jerusalem and the third Temple will be built as per Ezekiel 40 - 48 and representative populations of ALL the tribes of Israel will return to the physical Promised Land. Then those who have been humbled and had their pride broken to contrition and sincere repentance will be saved.

147:2 The LORD doth build up Jerusalem: he gathereth together the outcasts of Israel. **147:3** He healeth the broken in heart, and bindeth up their wounds.

God the Father knows every star in the heavens and he knows and loves all those who turn to Him to live by every Word of God. All the sincerely repentant who are meek, submissive and humble before God, turning in sincere repentance to diligently live by every Word of God; will be healed in spirit and delivered from bondage to Satan, sin and death; and the unrepentant wicked will be destroyed.

147:4 He telleth the number of the stars; he calleth them all by their names. **147:5** Great is our Lord, and of great power: his understanding is infinite. **147:6** The LORD lifteth up [delivers] the meek: he casteth the wicked down to the ground.

When Christ comes a repentant Israel and humanity will sing to God in rejoicing for their deliverance; singing out to the Great God, the Giver of Salvation and all Good Things.

147:7 Sing unto the LORD with thanksgiving; sing praise upon the harp unto our God: **147:8** Who covereth the heaven with clouds, who prepareth rain for the earth, who maketh grass to grow upon the mountains. **147:9** He giveth to the beast his food, and to the young ravens which cry.

God has all power and has no need of the help of horse or man.

147:10 He delighteth not in the strength of the horse: he taketh not pleasure in the legs of a man.

God will save all those who fear to sin and who love and respect God enough to live by every Word of God.

147:11 The LORD taketh pleasure in them that fear him, in those that hope in his mercy.

Jerusalem as the capital represents all the tribes and people of Israel, and when their Deliverer comes to save then they will all surely rejoice and praise God.

147:12 Praise the LORD, O Jerusalem; praise thy God, O Zion.

God will make Jerusalem the capital of Messiah over the whole earth and will greatly bless her, placing the Ezekiel Temple of God within her.

147:13 For he hath strengthened the bars of thy gates; he hath blessed thy children within thee. **147:14** He maketh peace in thy borders, and filleth thee with the finest of the wheat.

Micah 4:2 And many nations shall come, and say, Come, and let us go up to the mountain of the Lord, and to the house of the God of Jacob; and he will teach us of his ways, and we will walk in his paths [God's ways, Word]: for the law shall go forth of Zion, and the word of the Lord from Jerusalem.

Psalm 147:15 He sendeth forth his commandment upon earth: his word runneth very swiftly.

God the Creator made all things including the heat and the cold and the seasons of the earth.

God created the beautiful patterns of the night frost, scattering the hoarfrost like grey ashes on the ground; and God makes the snows to fall on the mountains in winter and causes them to melt in summer to water the land.

147:16 He giveth snow like wool: he scattereth the hoarfrost like ashes. **147:17** He casteth forth his ice like morsels: who can stand before his cold? **147:18** He sendeth out his word, and melteth them: he causeth his wind to blow, and the waters flow.

In that day, God's Spirit will be poured out on all flesh (Joel 2:28) and all nations which have not known God will be grafted into the New Covenant (Jer 31:31) and a new spiritual Israel.

147:19 He sheweth his word unto Jacob, his statutes and his judgments unto Israel. **147:20** He hath not dealt so with any nation: and as for his judgments, they have not known them. Praise ye the LORD.

Psalm 148

A song of praise to God and Messiah for making all things and for the deliverance of men from Satan, sin, death and the grave to eternal salvation. Let every person and every being praise the Mighty God of Jacob, forever and forever, Amen!

Psalm 148:1 Praise ye the LORD. Praise ye the LORD from the heavens: praise him in the heights.

148:2 Praise ye him, all his angels: praise ye him, all his hosts. **148:3** Praise ye him, sun and moon: praise him, all ye stars of light. **148:4** Praise him, ye heavens of heavens, and ye waters that be above the heavens.

God created all things and is worthy of praise and great glory!

148:5 Let them praise the name of the LORD: for he commanded, and they were created. **148:6** He hath also stablished them for ever and ever: he hath made a decree which shall not pass. **148:7** Praise the LORD from the earth, ye dragons [wild beasts], and all deeps [creatures in the sea]:

All things will be brought into subjection and under control by God the Almighty!

148:8 Fire, and hail; snow, and vapours; stormy wind fulfilling his word: **148:9** Mountains, and all hills; fruitful trees, and all cedars: **148:10** Beasts, and all cattle; creeping things, and flying fowl:

All men will be humbled and offered the gift of Eternal Salvation, and they shall praise the God of their Salvation forever and forever, Amen!

148:11 Kings of the earth, and all people; princes, and all judges of the earth: **148:12** Both young men, and maidens; old men, and children: **148:13** Let them praise the name of the LORD: for his name alone is excellent; his glory is above the earth and heaven.

148:14 He also exalteth the horn [life and strength] of his people, the praise of all his saints [the saints are those who live by every Word of God]; even of the children of [the sincerely repentant from all nations will be grafted into the New Covenant spiritual Israel] Israel, a people [New Covenant spiritual Israel (Jer 31:31) will be a people near unto God, and the Word of God will be written in their minds and on their hearts] near unto him. Praise ye the LORD.

Psalm 149

At the coming of Messiah the Christ, the resurrected saints will sing a new song of rejoicing in the deliverance of the Mighty Savior.

Psalm 149:1 Praise ye the LORD. Sing unto the LORD a new song, and his praise in the congregation of saints.

Just as Israel rejoiced when they came up out of the Red Sea and saw their pursuers destroyed, the saints of spiritual Israel will break out in song and will dance and shout in great rejoicing when the Savior comes and they are resurrected and delivered from the bondage of death and the grave!

149:2 Let Israel rejoice in him that made him: let the children of Zion be joyful in their King. **149:3** Let them praise his name in the dance: let them sing praises unto him with the timbrel and harp.

The Eternal will save his sincerely repentant people and will give the gift of eternal salvation to those who are meek and teachable before God the Great, the Almighty!

149:4 For the LORD taketh pleasure in his people: he will beautify the meek with salvation.

When Messiah comes with deliverance the resurrected saints will rejoice day and night for their deliverance from bondage to Satan, sin and death.

149:5 Let the saints be joyful in glory: let them sing aloud upon their beds.

The resurrected servants of God will be full of the TRUTH of every Word of God, and the sword of truth will continually be in their mouths to destroy all wickedness and sin from off the earth!

149:6 Let the high praises of God be in their mouth, and a two-edged sword in their hand;

Messiah the Christ and all his resurrected saints - the bride of the New Covenant - will come to rule all nations with the truth and righteousness of every Word of God, and they will correct the unrepentant and cleanse the earth of wickedness and sin.

149:7 To execute vengeance upon the heathen [the unrepentant wicked], and punishments upon the [upon unrepentant wicked people] people;

The king of wickedness is Satan and his kings are his spirit followers who have enslaved the nations; they will be bound and imprisoned for one thousand years and will then be defeated one last time and judged to destruction. See the Fall Festivals studies.

149:8 To bind their kings with chains, and their nobles with fetters of iron;

The resurrected saints will have the honour, with Christ; of executing the judgment of God and destroying Satan and his demonic followers on the Fast of Atonement.

149:9 To execute upon them the judgment written: this honour have all his saints. Praise ye the LORD.

Psalm 150

God our Maker the God of our Salvation will save humanity from bondage to Satan, demons, sin, sorrows, suffering and death; to give the gift of eternal life to all those who live by every Word of God.

Then as pictured by The Feast of The Eighth Day, all sincerely repentant humanity will inherit the entire universe and will go forward in peace and unity with God for everlasting eternity!

Praise God forever and forever, for all that he does for the sins of men!

Psalm 150:1 Praise ye the LORD. Praise God in his sanctuary: praise him in the firmament of his power. **150:2** Praise him for his mighty acts: praise him according to his excellent greatness. **150:3** Praise him with the sound of the trumpet: praise him with the psaltery and harp. **150:4** Praise him with the timbrel and dance: praise him with stringed instruments and organs. **150:5** Praise him upon the loud cymbals: praise him upon the high sounding cymbals. **150:6** Let every thing that hath breath praise the LORD. Praise ye the LORD.

Purim

Introduction

Ezra records the decree of Cyrus to build the temple, and the history of building the Temple, but Ezra did NOT go to Judea until many years later and AFTER the Temple was completed! It was "the chief of the fathers [Elders and family leaders] of Judah and Benjamin, and the priests, and the Levites" who went to Judea at the decree of Cyrus, NOT Ezra!

The Decree of Cyrus

Ezra 1:1 Now in the first year of Cyrus [c536 B.C.] king of Persia, that the word of the LORD by the mouth of Jeremiah might be fulfilled, the LORD stirred up the spirit of Cyrus king of Persia, that he made a proclamation throughout all his kingdom, and put it also in writing, saying,

1:2 Thus saith Cyrus king of Persia, **The LORD God of heaven hath given me all the kingdoms of the earth; and he hath charged me to build him an house at Jerusalem, which is in Judah. 1:3 Who is there among you of all his people? his God be with him, and let him go up to Jerusalem, which is in Judah, and build the house of the LORD God of Israel, (he is the God,) which is in Jerusalem.**

1:4 And whosoever remaineth in any place where he sojourneth, let the men of his place help him with silver, and with gold, and with goods, and with beasts, beside the freewill offering for the house of God that is in Jerusalem.

King Cyrus decreed that those who wanted to; could go back and begin to build the Temple in Jerusalem. Then the sincerely repentant in the captivity arose to return to Judea. In spite of their numbers they were only a very small portion of those in captivity, the vast majority remaining in Babylon.

However the construction of the Temple suffered long delays and the Temple was not completed until c 517-516 B.C.

Over one hundred years after Cyrus, in his third year; King Ahasuerus Longimanus [this particular Artaxerxes being Artaxerxes Longimanus mentioned in Nehemiah chapters 1 and 2] who became the husband of Esther, put away Vashti (461 B.C.), and in his seventh year (457 B.C.) sent Ezra to rebuild the city Jerusalem then in his twelfth year (c452 B.C.) he saved the Jews from Haman.

Ahasuerus was the King Artaxerxes [both these words were general titles of the kings of Persia, this particular Artaxerxes being Artaxerxes Longimanus] who in his seventh year (457 B.C.) authorized Ezra to restore godly religion in Jerusalem and rebuild the city.

Then in his twentieth year (444 B.C.) Artaxerxes Longimanus also sent Nehemiah to help build the city.

Artaxerxes Longimanus put away Vashti in 461 B.C. and over the next few years paid attention to finding a new Queen. Haman's attempt to destroy Judah, was motivated by jealousy that Mordecai would not bow to him and also by the fact that Artaxerxes had ordered the rebuilding of the city Jerusalem in 457 B.C. which fulfilled the Seventy Weeks Prophecy by issuing a decree to build the city of Jerusalem, beginning the count to and dating the ministry of Jesus Christ.

Then King Artaxerxes Longimanus saved Judah and Queen Esther from Haman's attack in the king's twelfth year (452 B.C.)

Later Artaxerxes Longimanus in the seventh year of his reign (457 B.C.), authorized Ezra the priest and scribe, and all who wished to join him, to go to Jerusalem.

It was Ezra's desire to instruct the Jews in the laws of God and to restore true religion.

Artaxerxes granted him large amounts of silver and gold to furnish the temple, and gave instruction that his treasurers on that side of the river should provide whatever was needed to beautify the Lord's house.

Ezra enters with king Artaxerxes Longimanus in Ezra 7 some years AFTER the Temple is completed.

It was Ezra who set up the temple worship system existing at the time of Christ, including the water pouring and light ceremonies during the Feast of Tabernacles which Jesus used to demonstrate his teachings.

In the decree, Artaxerxes Longimanus commanded Ezra to "set magistrates and judges, which may judge all the people that are beyond the river, **all such as know the laws of thy God; and teach ye them that know them not. And whosoever will not do the law of thy God, and the law of the king, let judgment be executed speedily upon him, whether it be unto death, or to banishment, or to confiscation of goods, or to imprisonment.**" (Ezra 7:25, 26).

The story of Nehemiah began in the 20th year of Artaxerxes' Longimanus reign. Nehemiah, was the king's cupbearer. One day some of his brethren from Judah arrived in Shushan where king's palace was. Nehemiah inquired of them about the condition of things in Jerusalem.

"The remnant that are left of the captivity there in the province are in great affliction and reproach," they replied. "The wall of Jerusalem also is broken down, and the gates thereof are burned with fire."

Nehemiah sat down and wept. For several days he mourned and fasted and prayed. His prayer is remarkably similar to that of Daniel in Daniel 9. He prayed that somehow God would "grant him mercy in the sight of" the king.

Four months later, Nehemiah was serving wine to the king, and Artaxerxes noticed a sadness in Nehemiah's countenance. "Why is thy countenance sad?" the king asked.

Nehemiah explained that **Jerusalem was still in ruins**, the wall and the gates were still not repaired. When the king asked what he would like to do, Nehemiah answered, "If it please the king, and if thy servant have found favour in thy sight, that thou wouldest send me unto Judah, unto the city of my fathers' sepulchres, that I may build it."

Artaxerxes consented, and sent with him letters for the governors of the region, authorizing Nehemiah to rebuild the city of Jerusalem.

This commission to BUILD THE CITY, was issued in the spring of 457 B.C., and in 444 B.C. in Artaxerxes Longimanus' 20th year of reign, Nehemiah was also sent to Jerusalem.

The Seventy Weeks prophecy of Daniel reveals that it was the decree to **build the City of Jerusalem,** and not a decree to build the Temple, which began the countdown to the revealing of Messiah.

Daniel 9:25 says, "Know therefore and understand, that from the going forth of **the commandment to restore and to build Jerusalem** [the CITY, not the temple] unto the Messiah the Prince shall be seven weeks, and threescore and two weeks: the street shall be built again, and the wall, even in troublous times."

Purim

The scriptures establish that Purim was on Adar 13, 14 and 15. Esther 9 sets Purim as the 15th day of the 12th month Adar 1.

We see in Esther **9:1** "Now in **the twelfth month**, that is, the month Adar". . . clearly meaning that Purim is to be in the 12th month.

In the years when an intercalary month is to be added, the Calendar has an Adar I [12th month] and an Adar 2 [13th month] is added.

Purim is celebrated with the reading of Esther; feasting and festivities, often including a performance of the story by costumed actors or youth.

Much of scriptural history is prophetic allegory: for example, physical Israel coming out of Egypt, is a type of a spiritual Israel to be called out of the spiritual Egypt of bondage to sin and this society's pharaoh god-king, Satan.

That does not mean that every detail is a part of the allegory; even as every detail of Abraham's life was not a perfect example of faith. Yet many of the main events can be pointed out as allegory.

For far too long the Book of Esther has been sidelined as a mere historical book intended to show why Jews observe Purim; or to show the faithfulness of Esther [Hebrew: Hadassah].

There is far more to Esther than mere history, for ALL scripture is written for our instruction and edification, and all these things were recorded as examples for our good.

This is a short book full of allegory and prophetic significance revealing much about our God and his plan.

Esther is an allegory which can be understood only through understanding the roles of the main characters.

Cast of Characters

1) First is the great King who is king of all the known world and who cannot be approached, except the attendee first be "CALLED" to him.

This great king pictures Messiah [Yeshua, Jesus Christ] as Lord of all the earth, and people being called to him.

2) Vashti, who is like the first [Mosaic] bride of Christ, physical Israel; she goes to do her own thing, continually rebellious, disobedient and neglectful of her Lord. She refuses to be the example for all peoples that it is her duty and responsibility to be as the Queen.

3) Next is Hadassah [Myrtle], to whom the king gave the name Esther, which is Ishtar, or Queen of Heaven. While this is the name of a pagan goddess, please consider that, as an allegory; the bride of Christ, the collective saints; will be a true Queen of Heaven.

Now consider that this Esther is called out to an opportunity to become the bride of the Great King and is a Jew indeed [spiritually]. As such Esther is a picture of the called out saints. She then becomes Queen, picturing the resurrected saints married to the Great King of the whole earth.

Esther was incomparable in beauty, faithfulness, wisdom and righteousness, without any blemish, as befits the bride of Christ.

4) Physical Judah is a portrayal of those who are the faithful spiritual Judah, faithful to all the ways and commandments of God and hated by Satan, pictured by Haman.

5) Haman, clearly a picture of Satan, the enemy of physical and spiritual Judah [Satan the Adversary of God and God's called out faithful]. As Haman has access to the king and tries to use that access to destroy the

physical Judah [Israel]; so Satan has access to the throne of God and works to destroy God's spiritual faithful, Job 1-2.

6) Mordecai, who is a type of God's leading guiding spirit of wisdom; which Hadassah follows and is subject to.

Outline

Hadassah is orphaned and has no attachments to this world, being raised by her uncle Mordecai. She is one of the humble lowly of this world; who is to be called out to an espousal to marry the Great King and become the Queen of all the earth.

Hadassah is an example of the lowly of this world being called out to Christ, to become the bride of the Lamb of God; who will come to this earth to rule all nations.

The King has a wife, Vashti; who refuses the king's command to be an proper example for the nations and citizens of the world, and who brings disrepute and shame on the great King. For her rebellion and terrible example of preferring her own ways to serving her husband the king she is rejected from being Queen, and is replaced by others called to train to receive that dignity.

Vashti is a type of physical Israel who for her continual rebellion against her LORD was rejected and a new spiritual bride was called out to him.

The many women called to the king typifies the many persons called out to become part of the collective spiritual bride; while once chosen Hadassah pictures that bride herself.

Hadassah is called along with many others to be a part of the bride of the King as a type of the bride of Christ; and is raised and taught [made perfect] by God's Spirit, represented by Mordecai, having nothing in this world.

Esther 2:17 And the king loved Esther above all the women, and she obtained grace and favour in his sight more than all the virgins; so that he set the royal crown upon her head, and made her queen instead of Vashti.

Even so, many are called but few will be chosen to become a part of the collective resurrected bride, the Queen of God's Kingdom.

Hadassah overcomes and by her perfection and zeal to serve and please the king she is made Queen; She does not love her life, but is willing to give herself for her people [which is also for the king's good].

Hadassah sought advice from Mordecai and he responded: this is a type of the New Covenant called out seeking God and the wisdom of the Holy Spirit. Hadassah then followed Mordecai's instruction, just like the New covenant faithful will follow God's Spirit to diligently live by every Word of God.

Esther 4:13 Then Mordecai commanded to answer Esther, Think not with thyself that thou shalt escape in the king's house, more than all the Jews.

4:14 For if thou altogether holdest thy peace at this time, then shall there enlargement and deliverance arise to the Jews from another place; but thou and thy father's house shall be destroyed: and who knoweth whether thou art come to the kingdom for such a time as this?

Hadassah was advised to do good, regardless of personal cost; and the spiritually called out are guided by the Holy Spirit to live by every Word of God regardless of the cost in physical terms.

Now Haman [Satan] comes along to try and destroy all Judah. This speaks of Satan's attempts to destroy God's elect from the very beginning and especially at the latter day tribulation when physical and much of spiritual Israel are given over to him.

Because of the faith, love, obedient service, courage, blamelessness and spiritual beauty of Hadassah, representative of the beauty and purity from all blemish of sin of the bride at the marriage of the Lamb; she is chosen to be the Queen, and Haman is removed and all Judah is saved.

Spiritually this pictures the faithfulness and spiritual beauty of those finally chosen to be resurrected as part of the collective bride of Christ, and the removal of Satan [Haman] at Christ's coming.

Romans 11:26 And so all Israel shall be saved: as it is written, There shall come out of Sion the Deliverer, and shall turn away ungodliness from Jacob: **11:27** For this is my covenant unto them, when I shall take away their sins.

The Great King intervenes to destroy Haman, a type of Satan by strengthening Judah to rise up and fight against her enemies; overcoming all evil.

The great spirit king, Jesus Christ, also gives his faithful strength to overcome Satan and sin, and complete victory over Satan and sin through HIS power!

This Ahasuerus, husband of Esther in his third year [Purim c 460 B.C.], was the king Artaxerxes who would send Ezra in his seventh year [c 457 B.C.] to restore true religion, and later send Nehemiah in his twentieth year [c 444 B.C.] with the commission to build the city Jerusalem [and thereby begin the countdown to the advent of the physical ministry of Jesus Christ [Hebrew: Yeshua Mashiach] in 27 A.D.

Please consider these things with prayer and then read through the book of Esther, carefully considering each detail. The allegory will open up to you as a beautiful flower opens with the light of dawn.

Purim is NOT a commanded High Holy Day, yet it is an event in Holy Scripture worthy of remembrance and observing by Spiritual Judah; in honour of the wonders God has done, and as instruction in spiritual things. Remember that ALL scripture is written for our example and instruction.

Esther is a physical history of physical Judah, and is an allegory of the deliverance of the spiritual Bride of Christ, when the Kingdom of God shall destroy all evil and flourish over all the earth

Esther

Esther 1:1 Now it came to pass in the days of Ahasuerus, (this is Ahasuerus which reigned, from India even unto Ethiopia, over an hundred and seven and twenty provinces:) **1:2** That in those days, when the king Ahasuerus sat on the throne of his kingdom, which was in Shushan the palace, **1:3 In the third year of his reign**, he made a feast unto all his princes and his servants; the power of **Persia and Media**, the nobles and princes of the provinces, being before him: **1:4** When he shewed the riches of his glorious kingdom and the honour of his excellent majesty many days, even an hundred and fourscore days.

1:5 And when these days were expired, the king made a feast unto all the people that were present in Shushan the palace, both unto great and small, seven days, in the court of the garden of the king's palace; **1:6** Where were white, green, and blue, hangings, fastened with cords of fine linen and purple to silver rings and pillars of marble: the beds were of gold and silver, upon a pavement of red, and blue, and white, and black, marble.

1:7 And they gave them drink in vessels of gold, (the vessels being diverse one from another,) and royal wine in abundance, according to the state of the king.

1:8 And the drinking was according to the law; none did compel: for so the king had appointed to all the officers of his house, that they should do according to every man's pleasure.

Vashti the Queen refuses to perform her royal duty and appear in her royal attire before the gathered leaders of the known world. This is a type that physical Israel, called out of Egypt to be an example for all nations for good, rebelled and became an example for all nations of rebellion and sin. As Vashti insisted on doing her own thing rather than obeying the king, so physical [and spiritual] Israel has insisted on her own ways rather than obeying her LORD.

1:9 Also Vashti the queen made a feast for the women in the royal house which belonged to king Ahasuerus.

1:10 On the seventh day, when the heart of the king was merry with wine, he commanded Mehuman, Biztha, Harbona, Bigtha, and Abagtha, Zethar, and Carcas, the seven chamberlains that served in the presence of Ahasuerus the king, **1:11** To bring Vashti the queen before the king with the crown royal, to shew the people and the princes her beauty: for she was fair to look on.

1:12 But **the queen Vashti refused to come at the king's commandment by his chamberlains:** therefore was the king very wroth, and his anger burned in him.

When physical Israel refused to be an example for good and rebelled against God; God was very angry with them and rejected them. Our God does not change and he will also strongly correct those of the called out of spiritual Israel if they rebel against him to follow their own ways.

1:13 Then the king said to the wise men, which knew the times, (for so was the king's manner toward all that knew law and judgment: **1:14** And the next unto him was Carshena, Shethar, Admatha, Tarshish, Meres, Marsena, and Memucan, the seven princes of Persia and Media, which saw the king's face, and which sat the first in the kingdom;)

The king did not act out of anger but sought advice from his wise men.

1:15 What shall we do unto the queen Vashti according to law, because she hath not performed the commandment of the king Ahasuerus by the chamberlains? **1:16** And Memucan answered before the king and the princes, Vashti the queen hath not done wrong to the king only, but also to all the princes, and to all the people that are in all the provinces of the king Ahasuerus.

The issue was rebellion, and the example of rebellion.

1:17 For this deed of the queen shall come abroad unto all women, so that they shall despise their husbands in their eyes, when it shall be reported, The king Ahasuerus commanded Vashti the queen to be brought in before him, but she came not.

1:18 Likewise shall the ladies of Persia and Media say this day unto all the king's princes, which have heard of the deed of the queen. Thus shall there arise too much contempt and wrath.

This is all about example

1:19 If it please the king, let there go a royal commandment from him, and let it be written among the laws of the Persians and the Medes, that it be not altered, That **Vashti come no more before king Ahasuerus; and let the king give her royal estate unto another that is better than she.**

1:20 And when the king's decree which he shall make shall be published throughout all his empire, (for it is great,) all the wives shall give to their husbands honour, both to great and small.

1:21 And the saying pleased the king and the princes; and the king did according to the word of Memucan: **1:22** For he sent letters into all the king's provinces, into every province according to the writing thereof, and to every people after their language, that every man should bear rule in his own house, and that it should be published according to the language of every people.

Esther 2

Esther 2:1 After these things, when the wrath of king Ahasuerus was appeased, he remembered Vashti, and what she had done, and what was decreed against her.

The king is advised to seek out another Queen; spiritually this refers to God putting away his wife of collective Israel [and later dying to end his marriage covenant], and many people being called out to espousal to Christ to see if they can qualify to become part of a new collective bride for the Lamb of God.

2:2 Then said the king's servants that ministered unto him, Let there be fair young virgins sought for the king: **2:3** And let the king appoint officers in all the provinces of his kingdom, that they may gather together all the fair young virgins unto Shushan the palace, to the house of the women, unto the custody of Hege the king's chamberlain, keeper of the women; and let their things for purification be given them: **2:4** And **let the maiden which pleaseth the king be queen instead of Vashti.** And the thing pleased the king; and he did so.

2:5 Now in Shushan the palace there was a certain Jew, whose name was Mordecai, the son of Jair, the son of Shimei, the son of Kish, a Benjamite; **2:6** Who [Kish had been taken from Judea March 15/16th, 597 B.C.] had been carried away from Jerusalem with the captivity which had been carried away with Jeconiah king of Judah, whom Nebuchadnezzar the king of Babylon had carried away.

2:7 And **he brought up Hadassah, that is, Esther, his uncle's daughter: for she had neither father nor mother**, and the maid was fair and beautiful; whom Mordecai, when her father and mother were dead, took for his own daughter.

2:8 So it came to pass, when the king's commandment and his decree was heard, and when many maidens were gathered together unto Shushan the palace, to the custody of Hegai, that Esther was brought also unto the king's house, to the custody of Hegai, keeper of the women.

2:9 And the maiden pleased him, and she obtained kindness of him; and he speedily gave her her things for purification, with such things as belonged to her, and seven maidens, which were meet to be given her, out of the king's house: and he preferred her and her maids unto the best place of the house of the women.

2:10 Esther had not shewed her people nor her kindred: for Mordecai had charged her that she should not shew it.

Today there is no race with God when it comes to the calling out of prospectives for his new spiritual bride. Mordecai was very attentive to his charge that she do well, as God's spirit I s very attentive to lead the spiritually called out into all truth, to become pleasing to our LORD; if we would only follow it.

2:11 And Mordecai walked every day before the court of the women's house, to know how Esther did, and what should become of her.

2:12 Now when every maid's turn was come to go in to king Ahasuerus, after that she had been twelve months, according to the manner of the women, (for so were the days of their purifications accomplished, to wit, six months with oil of myrrh, and six months with sweet odours, and with other things for the purifying of the women;) **2:13** Then thus came every maiden unto the king; whatsoever she desired was given her to go with her out of the house of the women unto the king's house.

2:14 In the evening she went, and on the morrow she returned into the second house of the women, to the custody of Shaashgaz, the king's chamberlain, which kept the concubines: she came in unto the king no more, except the king delighted in her, and that she were called by name.

2:15 Now when the turn of Esther, the daughter of Abihail the uncle of Mordecai, who had taken her for his daughter, was come to go in unto the king, she required nothing but what Hegai the king's chamberlain, the keeper of the women, appointed. And Esther obtained favour in the sight of all them that looked upon her.

2:16 So Esther was taken unto king Ahasuerus into his house royal in the tenth month, which is the month Tebeth, in the seventh year of his reign.

Hadassah was highly favoured by the king for her beauty of person and spirit. This is an example that we are to fully internalize the nature of God and we are to remove all blemishes and uncleanness of sin, that we may be highly favoured by our LORD and be called as a part of his collective spiritual bride and Queen of the earth..

2:17 And the king loved Esther above all the women, and she obtained grace and favour in his sight more than all the virgins; so that **he set the royal crown upon her head, and made her queen instead of Vashti.**

The king's marriage feast is typical of the Marriage of the Lamb in heaven to his chosen bride. Truly Jesus said: "Many are called, but few are [will be} chosen." Only the choicest who are dedicated to pleasing him will be among the chosen of the first resurrection to spirit.

2:18 Then the king made a great [marriage] feast unto all his princes and his servants, even Esther's feast; and he made a release to the provinces, and gave gifts, according to the state of the king.

2:19 And when the virgins were gathered together the second time, then Mordecai sat in the king's gate.

2:20 Esther had not yet shewed her kindred nor her people; as Mordecai had charged her: for Esther did the commandment of Mordecai, like as when she was brought up with him.

2:21 In those days, while Mordecai sat in the king's gate, **two of the king's chamberlains, Bigthan and Teresh, of those which kept the door, were wroth, and sought to lay hands on the king Ahasuerus.**

Esther warns the king from Mordecai and gains even more favour.

2:22 And the thing was known to Mordecai, who told it unto Esther the queen; and Esther certified the king thereof in Mordecai's name.

2:23 And when inquisition was made of the matter, it was found out; therefore they were both hanged on a tree: and it was written in the book of the chronicles before the king.

Esther 3

Esther 3:1 After these things did king Ahasuerus promote Haman the son of Hammedatha the Agagite, and advanced him, and set his seat above all the princes that were with him.

3:2 And all the king's servants, that were in the king's gate, bowed, and reverenced Haman: for the king had so commanded concerning him. But Mordecai bowed not, nor did him reverence.

3:3 Then the king's servants, which were in the king's gate, said unto Mordecai, Why transgressest thou the king's commandment? **3:4** Now it came to pass, when they spake daily unto him, and he hearkened not unto them, that they told Haman, to see whether Mordecai's matters would stand: for he had told them that he was a Jew.

Haman was filled with wrath because he wanted to be exalted as much as or more than the king. The same attitude exists today in may elders and leaders of the Ekklesia who love the high sounding titles and chief seats.

3:5 And when Haman saw that Mordecai bowed not, nor did him reverence, then was Haman full of wrath.

3:6 And he thought scorn to lay hands on Mordecai alone; for they had shewed him the people of Mordecai: wherefore Haman sought to destroy all the Jews that were throughout the whole kingdom of Ahasuerus, even the people of Mordecai.

3:7 In the first month, that is, the month Nisan, in the twelfth year of king Ahasuerus, they cast Pur, that is, the lot, before Haman from day to day, and from month to month, to the twelfth month, that is, the month Adar.

Haman conspires against the Jews and against the king for he knows that the Jews exalt the king above himself and getting rid of them he seeks to exalt himself. It is exactly they same with Satan who seeks to destroy all those faithful to God [spiritual Israel].

3:8 And Haman said unto king Ahasuerus, There is a certain people scattered abroad and dispersed among the people in all the provinces of thy kingdom; and their laws are diverse from all people; neither keep they the king's laws: therefore it is not for the king's profit to suffer them.

3:9 If it please the king, let it be written that they may be destroyed: and I will pay ten thousand talents of silver to the hands of those that have the charge of the business, to bring it into the king's treasuries.

3:10 And the king took his ring from his hand, and gave it unto Haman the son of Hammedatha the Agagite, the Jews' enemy.

3:11 And the king said unto Haman, The silver is given to thee, the people also, to do with them as it seemeth good to thee.

3:12 Then were the king's scribes called on the thirteenth day of the first month, and there was written according to all that Haman had commanded unto the king's lieutenants, and to the governors that were over every province, and to the rulers of every people of every province according to the writing thereof, and to every people after their language; in the name of king Ahasuerus was it written, and sealed with the king's ring.

3:13 And the letters were sent by posts into all the king's provinces, to destroy, to kill, and to cause to perish, all Jews, both young and old, little children and women, in one day, even upon the thirteenth day of the twelfth month, which is the month Adar, and to take the spoil of them for a prey.

3:14 The copy of the writing for a commandment to be given in every province was published unto all people, that they should be ready against that day.

3:15 The posts went out, being hastened by the king's commandment, and the decree was given in Shushan the palace. And the king and Haman sat down to drink; but the city Shushan was perplexed.

Esther 4

Esther 4:1 When Mordecai perceived all that was done, Mordecai rent his clothes, and put on sackcloth with ashes, and went out into the midst of the city, and cried with a loud and a bitter cry; **4:2** And came even before the king's gate: for none might enter into the king's gate clothed with sackcloth.

4:3 And in every province, whithersoever the king's commandment and his decree came, there was great mourning among the Jews, and fasting, and weeping, and wailing; and many lay in sackcloth and ashes.

4:4 So Esther's maids and her chamberlains came and told it her. Then was the queen exceedingly grieved; and she sent raiment to clothe Mordecai, and to take away his sackcloth from him: but he received it not.

4:5 Then called Esther for Hatach, one of the king's chamberlains, whom he had appointed to attend upon her, and gave him a commandment to Mordecai, to know [to learn the cause of the mourning] what it was, and why it was.

4:6 So Hatach went forth to Mordecai unto the street of the city, which was before the king's gate.

4:7 And Mordecai told him of all that had happened unto him, and of the sum of the money that Haman had promised to pay to the king's treasuries for the Jews, to destroy them.

4:8 Also he gave him the copy of the writing of the decree that was given at Shushan to destroy them, to shew it unto Esther, and to declare it unto her, and to charge her that she should go in unto the king, to make supplication unto him, and to make request before him for her people.

4:9 And Hatach came and told Esther the words of Mordecai.

4:10 Again Esther spake unto Hatach, and gave him commandment unto Mordecai; **4:11** All the king's servants, and the people of the king's provinces, do know, that whosoever, whether man or women, shall come unto the king into the inner court, who is not called, there is one law of his to put him to death, except such to whom the king shall hold out the golden sceptre, that he may live: but I have not been called to come in unto the king these thirty days.

4:12 And they told to Mordecai Esther's words.

4:13 Then Mordecai commanded to answer Esther, Think not with thyself that thou shalt escape in the king's house, more than all the Jews.

Brethren, we are not to keep silent about the evils in the Ekklesia today; we are to mourn over them and cry out against them in the hope that some might be saved. Knowing that God hears us and delights is those who love him and mourn [sigh and cry, Ezekiel 9] over the evil. If you cannot cry out, then support those who are sounding the warning.

4:14 For if thou altogether holdest thy peace at this time, then shall there enlargement and deliverance arise to the Jews from another place; but thou and thy father's house shall be destroyed: and who knoweth whether thou art come to the kingdom for such a time as this?

4:15 Then Esther bade them return Mordecai this answer, **4:16** Go, gather together all the Jews that are present in Shushan, and fast ye for me, and neither eat nor drink three days, night or day: I also and my maidens will fast likewise; and so will I go in unto the king, which is not according to the law: and if I perish, I perish.

4:17 So Mordecai went his way, and did according to all that Esther had commanded him.

Esther 5

Esther 5:1 Now it came to pass on the third day, that Esther put on her royal apparel, and stood in the inner court of the king's house, over against the king's house: and the king sat upon his royal throne in the royal house, over against the gate of the house.

5:2 And it was so, when the king saw Esther the queen standing in the court, that she obtained favour in his sight: and the king held out to Esther the golden sceptre that was in his hand. So Esther drew near, and touched the top of the sceptre.

5:3 Then said the king unto her, What wilt thou, queen Esther? and what is thy request? it shall be even given thee to the half of the kingdom.

5:4 And Esther answered, If it seem good unto the king, let the king and Haman come this day unto the banquet that I have prepared for him.

5:5 Then the king said, Cause Haman to make haste, that he may do as Esther hath said. So the king and Haman came to the banquet that Esther had prepared.

5:6 And the king said unto Esther at the banquet of wine, What is thy petition? and it shall be granted thee: and what is thy request? even to the half of the kingdom it shall be performed.

5:7 Then answered Esther, and said, My petition and my request is; **5:8** If I have found favour in the sight of the king, and if it please the king to grant my petition, and to perform my request, let the king and Haman come to the banquet that I shall prepare for them, and I will do to morrow as the king hath said.

5:9 Then went Haman forth that day joyful and with a glad heart: but when Haman saw Mordecai in the king's gate, that he stood not up, nor moved for him, he was full of indignation against Mordecai.

5:10 Nevertheless Haman refrained himself: and when he came home, he sent and called for his friends, and Zeresh his wife.

5:11 And Haman told them of the glory of his riches, and the multitude of his children, and all the things wherein the king had promoted him, and how he had advanced him above the princes and servants of the king.

Haman is filled with pride in his opinion of himself as many elders and leaders of the Ekklesia are today. Yet he was blindly going to his own destruction as are all those filled with pride in themselves, their idols of men and their own ways

5:12 Haman said moreover, Yea, Esther the queen did let no man come in with the king unto the banquet that she had prepared but myself; and to morrow am I invited unto her also with the king.

5:13 Yet all this availeth me nothing, so long as I see Mordecai the Jew sitting at the king's gate.

5:14 Then said Zeresh his wife and all his friends unto him, Let a gallows be made of fifty cubits high, and to morrow speak thou unto the king that Mordecai may be hanged thereon: then go thou in merrily with the king unto the banquet. And the thing pleased Haman; and he caused the gallows to be made.

Doubtless God's spirit stirred the king to remember Mordecai and his service to the king. God can deliver his faithful if we will be diligent to learn of him and to live by his every Word and to put our trust in him.

Esther 6

Esther 6:1 On that night could not the king sleep, and he commanded to bring the book of records of the chronicles; and they were read before the king.

6:2 And it was found written, that Mordecai had told of Bigthana and Teresh, two of the king's chamberlains, the keepers of the door, who sought to lay hand on the king Ahasuerus.

6:3 And the king said, What honour and dignity hath been done to Mordecai for this? Then said the king's servants that ministered unto him, There is nothing done for him.

6:4 And the king said, Who is in the court? Now Haman was come into the outward court of the king's house, to speak unto the king to hang Mordecai on the gallows that he had prepared for him.

6:5 And the king's servants said unto him, Behold, Haman standeth in the court. And the king said, Let him come in.

Haman's great pride got the better of him and the sentence he pronounced thinking it was for himself was given to another.

6:6 So Haman came in. And the king said unto him, What shall be done unto the man whom the king delighteth to honour? Now **Haman thought in his heart, To whom would the king delight to do honour more than to myself?**

6:7 And Haman answered the king, For the man whom the king delighteth to honour, **6:8** Let the royal apparel be brought which the king useth to wear, and the horse that the king rideth upon, and the crown royal which is set upon his head: **6:9** And let this apparel and horse be delivered to the hand of one of the king's most noble princes, that they may array the man withal whom the king delighteth to honour, and bring him on horseback through the street of the city, and proclaim before him, Thus shall it be done to the man whom the king delighteth to honour.

6:10 Then the king said to Haman, Make haste, and take the apparel and the horse, as thou hast said, and do even so to Mordecai the Jew, that sitteth at the king's gate [sitting in the king's gate is a reference to being a judge on the king's authority, and in this case Mordecai would have been a judge of the Jews]: let nothing fail of all that thou hast spoken.

Haman must have been really galled but had no choice to honour his avowed enemy as he had thought to be honoured himself.

6:11 Then took Haman the apparel and the horse, and arrayed Mordecai, and brought him on horseback through the street of the city, and proclaimed before him, Thus shall it be done unto the man whom the king delighteth to honour.

6:12 And Mordecai came again to the king's gate. But Haman hasted to his house mourning, and having his head covered [hiding his face in shame].

6:13 And Haman told Zeresh his wife and all his friends every thing that had befallen him. Then said **his wise men and Zeresh his wife unto him, If Mordecai be of the seed of the Jews, before whom thou hast begun to fall, thou shalt not prevail against him, but shalt surely fall before him**.

6:14 And while they were yet talking with him, came the king's chamberlains, and hasted to bring Haman unto the banquet that Esther had prepared.

Esther 7

Esther 7:1 So the king and Haman came to banquet with Esther the queen.

7:2 And the king said again unto Esther on the second day at the banquet of wine, What is thy petition, queen Esther? and it shall be granted thee: and what is thy request? and it shall be performed, even to the half of the kingdom.

7:3 Then Esther the queen answered and said, If I have found favour in thy sight, O king, and if it please the king, let my life be given me at my petition, and my people at my request: **7:4** For we are sold, I and my people, to be destroyed, to be slain, and to perish. But if we had been sold for bondmen and bondwomen, I had held my tongue, although the enemy could not countervail the king's damage.

7:5 Then the king Ahasuerus answered and said unto Esther the queen, Who is he, and where is he, that durst presume in his heart to do so? **7:6** And Esther said, **The adversary and enemy is this wicked Haman. Then Haman was afraid before the king and the queen.**

7:7 And the king arising from the banquet of wine in his wrath went into the palace garden: and Haman stood up to make request for his life to Esther the queen; for he saw that there was evil determined against him by the king.

7:8 Then the king returned out of the palace garden into the place of the banquet of wine; and Haman was fallen upon the bed whereon Esther was. [Haman had fallen down to beg for his life and the king misinterpreted the scene, but did justice to this wicked person] Then said the king, Will he force the queen also before me in the house? As the word went out of king's mouth, they covered Haman's face [it was the custom to cover the face of the condemned].

7:9 And Harbonah, one of the chamberlains, said before the king, Behold also, the gallows fifty cubits high, which Haman had made for Mordecai, who spoken good for the king, standeth in the house of Haman. Then the king said, Hang him thereon.

7:10 So they hanged Haman on the gallows that he had prepared for Mordecai. Then was the king's wrath pacified.

Esther 8

Esther 8:1 On that day did the king Ahasuerus give the house of Haman the Jews' enemy unto Esther the queen. And Mordecai came before the king; for Esther had told what he was unto her.

8:2 And the king took off his ring, which he had taken from Haman, and gave it unto Mordecai [the king made Mordecai prime minister, the ring symbolizing the king's seal of authority]. And Esther set Mordecai over the house of Haman.

8:3 And Esther spake yet again before the king, and fell down at his feet, and besought him with tears to put away the mischief of Haman the Agagite, and his device that he had devised against the Jews.

8:4 Then the king held out the golden sceptre toward Esther. So Esther arose, and stood before the king, **8:5** And said, If it please the king, and if I have favour in his sight, and the thing seem right before the king, and I be pleasing in his eyes, let it be written to reverse the letters devised by Haman the son of Hammedatha the Agagite, which he wrote to destroy the Jews which are in all the king's provinces: **8:6** For how can I endure to see the evil that shall come unto my people? or how can I endure to see the destruction of my kindred? **8:7** Then the king Ahasuerus said unto Esther the queen and to Mordecai the Jew, Behold, I have given Esther the house of Haman, and him they have hanged upon the gallows, because he laid his hand upon the Jews.

8:8 Write ye also for the Jews, as it liketh you, in the king's name, and seal it with the king's ring: for the writing which is written in the king's name, and sealed with the king's ring, may no man reverse.

8:9 Then were the king's scribes called at that time in the third month, that is, the month Sivan, on the three and twentieth day thereof; and it was written according to all that Mordecai commanded unto the Jews, and to the lieutenants, and the deputies and rulers of the provinces which are from India unto Ethiopia, an hundred twenty and seven provinces, unto every province according to the writing thereof, and unto every people after their language, and to the Jews according to their writing, and according to their language.

8:10 And he wrote in the king Ahasuerus' name, and sealed it with the king's ring, and sent letters by posts on horseback, and riders on mules, camels, and young dromedaries: **8:11** Wherein the king granted the Jews which were in every city to gather themselves together, and to stand for their life, to destroy, to slay and to cause to perish, all the power of the people and province that would assault them, both little ones and women, and to take the spoil of them for a prey, **8:12** Upon one day in all the provinces of king Ahasuerus, namely, upon the thirteenth day of the twelfth month, which is the month Adar.

The king commanded the Jews to fight all those who would do them harm.

Brethren we also have a command from our King to fight the Adversary with all of the might that God will give us! Yet our fight is not with flesh and blood but with spiritual forces and our weapon is the sharp two edged sword of TRUTH!

8:13 The copy of the writing for a commandment to be given in every province was published unto all people, and that the Jews should be ready against that day to avenge themselves on their enemies.

8:14 So the posts that rode upon mules and camels went out, being hastened and pressed on by the king's commandment. And the decree was given at Shushan the palace.

8:15 And Mordecai went out from the presence of the king in royal apparel of blue and white, and with a great crown of gold, and with a garment of fine linen and purple: and the city of Shushan rejoiced and was glad.

8:16 The Jews had light, and gladness, and joy, and honour.

8:17 And in every province, and in every city, whithersoever the king's commandment and his decree came, the Jews had joy and gladness, a feast and a good day. And many of the people of the land became Jews; for the fear of the Jews fell upon them.

Esther 9

Esther 9:1 Now in **the twelfth month**, that is, the month Adar, on **the thirteenth day** of the same, when the king's commandment and his decree drew near to be put in execution, in the day that the enemies of the Jews hoped to have power over them, (though it was turned to the contrary, that the Jews had rule over them that hated them;) **9:2** The Jews gathered themselves together in their cities throughout all the provinces of the king Ahasuerus, to lay hand on such as sought their hurt: and no man could withstand them; for the fear of them fell upon all people.

9:3 And all the rulers of the provinces, and the lieutenants, and the deputies, and officers of the king, helped the Jews; because the fear of Mordecai fell upon them.

9:4 For Mordecai was great in the king's house, and his fame went out throughout all the provinces: for this man Mordecai waxed greater and greater.

9:5 Thus the Jews smote all their enemies with the stroke of the sword, and slaughter, and destruction, and did what they would unto those that hated them.

9:6 And in Shushan the palace the Jews slew and destroyed five hundred men.

9:7 And Parshandatha, and Dalphon, and Aspatha, **9:8** And Poratha, and Adalia, and Aridatha, **9:9** And Parmashta, and Arisai, and Aridai, and

Vajezatha, **9:10** The ten sons of Haman the son of Hammedatha, the enemy of the Jews, slew they; but on the spoil laid they not their hand.

9:11 On that day the number of those that were slain in Shushan the palace was brought before the king.

9:12 And the king said unto Esther the queen, The Jews have slain and destroyed five hundred men in Shushan the palace, and the ten sons of Haman; what have they done in the rest of the king's provinces? now what is thy petition? and it shall be granted thee: or what is thy request further? and it shall be done.

9:13 Then said Esther, If it please the king, let it be granted to the Jews which are in Shushan to do to morrow [the 14th day of the 12th month] also according unto this day's decree, and let Haman's ten sons be hanged upon the gallows.

9:14 And the king commanded it so to be done: and the decree was given at Shushan; and they hanged Haman's ten sons.

9:15 For the Jews that were in Shushan gathered themselves together on the fourteenth day also of the month Adar, and slew three hundred men at Shushan; but on the prey they laid not their hand.

9:16 But the other Jews that were in the king's provinces gathered themselves together, and stood for their lives, and had rest from their enemies, and slew of their foes seventy and five thousand, but they laid not their hands on the prey,

Purim is the 14th and 15th days of the 12th month; Adar 1.

9:17 On the thirteenth day of the month Adar; and on the fourteenth day of the same rested they, and made it a day of feasting and gladness.

9:18 But **the Jews that were at Shushan assembled together on the thirteenth day thereof, and on the fourteenth thereof; and on the fifteenth day of the same they rested, and made it a day of feasting and gladness.**

9:19 Therefore the Jews of the villages, that dwelt in the unwalled towns, made the fourteenth day of the month Adar a day of gladness and feasting, and a good day, and of sending portions one to another.

9:20 And Mordecai wrote these things, and sent letters unto all the Jews that were in all the provinces of the king Ahasuerus, both nigh and far, **9:21** To stablish this among them, **that they should keep the fourteenth day of the month Adar, and the fifteenth day of the same, yearly, 9:22** As the days wherein the Jews rested from their enemies, and the month which was turned unto them from sorrow to joy, and from mourning into a good day: **that they should make them days of feasting and joy, and of sending portions one to another, and gifts to the poor.**

9:23 And the Jews undertook to do as they had begun, and as Mordecai had written unto them; **9:24** Because Haman the son of Hammedatha, the Agagite, [a descendant of Agag the Amalekite] the enemy of all the Jews, had devised against the Jews to destroy them, and had cast Pur, that is, the lot, to consume them, and to destroy them; **9:25** But when Esther came before the king, he commanded by letters that his wicked device, which he devised against the Jews, should return upon his own head, and that he and his sons should be hanged on the gallows.

9:26 Wherefore they called these days Purim after the name of Pur.

Therefore for all the words of this letter, and of that which they had seen concerning this matter, and which had come unto them, **9:27** The Jews ordained, and took upon them, and upon their seed, and upon all such as joined themselves unto them, so as it should not fail, that they would keep these two days according to their writing, and according to their appointed time every year; **9:28** And that these days should be remembered and kept throughout every generation, every family, every province, and every city; and that these days of Purim should not fail from among the Jews, nor the memorial of them perish from their seed.

9:29 Then Esther the queen, the daughter of Abihail, and Mordecai the Jew, wrote with all authority, to confirm this second letter of Purim.

9:30 And he sent the letters unto all the Jews, to the hundred twenty and seven provinces of the kingdom of Ahasuerus, with words of peace and truth, **9:31** To confirm these days of Purim in their times appointed, according as Mordecai the Jew and Esther the queen had enjoined them, and as they had decreed for themselves and for their seed, the matters of the fastings and their cry.

9:32 And the decree of Esther confirmed these matters of Purim; and it was written in the book.

Esther 10

Esther 10:1 And the king Ahasuerus laid a tribute upon the land, and upon the isles of the sea.

10:2 And all the acts of his power and of his might, and the declaration of the greatness of Mordecai, whereunto the king advanced him, are they not written in the book of the chronicles of the kings of Media and Persia? **10:3** For Mordecai the Jew was next unto king Ahasuerus, and great among the Jews, and accepted of the multitude of his brethren, seeking the wealth of his people, and speaking peace to all his seed.

In conclusion although it Is not a High Holy Day of God, it would be well for all those of spiritual Israel to observe the Feast of Purim. It is scripture and it is full of powerful lessons in God's deliverance.

Visit Our Website

theshininglight.info

www.ingramcontent.com/pod-product-compliance
Lightning Source LLC
Chambersburg PA
CBHW082035230426
43670CB00016B/2658